THE GOVERNMENT OF
THE ROMAN EMPIRE

THE GOVERNMENT OF THE ROMAN EMPIRE

A Sourcebook

Barbara Levick

BARNES & NOBLE BOOKS
Totowa, New Jersey

© 1985 Barbara Levick

First published in the USA 1985 by
Barnes and Noble Books
81 Adams Drive
Totowa, New Jersey, 07512

Library of Congress Cataloging in Publication Data

Levick, Barbara.
The government of the roman empire.

Bibliography:p.
Includes index.
1. Rome — Politics and Government —
Sources. I. Title.
DG83.L62   1985   937'.06   85-4014
ISBN 0-389-20572-9

Printed and bound in Great Britain

Contents

TO
K.A.F.

Acknowledgements

The pleasure of thanking friends and colleagues for help and advice is tempered by the need to protect them from being held responsible for persistent errors of the author. If I thank Dr I. Ault, Dr K. Forsyth, Dr N. Mackie, Dr J. Matthews, Dr D. Nash, Dr M. Rayner, Mr and Mrs M. Shortland-Jones and Mr A. Woolley, without specifying their contributions (each knows his or her own and how grateful I am for it), that attains both ends. For the typing of much of the MS and for bibliographical help I am greatly indebted respectively to Mrs H. Hyder and Ms V. Magyar, and for his patience to my editor, Dr R. Stoneman. The cartography is by Jane Lewin.

B.M.L.

Abbreviations

AE	R. Cagnat *et al.* (eds.), *L'Année épigraphique* (Paris, 1893-)
AJ	F.F. Abbott and A.C. Johnson, *Municipal Administration in the Roman Empire* (Princeton, 1926; repr. New York, 1968)
AJP	*American Journal of Philology*
ANRW	H. Temporini *et al.* (eds.), *Aufstieg und Niedergang der römischen Welt* (Berlin, 1972-)
Aphrodisias	J. Reynolds, *Aphrodisias and Rome, Documents from the . . . Theatre . . . with some related Texts, JRS Monographs* 1 (London, 1982)
CIL	Th. Mommsen *et al.* (eds.), *Corpus Inscriptionum Latinarum* (Berlin, 1863-)
EJ	V. Ehrenberg and A.H.M. Jones, *Documents illustrating the Reigns of Augustus and Tiberius*, ed. by D.L. Stockton (Oxford, 1976)
FIRA	S. Riccobono *et al.* (eds.), *Fontes iuris Romani anteiustiniani* (three vols., 2nd edn of vol. I, Florence 1940-3)
IG	*Inscriptiones Graecae* (Berlin, 1873-)
IGR	R. Cagnat *et al.* (eds.), *Inscriptiones Graecae ad res Romanas pertinentes* (vols. 1, 3, 4, Paris, 1906-27)
ILS	H. Dessau (ed.), *Inscriptiones Latinae Selectae* (Berlin, 1892-1916)
Inscr.Ital.	*Academicae Italicae consociatae ediderunt Inscriptiones Italiae* (Rome, 1931-)
JRS	*Journal of Roman Studies*
LR	N. Lewis and M. Reinhold, *Roman Civilization: the Empire* (New York, 1955; paperback 1966)
MAMA	*Monumenta Asiae Minoris Antiqua* (Manchester, 1928-)
MW	M. McCrum and A.G. Woodhead, *Select Documents of the Principates of the Flavian Emperors including the Year of Revolution, A.D. 68-96* (Cambridge, 1961)

Musurillo, *Christian Acts*	H.A. Musurillo, *The Acts of the Christian Martyrs.* *Oxford Early Christian Texts* (Oxford, 1972)
Musurillo, *Pagan Acts*	H.A. Musurillo, *The Acts of the Pagan Martyrs* (Acta Alexandrinorum) (Oxford, 1954)
Pflaum, *Carrières*	H.-G. Pflaum, *Les Carrières procuratoriennes équestres sous le Haut-Empire romain* (4 vols., Paris, 1960-1)
P. Got.	H. Frisk, *Papyrus grecs de la Bibliothèque municipale de Gothembourg* (Gothenburg, 1929)
PIR	E. Klebs *et al.* (eds.), *Prosopographia Imperii Romani* (3 vols., Berlin, 1897-8); 2nd edn by E. Groag, A. Stein *et al.* (Berlin & Leipzig, 1933-)
P. Oxy.	S.P. Grenfell, A.S. Hunt *et al.* (eds.), *The Oxyrhynchus Papyri* (London, 1898-)
P. Teb.	S.P. Grenfell, A.S. Hunt, J.G. Smyly, *et al.* (eds.), *The Tebtunis Papyri* (London, 1902-)
RIC	E.H. Mattingly, A. Sydenham *et al.* (eds.), *The Roman Imperial Coinage* (London 1923-)
SEG	J.J.E. Hondius *et al.* (eds.), *Supplementum Epigraphicum Graecum* (Leiden, 1923-)
Sherk, *Docs.*	R.K. Sherk, *Roman Documents from the Greek East*: Senatus Consulta *and* Epistulae *to the Age of of Augustus* (Baltimore, 1969)
Smallwood, *Nerva-Hadrian*	E.M. Smallwood (ed.), *Documents illustrating the Principates of Gaius Claudius and Nero* (Cambridge, 1967)
Smallwood *Nerva-Hadrian*	E.M. Smallwood (ed.), *Documents illustrating the Principates of Nerva Trajan and Hadrian* (Cambridge, 1966)
SP	A.S. Hunt and C.C. Edgar (eds.), *Select Papyri: Non-Literary Papyri* (2 vols., Cambridge, Mass., 1932-4)
ZPE	*Zeitschrift für Papyrologie und Epigraphik* (Cologne)

Passages from collections of documents are cited by number.
Numbers in **bold type** refer to excerpts included in this book.
Square brackets [] represent a lacuna in the text; - - - indicates where it has not been restored.
Points . . . represent passages omitted by the editor.
All dates are AD except where indicated.

Weights, Measures, Currency and Wealth

Greek:

Attic talent	=	60 *minae*	26.196 kg (57.8 lb)
mina	=	100 *drachmae*	436.6 gr (15½ oz)
stater	=	2 *drachmae*	8.73 gr
drachma	=	6 obols	4.36 gr
obol	=	12 chalcia ('coppers')	0.73 gr
Egyptian drachma	=	¼ Attic drachma	
stade			178.6 m (202.25 yds)

Roman:

libra ('pound')	=	12 *unciae* ('ounces')	327.5 gr (11.5 oz)
uncia	=	6 *denarii*	27.3 gr (0.963 oz)
aureus ('gold piece')	=	25 *denarii*	8.19 gr
denarius ('ten *as* piece')	=	4 sesterces	3.72 gr (*c.* 98% silver until Nero; then 93%; by 250 the double *denarius* was 3.97 gr, with *c.* 41% silver: Walker, 1976-8 (5), 1, 18; 3, 50)

(The Attic drachma and the *denarius* were equivalent)

sestertius or HS	=	originally '2½ *asses*', later 4
mile ('thousand paces')		*c.*1500 m (1618 yds)
iugerum		0.25 ha (0.66 acre)
modius		8.62 1 (15.17 pints or 6.65 kg): L. Foxhall and H.A. Forbes, *Chiron* 12 (1982), 88f.

Property qualification for a senator:	1,000,000 sesterces
a knight:	400,000
a municipal councillor (of Comum):	100,000
Salary of a senatorial governor:	400,000
an equestrian procurator:	60,000-300,000
Pay of a legionary (before Domitian):	900
(after Domitian):	1,200

Distributions of grain at Rome: 5 *modii* of wheat per man per month
(monetary value *c.* 300-360 sesterces
per year, and supplying 130 per cent
of calories required by a moderately
active adult male: see Hopkins 1978
(6), 49 n.36; Foxhall and Forbes,
above)

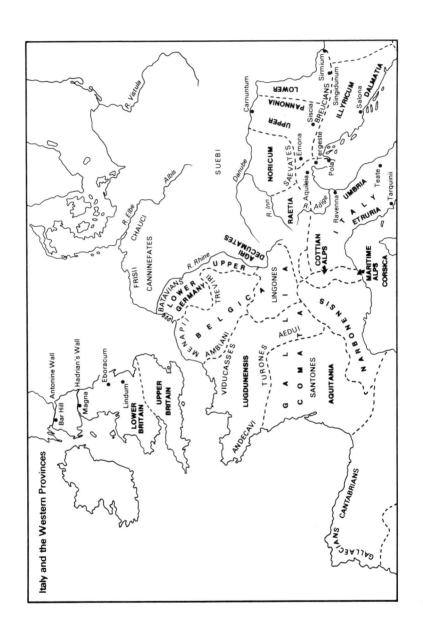

Italy and the Western Provinces

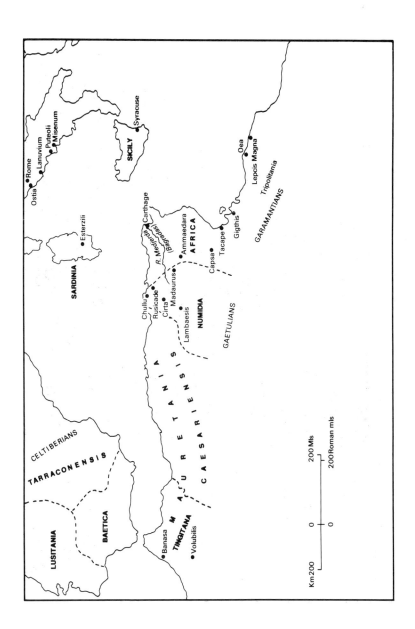

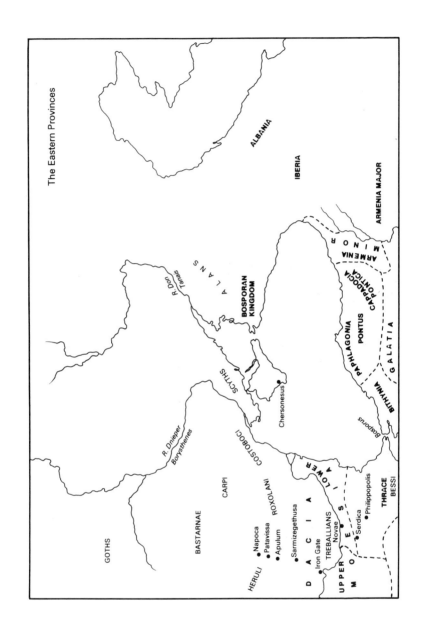

The Eastern Provinces

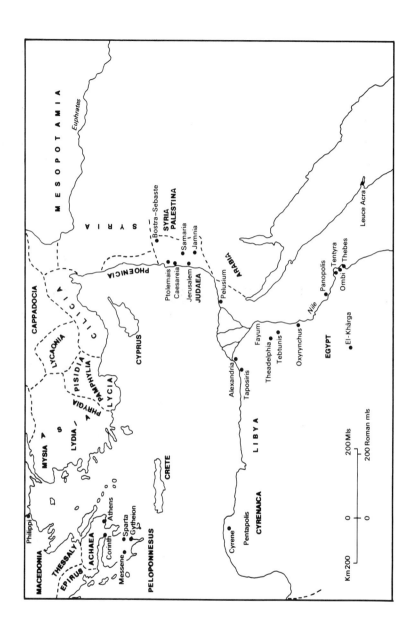

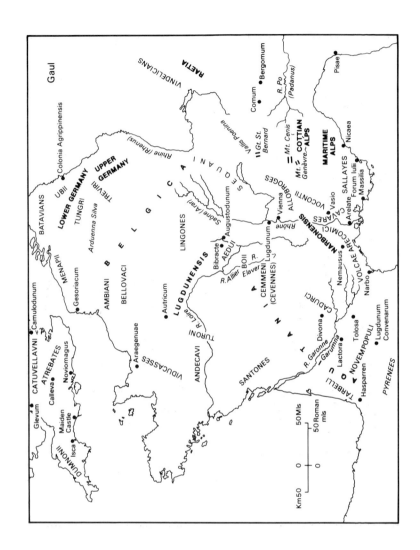

Gaul

RAETIA
VINDELICIANS

Bergomum
Comum
R. Po
(Padanus)
Pisae

COTTIAN
ALPS
MARITIME
ALPS
Nicaea

Gt. St.
Bernard
Mt. Cenis
Vallis Poenina
Mt.
Genève
SALLAYES
Forum Iulii
Arelate
Massilia
CAVARES
Vasio
VOCONTII
ALLOBROGES
Vienna
NARBONENSIS
SEQUANI

Rhine (Rhenus)
Colonia Agrippinensis
UBII
UPPER
GERMANY
LOWER GERMANY
TREVIRI
Arduenna Silva
BATAVIANS
MENAPII
Gesoriacum
AMBIANI
BELLOVACI
B
E
L
G
I
C
A
LINGONES
Augustodunum
Saône (Arar)
Rhône
VOLCAE ARECOMICI
Nemausus
Narbo
Tolosa
Lugdunum Convenarum
NOVEMPOPULI
TARBELLI
Hasparren
PYRENEES
Lactora
Divona
R. Garonne
Garumna
CADURCI
CEMMENI
(CEVENNES)
R. Allier
R. Elaver
BOII
Lugdunum
Bibracte
AEDUI
LUGDUNENSIS
A
Q
U
I
T
A
N
I
A
Autricum
R. Loire
TURONI
ANDECAVI
VIDUCASSES
Araegenuae
SANTONES

Camulodunum
CATUVELLAVNI
ATREBATES
Noviomagus
Calleva
Glevum
Maiden
Castle
Isca
DUMNONII

50 Mls
50 Roman
mls
Km 50   0
0

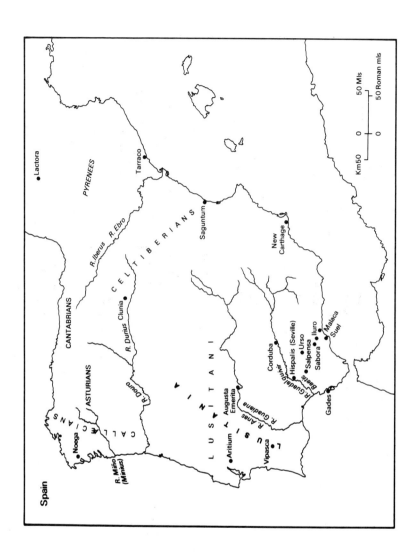

Spain

Lactora

PYRENEES

Tarraco

CANTABRIANS

R. Iberus *R. Ebro*

Saguntum

C E L T I B E R I A N S

R. Durius Clunia

New
Carthage

ASTURIANS

R. Douro

*R. Miño
(Minius)*

Noega

C A L L E C I A N S

L U S I T A N I

Aritium

Augusta
Emerita

R. Anas

Vipasca

R. Guadiana

Corduba

R. Guadalquivir

Hispalis (Seville)

Urso

Baetis

Salpensa

Sabora

Iluro

Malaca

Suel

Gades

Km50   0

50 Mls

0

50 Roman mls

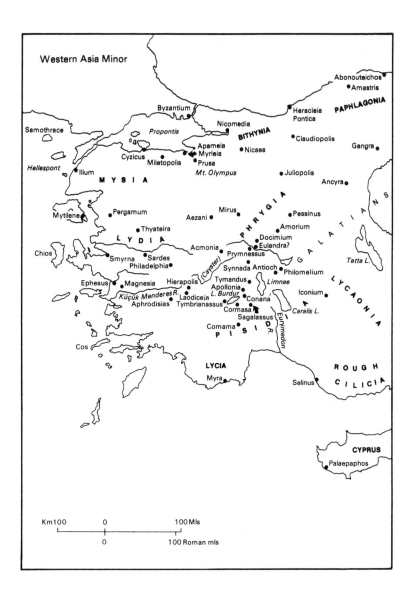

Western Asia Minor

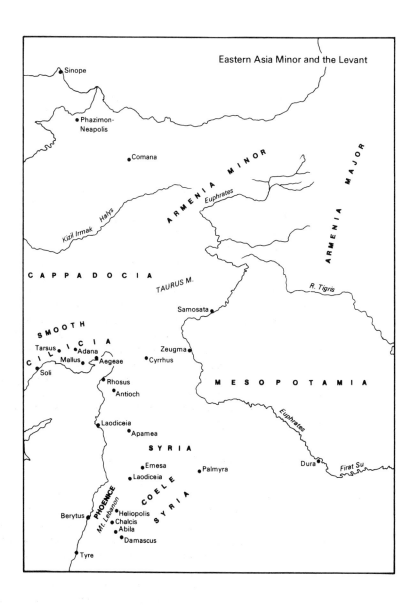

Eastern Asia Minor and the Levant

1

Introduction: The Power of Rome

The power of Rome, *imperium Romanum*, lasted from the traditional foundation date of the city in 753 BC until AD 476, the conventional date of its end in the west, and until the fall of Constantinople to the Turks in AD 1453 in the east. The documents in this book show the Empire at its greatest extent, and at its most confident, during the three centuries from the permanent establishment of one-man rule in 27 BC to the onset of acute problems, military, political and economic, in the third century AD. The establishment of the Principate at the end of the Civil Wars of 49-30 made it possible to adapt existing institutions to the needs of the Empire and to set up new ones, and it was able to emerge through another period of reform and renewal into the fourth century.

Repugnant though many of its features are (the rigid class structure, slaves at the bottom of the heap), the Empire commands respect for its durability and for the effect its existence has had on the language, literature, architecture and law of Europe and elsewhere; it is worth asking how it survived so long. Some answers may be found by examining the machinery devised by the Romans for controlling the Empire (Chapters 2-4); more by considering changing attitudes towards Rome's subjects and the way some of them came to feel about Rome (Chapters 7-9).

In itself, the machinery of government looks grossly inadequate even if we allow for the diplomacy that exploited inter-tribal and inter-city hostility and remember that the tribes were badly placed to organise a durable resistance, while much of the eastern half of the Empire had long been under alien rule. From Hadrian's Wall in the north to Leuce Acra on the Red Sea was 4,654 km (2,890 miles), and the population of the Empire has been estimated at between fifty and sixty million. Yet the army that kept it was only thirty legions strong in the later second century, about 150,000-180,000 men, with a force of about 253,690 auxiliary troops and sailors (Birley in King and Henig 1981 (12), 40ff.; for lower estimates see Mitchell 1983 (6), 147 n.14) and the members of the Roman upper class (members of the senate and of the equestrian order, the 'Knights', that ranked immediately below it) actively involved in its administration at any one time has been put as low as 150 (Hopkins 1980 (5), 121). True, the respect that the army inspired in enemies and

1

subjects was enhanced by strategic positioning of the troops (the Rhine legions more than once showed that they were as well placed to deal with revolt in Gaul as with German tribes (**196**), and those in Syria kept as much of an eye on the inhabitants of Antioch and Laodiceia as they did on the Parthians beyond the Euphrates (cf. **39**) and by their mobility. As the army settled to a relatively static role, the legions moving towards the hardening periphery of the Empire (Luttwak 1976 (3) 55ff.), the habit of obedience prevailed among Rome's subjects (with notorious exceptions, such as the Jews in Judaea (**199f.**)).

Whether this apparent inadequacy is something that needs explanation or whether it rather helps to explain Roman success (as Dr Nash has suggested to me), in that only such economy of means made expansion and the maintenance of the Empire possible, there is no doubt that expansion was intended to pay, in booty, land for settlement and leasing out, and taxation. That was made clear when Italy was exempted from the payment of direct taxation in 167 BC. Not only the state was to benefit: the careers and reputation of individuals depended largely on military glory and they were often readier to take decisive and aggressive military action than the senate as a whole (hence divergent views as to the nature, offensive or defensive, of Roman wars under the Republic and the way Rome came by her Empire); the minimum cost of wars in money and manpower was calculable, while the outcome was uncertain and the profitability of acquisitions variable. Calculations were made about it, even if only after a decision had been taken, probably on quite other grounds, as it had about Britain before Strabo wrote, justifying it.

1. Strabo, *Geography*, 4, 5, 3, p. 200f.; Greek

At the present time, however, some of the chieftains there, who have sent embassies to make overtures to Caesar Augustus and have secured his friendship, have set up offerings on the Capitol and have made the island virtually a Roman possession in its entirety. They are also so ready to put up with heavy duties on what is imported into Gaul from there and on exports from here . . . that there is no need for a garrison on the island. It would require at least one legion and some cavalry to take tribute off them, and the expenditure on the troops would equal the sums they contributed: (p. 201) the customs duties would have to be lowered if tribute were imposed on them, besides which there would be a certain amount of danger involved in using force.

Profits fell after the Republican era: less territory was acquired and the pickings were less rich (Dacia with its gold is an exception); what had already been acquired had to be garrisoned at a high cost in money and men. Even with extensive use of non-citizen troops, it put a strain on imperial finances (**80**) and Italian manpower (**28**). Eventually the aristocracies of Italy and the provinces became a united ruling class and the imperialism of Rome and Italy gave way to an Empire-wide structure of rulers and ruled, 'men of standing' and 'those of the humbler classes' (cf. **184f.**), and the distinction between citizen and non-citizen became less important than that between privileged and unprivileged. No less than before the Empire marked the 'in-out' categories that both helped to give it coherence and endangered its stability; but they were categories transformed.

The pressures that caused the change must have been strong: the original attitude of Romans to peoples outside the Empire, especially to the tribal, non-Greek speaking societies of the west, and to the recalcitrant within it, would have led one to expect them to try maintaining their supremacy in isolation and by brute force. By the time of Augustus the Romans had discovered that their destiny was to rule; they had become open imperialists and set no limit to what they might attempt (Virgil, *Aeneid* 1, 279; Brunt, 1978). Conquests were often spectacularly bloody (5,000 dead qualified a general for a triumph) and followed up by enslavement and pillage to defray the costs of the campaign, fill the pockets of the commander, and give the rank and file something to take back into civil life. Not surprisingly the Roma of the coinage is a helmeted warrior.

But it was precisely the army and its manpower needs that provided the most important piece of machinery for turning aliens into Romans. In theory only Roman citizens served in the legions. Originally, the Roman citizen body, barring those disqualified by sex or age, *was* the Roman army. It met as an assembly in the Field of Mars outside the city boundary to elect magistrates with the power to command (*imperium*), potential generals. When it was in session a flag flew on a hill over the Tiber. If the flag was lowered it meant that the enemy were in sight; the assembly came to an end for the participants to prepare for battle. This ritual went on until at least the third century AD (Cassius Dio, *Roman History* 37, 28, 1ff.). For the endless supplies of manpower they needed the Romans relied until the end of the Republic mainly on the resources of Italy, which had become available to the legions proper when the Italian allies were enfranchised as a result of the Social War of 91 BC. Under the Principate the Romans solved two problems at once by (for example) sending potentially rebellious mountaineers of Spain to serve as auxiliary troops in the Balkan provinces (**152**, cf. **34**). That did not replenish the gaps in the legions that Tiberius complained of (**28**), but auxiliaries who had served 25 years and received honourable discharge were enfranchised and their sons might enlist in the legions (**152**; cf. **153f.**). By granting citizenship in the provinces to these and other men of good standing and well disposed to Rome the Emperors gradually created a new pool of potential legionaries, especially in Spain and Gaul and later in the Balkans. By 68 more than half the men in the legions seem to have been of provincial origin (Webster 1974 (3), 108; Forni 1974 (9); Mann 1983 (9), 49ff.).

Until 107 BC only men of a certain property qualification were enlisted in the legions, in theory at least. Even afterwards recruiting officers continued to prefer them, and under the Principate that prejudice contributed to the provincialisation of the legions (**28**). The Augustan peace guaranteed by the army, and the new markets that the expanding Empire provided, with developing areas crying out for the amenities of civilised life such as improved housing, wine and table-ware, gave enterprising provincials unprecedented chances of making money. As the provinces came to be better recruiting grounds than Italy, so well-off men might enter as officers and pass on to service as tax-officials or governors of minor provinces, as Italian knights were also doing (**11ff.**). Some of the wealthiest entered the senate (cf. **133**, **159ff.**), finally and irretrievably identifying themselves with the conquerors. In the senate their votes, voice and money would be welcome, if not to their older established peers then to the Emperor.

The change of government from senatorial oligarchy to disguised autocracy worked in favour of the provinces too, at least in favour of men of wealth and power. The power they wielded locally could be deployed in favour of the Emperor and offset any republican resentment of ancient Roman families. An Emperor neglected the provinces at his peril, as Nero discovered in 68; most paid them attention and courted their upper classes.

Only those members of the upper classes who had failed to maintain their position or who had lost their property in the transition from independence to Roman rule or from Republic to Principate would point out the difference between real independence and what Rome allowed (cf. **196**). In the main, the classes who were put into power in the cities and tribes, or kept in it, had a vested interest in the continuance of Roman suzerainty. In return for helping to secure tranquillity magnates and client princes were allowed to rule and exploit their local territories in their own interests. Their own income and whatever taxes and tribute accrued to Rome came ultimately from the workers under their control and from the artisans who made up their produce or the raw materials they provided into manufactured goods.

The documents in this book mostly present the Empire from the points of view of the Italian or provincial aristocracy. They are the work of emperors, officials and successful literary men, those in whose interest the structure had been set up and was maintained. The voices of those lower in the pile are rarely to be heard (but cf. **196**, **54**, **226**); they were poor and illiterate. Their rulers made professions of benevolence when acts of injustice came to light (cf. **91**, **167**, **184**), but took little interest in them except as soldiers, food-producers or tax-payers. Their collective voice is heard when they rebel (Chapter 11) and invoke pre-Roman culture, experience and religion against the power of Rome.

The chapters may be used in combination as part of a chain: 2, 3 and 4 are particularly closely linked; 5 is connected with 6; 7, 8 and 9 belong together; and 10 is linked to 11; but 3 and 11, 4 and 10 form two further pairs.

2

Structure

At the apex of power was the Emperor, emerging from senatorial struggles for supremacy only after the Roman Republic had existed for nearly five centuries; he could be seen as a senator by his peers but his subjects recognised the monarch and in the East openly gave him the name (see **227**).

From 19 BC the Emperor had power (*imperium*) in Rome, Italy and the Empire which was effectively his for life and which had already, in 23, been defined as superior to any other; he had also been in possession of a large part of the Empire, including Egypt, Syria, Gaul and the Iberian peninsula, to rule it directly as its governor, since 27. There is no need for passages to illustrate his power; he will be seen throughout, in command of armies, controlling finance, exercising supreme jurisdiction, issuing edicts and taking decisions that had the force of law, the constant object of appeals, queries, petitions and homage from governors, communities and private individuals, offered in person, by embassy or by letter (or by both methods at once); but one anecdote vividly illustrates its ultimate basis.

2. *The Augustan History: Hadrian*, 15, 12f.

And Favorinus once had an expression he used criticised by Hadrian and conceded the point. When his friends found fault with him for wrongly conceding the point to Hadrian about a word in common use with reputable writers, he raised a hearty laugh (13) by saying, 'You are giving me bad advice, my friends, when you don't allow me to regard a man with thirty legions as more learned than anyone else.'

That Favorinus was a sophist (see on **163**) and came from Gaul was one of the three paradoxes about him; another was that (in less circumspect mood) he had 'quarrelled with an Emperor and lived' (Philostratus, *Lives of the Sophists*, 1, 8 (489)).

The Emperor made himself responsible for pay and bounty (**74f**), and it was through the relations that he was entitled to establish with the gods (auspices) that victories were assured; for legions named after Emperors, see **30f**.

6

3. EJ 43; from Lepcis Magna

Sacred to the god Mars-Augustus: the community of Lepcis (made the dedication) after Africa had been freed from the Gaetulian war under the auspices of Imperator Caesar Augustus, Supreme Pontiff, Father of his Country, and by the generalship of Cossus Lentulus, consul, member of the board of fifteen for religious ceremonies, proconsul.

The Gaetulians were one of the tribes that the Romans encountered as they advanced south and west into Africa; territory, freedom and livelihood were all threatened as settlement inhibited the annual north-south movement of flocks and herds. Cossus' campaigns, which were important enough to win his descendants the surname Gaetulicus, were conducted in 5-6; he had been consul in 1 BC. They did not bring warfare in Africa to an end (see **12**, for example). Later, only imperial victories were recognised, in the titulature of the Emperor (see **216**).

The following account of the Empire, bringing Strabo's *Geography* to an end, is the work of a contemporary Greek admirer more concerned with the realities of power than with constitutional niceties. (It is a matter of debate whether in the first century of the Principate Emperors had the legal right to make peace and war.)

4. Strabo, *Geography*, 17, 3, 24f., p. 839f.; Greek

Of the entire area which is subject to the Romans, some is ruled by kings, some they rule directly under the designation 'provincial' territory, appointing governors and tax collectors to the inhabitants. There are also free cities, some of which attached themselves to the Romans as friends from the outset, while to others the Romans themselves granted freedom as a mark of honour. Some dynasts, tribal chieftains and priestly rulers are also subject to the Romans; these people regulate their lives along their traditional lines.

(25, p. 480) But the provinces, which have been differently divided at various times, are arranged at the present time as Caesar Augustus laid down. For when his country entrusted him with supreme authority in the Empire and he became established as lord for life of peace and war, he divided the whole territory into two parts, assigning one to himself, the rest to the people. The part he assigned to himself was whatever has need of a military garrison: the uncivilised territory bordering on the peoples that have not yet been subdued, or poor territory that resists cultivation, so that, making up with plenty of strongholds for its lack of other resources, it is restless and rebellious. To the people he assigned the remainder, all that is peaceful and easy to govern without force.

Each part he divided into several provinces, which are known respectively as 'Caesar's' and 'the people's' provinces. To the former Caesar sends governors and administrators, dividing the country differently at various times and adapting the administration to circumstances; to the public provinces the people send praetors and consuls, but these too are assigned to different categories whenever the situation calls for it.

In his original allocation, however, Augustus made two consular provinces: the part of Africa that was subject to the Romans, excluding what was formerly subject to Juba and now to his son Ptolemy; and Asia on the nearer side of the river Halys and the Taurus range, excluding the Galatians and the tribes that had been subject to Amyntas and also excluding Bithynia and the Propontis. Ten public provinces he made praetorian: in Europe and the adjacent islands (1) Further Spain, as it is called, the territory round the rivers Baetis and Anas, and (2) Narbonensian Gaul; (3) Sardinia and Corsica; (4) Sicily; (5) the part of Illyria bordering on Epirus, and (6) Macedonia; (7) Achaea including Thessaly, the Aetolians, Acarnanians and some tribes of Epirus (those bordering on Macedonia); (8) Crete, together with Cyrenaica; (9) Cyprus; (10) Bithynia with the Propontis and certain parts of Pontus. The other provinces Caesar holds and to some he sends men of consular rank to look after them, to others men of praetorian rank; to others again men of equestrian rank. Kings, dynasts and principalities are and always have been at his disposal.

In the late Republic the senate had sent out members who had held the highest magistracy, the consulship, or the next highest, the praetorship, on a system of seniority combined with the drawing of lots, to the various provinces (a word which in Latin originally meant 'job' or 'function'). Under the Principate it was still senators for the most part who governed in the area assigned to the Emperor (what Strabo calls 'Caesar's', nowadays usually called 'imperial' provinces); he chose them, their power was delegated to them by him, and they were known, whether they had held the consulship or only the praetorship, as 'praetorian legate of Augustus'. For the remaining, Strabo's 'people's' provinces, nowadays usually called 'public' or, as in this book, 'senatorial', governors were still normally selected in the old way and they all bore the title proconsul whatever their seniority in the senate. The titulature shows Augustus' legates as his subordinates, the proconsuls as possessors of independent power and of a dignity that (considering the number of legions they controlled: two altogether) need cause him no anxiety.

Strabo's emphasis on flexibility is important: Galatia, for instance, conventionally regarded as an imperial province for ex-praetors without a garrison, was more than once governed by an ex-consul under

Augustus, and had a garrison of at least one legion. The system took time to settle down. But Strabo's account of Augustus' original disposition is not entirely accurate: Narbonensian Gaul and Cyprus were returned to the senate only in 23 BC, further Spain (Baetica) perhaps two years earlier. He also simplifies the distinction between peaceful senatorial and armed imperial provinces (see **3**): it was only in the reign of Gaius that proconsuls finally lost control of legions when the Third Legion, Augustan, in Africa was assigned to a separate commander.

In the third century another writer described the system and some developments.

5. Cassius Dio, *Roman History*, 53, 12, 7-9; 14, 1-4; Greek

Later he gave Cyprus and Narbonensian Gaul back to the people and took Dalmatia instead. (8) This was also done in the case of other provinces on later occasions, as the course of my narrative will show. These provinces I have listed in this way because each of them is administered separately while at the outset and for a considerable period the provinces were governed two or three together. (9) I have not mentioned the rest because some of them were acquired later, while others, even if they had already been made subject, were not under Roman administration but were allowed autonomy or had been assigned to various dependent kingdoms. And all of them that came into the Roman Empire after that were allocated to the reigning Emperor . . .

(14, 1) It was in this way and on these conditions that the practice of sending ex-praetors and ex-consuls to both types of province became established. When one of them was despatched by the Emperor, province and timing were at his discretion; some were holding governorships while they were still in office as praetor or consul, which is something that happens even now. (2) As for the senate's part, he had a particular regulation about Africa and Asia, allocating them to ex-consuls and leaving the rest to ex-praetors; but he made a general regulation forbidding men to draw lots for a province for five years after holding the domestic magistracy.

(3) For some time all men thus qualified went on drawing lots for the provinces even if they were too many for the number of provinces available. Later, when some of them proved unsatisfactory, the appointment of governors of these provinces was also put in the hands of the Emperor. And so in a sense the Emperor gives them their commands too, (4) by ordering the same number of men (and men chosen by him) as there are provinces to draw lots. Some Emperors have sent their own nominees to those provinces too and have allowed some of them to hold office for more than a year, and have assigned some provinces to knights in place of senators.

Dio is correct to point out that some provinces were administered as a group at first: it is not until 21 that the first governor of one of the separate parts of northern Gaul can be found; until four years before that the entire area had been under the supervision of members of the imperial family. As time went on provinces tended to be split, reducing the power but enhancing the control of the governor; it was a process that accelerated sharply in the third century (**223f.**).

The regulation enforcing a five-year gap between domestic and personnel in the provinces. Tacitus several times shows him intervening enacted by Pompey in 52 BC to inhibit electoral bribery (it delayed recovery of what one had spent).

Dio and Strabo show how closely the Emperor could control personnel in the provinces. Tacitus several times shows him intervening decisively in the choice of governors for senatorial provinces: in 21 the Emperor's observation that the senate should choose a proconsul of Africa capable of dealing with the rebel Tacfarinas, rather than leave the lot to decide between two senior consulars, led to their deciding between two nominees of his (*Annals* 3, 32 and 35); in 36 a candidate was deterred from standing for the province of Asia by a letter from the Emperor (6, 40, 3; cf. 3, 69, 1ff.); and Julius Agricola was given a hint that he should not come forward in about 90 (*Agricola* 42).

Note also the temporary transfer of provinces to direct imperial control, as that of Bithynia-Pontus in about 109, when Pliny the Younger was sent out as Trajan's legate (see index of passages cited). The senate received nothing in return, but in about 180, when Bithynia-Pontus became permanently imperial, they took in exchange the relative backwater of Lycia-Pamphylia.

In Domitian's reign a knight was allowed temporarily to take over a normally senatorial province (**85**); it caused a stir; by the end of the third century all armed provinces were in the hands of knights (see **225f.**).

The Emperor's legates received instructions from him when they went out to their provinces; Pliny's are attested in *Letters* 10, 22, and elsewhere (see Sherwin-White 1966 (1), 590); the real position of proconsuls was not very different, as the Emperor could intervene in their provinces at any time (see, e.g., **46** and Millar 1966); they seem to be receiving regular preliminary instructions at least as early as the Principate of Claudius.

6. J.H. Oliver, *AJP* 100 (1979), 551ff.; Greek, from Cos

[Gnaeus Dom]itius Corbulo, proconsul, sends greetings to the magistrates, council and people [of the Coans]. I have often considered it [not without profit] to draw the attention [even of cities], particularly with regard to such matters as lie within my jurisdiction, [to the fact] that it has been laid down [in the] instructions [that matters which] may be thought to merit the divine [decision] of the Emperor are [first to be submitted to] the provincial governors. [On the present occasion (a certain party)] has, on the basis of a decree passed by you, put in an appeal to [Augustus], and I was aware that he had done [this] as [an act] of defiance. Accordingly [it will be] necessary, if the appeal to the Emperor takes place, that I should first examine the reason; but if the case lies with me, the [quaestor] will have to exact adequate sureties of 2,500 *denarii*, as laid down by me in my edict dealing with those who fail to put in an appearance at judicial hearings. [If] he does not fulfil these requirements [- - -]

Before Burton's (1976) discussion of this badly damaged inscription, the reign of Hadrian was taken to offer the first known instance of regular instructions issued to a proconsul (**44**).

Scholars differ, but on Oliver's interpretation, a party appealing to the Emperor from a judicial decision (with the permission or support of Cos?) has failed to put down the deposit required of appellants by the governor to prevent their blackmailing litigants who could not afford the cost of a trial at Rome; nor has he submitted the appeal to the preliminary scrutiny of the governor, which was also required (for the governor's control of access to the Emperor see also Brunt 1961 (10), 207f.). The well-known general Corbulo was the last man to allow his prerogatives to be neglected (see Tacitus, *Annals*, 13, 8f., and R. Syme, *JRS* 60 (1970), 27 ff.).

Dio continues with a paragraph on the governor's staff (53 14, 5ff.), and Strabo shows the system working in the Spanish provinces.

7. Strabo, *Geography* 3, 4, 20, p. 166f.

At the present time . . . Baetica is assigned to the people, and a praetor is sent to it who has both a quaestor and a legate. The eastern boundary of this province they have set near Castulo and the rest of Spain is Caesar's. Two legates are sent there on his behalf, one an ex-praetor, the other an ex-consul. The former, who has a legate of his own with him, is to administer justice to the Lusitanians who border on Baetica and extend as far as the river Douro and its mouths — for Lusitania is the name they particularly apply to this region at the present time; this is where the city of Augusta Emerita is. But the rest, and this is the greater part of the Iberian peninsula, is under the consular governor, who has a considerable army of some three legions as well as three legates. One of them, who is in command of two legions, guards the frontier of the entire territory north of the Douro, whose inhabitants used to be called Lusitanians but are now known as Callaecians. (p. 167) Adjoining them are the northern mountains which contain the Asturians and Cantabrians. The river Melsus flows through the Asturians, and a little beyond it is the city of Noega and nearby an estuary, which divides the Asturians from the Cantabrians. The country immediately adjoining, which runs along the foot of the mountains as far as the Pyrenees, is guarded by the second legate with the other legion. The third legate supervises the interior and organises the affairs of those who are already coming to be called 'Togati' because they are peaceful and as they wear their Roman togas they are being brought over to civilisation on the Italian model. These are the Celtiberians and those who live next to them on either side of the river Ebro down to the coastal districts. The governor himself spends his winters dispensing justice in the districts by the sea, especially at New Carthage and Tarraco, while he goes on tour during the summer, continually keeping an eye on things that need improvement. There are also imperial procurators of equestrian rank, who are the officials who distribute to the troops all the supplies they need to run their daily life.

Besides legates with military and juridical functions (see below **45**), and (in senatorial provinces) a quaestor to look after finance, the governor would have an informal advisory body made up of friends, both local and from Rome and elsewhere (cf. **50**), as well as a considerable body of slaves.

8. Fronto, *Correspondence with Antoninus Pius* 8, 1

Fronto to Antoninus Pius Augustus. The actual facts bear witness, most sacred Emperor, that I have made every effort and that I was genuinely eager in my wish to perform my duties as proconsul: I stood out for my rights under the rules of the lot as long as I had a chance, and after another man was shown to have a prior claim because he had more children, I regarded the splendid province that remained to me in the same way as if it had been my own choice. I proceeded to make careful preparations for everything that had to do with equipping myself to deal with the province, so that the resources of my friends should put me in a better position to cope with the demanding business it involved. I summoned from home kinsmen and friends of known loyalty and integrity. I wrote to Alexandria to close friends telling them to make haste to Athens and wait for me there, and it was to those extremely learned men that I delegated the charge of my Greek correspondence. From Cilicia too I urged men of distinction to come (I have plenty of friends in that province, as I have constantly defended the interests of Cilicians before you, both communities and individuals). From Mauretania again I summoned to my side Julius Senex, a man who is extremely devoted to me and who is correspondingly dear, to enlist his help, not only because of his loyalty and willingness to work, but for his indefatigable energy as a soldier in flushing out brigands and crushing them.

Fronto ends his letter by explaining that in spite of abstemiousness and water-drinking, his health broke down and (temporarily or permanently: there is no evidence) ended his hopes of governing Asia, *c.* 157-8 (evidently he had hoped for Africa, where his 'home', Cirta, was). The letter naturally shows a prospective governor taking his duties seriously and doing what was expected of him. Fronto's plans to deal with brigandage shed light not only on his awareness of his personal limitations, but on conditions in the province (see **36, 42**). Fronto's friends in Alexandria included the historian Appian, for whom he asked an equestrian post from Pius (*Correspondence* 9).

The following inscription gives an idea of the retinue that might be found with a proconsul.

9. J.H. Oliver, *AJP* 87 (1966), 75ff.; P.R.C. Weaver, ibid. 457f.; from the Sanctuary of the Great Gods on Samothrace

(In Greek) Good Fortune! In the [kingship] of Aelius Epimachus, day [- - -] of the month of Munichion, (in Latin) in the consulship of [Orfitus] and Pudens, on the first of May, Publius Antius Orestes, son of Publius, proconsul of the province of Macedonia. Friends: Vibius Lupercianus, Septimius Tigranes, Flavius Theodorus (or Theodotus), Marcius Felix. Lictors: [- - -], Asconius, Vennus. Messengers: [- - -], Cleinia(s), Pompeianus. Devotees in prayer. Slaves of the said proconsul: [one name], Lydus, [two names, - - -]ius, Parthenopaeus, Dionysius, Abascantus, Lycorus, Zoticus, Zelotus, Phileus, Pam[- - -], Philo[-]sedius, Moschus. Soldiers: Numenius, ?Thracian archer, Pothinus, deputy centurion, [one name], ?Thracian archer, Junius, soldier on messenger duties, Cim[- - -]. Felix, home-bred slave of the Emperors; Onesimus, Vennus' ?attendant, Eutychus, slave of Septimius Tigranes, Pasiphilus, Atithreptio, [- - -]orius.

All, including the governor, had taken part in the mysteries celebrated at the sanctuary (as 'devotees in prayer') on 1 May, 165; the 'kingship' is a local magistracy, used for dating purposes.

The governor was accompanied by four friends, all Roman citizens; lictors to carry the rods and axes that symbolised his authority; messengers (the names of two of each survive); fifteen slaves; five auxiliary soldiers (none is a Roman citizen), one of them on special duty as a messenger, if Oliver's interpretation is correct, and one a junior officer; and an imperial slave precedes a list of servants belonging to the governor's companions, inserted as an afterthought.

The functions that a senator might perform in the course of service in the provinces are typically illustrated in the following inscription.

10. *ILS* 1070; Lambaesis

To Lucius Novius Crispinus Martialis Saturninus; designated to the
consulship; praetorian legate of Augustus in the province of Africa;
proconsul of Narbonensian Gaul; legate of Augustus of the First Legion,
Italica; legate of Augustus for the administration of justice in Asturia
and Callaecia; praetor; plebeian tribune; praetorian quaestor of the
province of Macedonia; military tribune of the Ninth Legion, Hispana;
member of the board of four charged with road maintenance; member of
the board of six in charge of the Roman knights; from the veterans of
the Third Legion, Augustan, who entered military service during the
consulships of Glabrio and Torquatus and also during those of Asiaticus
(for the second time) and Aquilinus.

The monument puts Saturninus' highest distinction, the consulship of
150 which he was about to take up, at the head of the list. After
preliminary civilian offices held by senators, Saturninus had been one of
the six military tribunes of the Ninth Legion, in Britain or on the
Danube; as quaestor he spent a year as a financial officer in Macedonia;
two further domestic posts followed, the praetorship of about 139-40
qualifying him to go to north-west Spain (now pacified) as one of the
subordinate juridical officers mentioned in **7**, *c.* 141-3; command of a
legion took Saturninus to Lower Germany for another three years. The
annual post of proconsul of Gallia Narbonensis belongs to about 145-6;
from Gaul Saturninus passed to Africa as commander of the Third
Legion and with responsibility for the military zone, 146-50. It was while
he was there that veterans of his army, recruited in the years 124-5,
erected the stone in the legionary camp to honour him.

Saturninus had seen service in six provinces for about a dozen years
and was a man of considerable experience when he came to the
consulship and qualified for Asia, Africa or one of the imperial consular
legateships. A few men were experienced beyond the average, such as
Aulus Caecina, Germanicus' legate in Gaul, who boasted of more than
forty years' service abroad (Tacitus, *Annals* 3, 33, 1, in **20**); others are
less so; Pliny the Younger is not known to have spent more than the
single season of his military service on official duties in any province
before he went to Bithynia; even for consular legateships in provinces
with several legions the qualifications required (beyond the trust of the
Emperor) were of the broadest (Campbell 1975 (**3**)).

There were equestrian as well as senatorial governors (see **4f.**). At the
head comes the prefect of Egypt, whose powers were equivalent to those
of proconsuls and who was charged with one of Rome's chief granaries.
The other prefects or, as these men were called from Claudius' time
onwards, 'praesidial' procurators, were in control of areas that might
prove intransigent but which were too small to require the attention of a

consular or praetorian legate. Such were Judaea (see **60** for its annexation in 6), Mauretania Tingitana (**153**) and Caesariensis (the early forties); and Thrace (**15**, annexed in 46). These prefectures were a natural extension of military service; others, of individual tribes or communities within a province, were part of it.

11. Smallwood, *Gaius-Nero*, 258; bronze from Iulium Carnicum, Venetia

To Gaius Baebius Atticus, son of Publius, of the Claudian Tribe; duovir with jurisdiction; leading centurion in the Fifth Legion, Macedonica; prefect of the communities of Moesia and Treballia; prefect of the communities of the Maritime Alps; military tribune in the Eighth Cohort of the Praetorian Guard; leading centurion for the second time; procurator of Tiberius Claudius Caesar Augustus Germanicus in Noricum: dedicated by the community of Saevates and Laianci.

Atticus began his military service (for his duovirate, or municipal magistracy, see on **25**) a step below equestrian rank, as leading centurion in a legion stationed at Oescus on the Danube. He was then given charge of certain communities in the hinterland of the province, south of the river; pacified in the reign of Augustus, they still required special supervision. Next, Atticus was transferred to the western side of the Alps to do a similar job of work. Service in the Praetorian Guard at Rome followed, and a second term as leading centurion, after which he obtained a real governorship of a province as a praesidial procurator. He is the first known governor of the former dependent kingdom of Noricum and the only one not to have had previous administrative experience as a procurator (cf. **15**). But all Atticus' service except his term with the Praetorian Guard had been in the Alpine or Danubian regions and his home town was not far distant. He had the experience to deal with the Celtic-speaking population and to commmand the garrison of auxiliaries. The administration of justice and securing of the revenue were also his responsibility and on a smaller scale had probably been part of his duties in dealing with the tribes on the Danube.

The Saevates and Laianci in the south-west of Noricum were communities probably attached to the municipality of Aguntum for administrative purposes but still aware of their separate identity (see G. Alföldy, *Noricum* (London, 1974), 96f.; and cf. **24f.**).

The same technique of supervision by a kind of 'resident' could be applied in a very different part of the Empire.

12. *ILS* 2721; from Comum, Cisalpine Gaul

Lucius Calpurnius Fabatus, son of Lucius, of the Oufentina Tribe:

member of the board of six; member of the board of four with jurisdiction; prefect of engineers; twice military tribune with the Twenty-First Legion, Rapax; prefect of the Seventh Cohort of Lusitanians and of the six tribes of Gaetulians in Numidia; priest of the deified Augustus; patron of the municipality: erected in accordance with his will.

After spells as military tribune in Germany, Fabatus commanded a unit of auxiliary troops in Africa, at the same time supervising the nomad tribes (see **3**). Control by prefect continued: *ILS* 9195.

The Emperors, as heirs of their relatives, their predecessors and many private citizens, acquired enormous wealth, much of it in land (cf. **48, 54, 73, 111, 221**). The power of the owner and the extent of the properties gave the manager effective standing and powers that came to be recognised in public law (**53n.**). Some estates were administered like small principalities.

13. Smallwood, *Gaius-Nero* 255; from Teate Marrucinorum, Italy

To Tiberius Caesar Augustus, son of the deified Augustus; Supreme Pontiff; in his thirty-eighth year of tribunician power; five times consul: dedicated in accordance with the will of Marcus Pulfennius, son of Sextus, of the Arnensis Tribe, centurion of the Sixth Legion, Ferrata, by Gaius Herennius Capito, son of Gaius, of the Arnensian Tribe; military tribune for three terms; prefect of a squadron of auxiliary cavalry; prefect of troops on the retirement list; procurator of Julia Augusta; of Tiberius Caesar Augustus; of Gaius Caesar Augustus Germanicus: ten pounds of silver.

After military service Capito acted as manager of an estate consisting of Jamnia and other districts which had been bequeathed to Augustus' wife by Salome, sister of Herod the Great (Josephus, *Antiquities of the Jews* 18, 31); it had passed to her son Tiberius and his successor Gaius, with Capito in charge of it for at least the period 29-37. In 35 or 36 Capito sent troops in pursuit of the future King Agrippa I of Judaea, who was in debt to the imperial family: perhaps he borrowed them from the procurator of Judaea, or he may have had some of his own (Josephus, ibid., 158). Even in the province of Asia a procurator of the Emperor's private estates had taken it on himself to commandeer the proconsul's troops (Tacitus, *Annals*, 4, 15, 3ff.); in 53 men with his job were specifically granted powers of jurisdiction in cases involving the Emperor's property (Tacitus, *Annals* 12, 60).

Another kind of procurator governed no territory but was engaged to manage the revenues in imperial provinces and to supply the troops there (**7, 91**); the first of these functions was equivalent to those of quaestors in senatorial provinces (**6, 10**).

14. EJ 224; Superaequum of the Paelignians, Italy

Quintus Octavius Sagitta, son of Lucius, grandson of Gaius, great-grandson of Lucius, of the Sergian Tribe; three times quinquennial duovir with jurisdiction; prefect of engineers; prefect of cavalry; military tribune elected by the people; procurator of Caesar Augustus among the tribes of the Vindalicians, Raetians, and in the Vallis Poenina for four years, in the province of Spain for ten, and in Syria for two.

Sagitta's monument was set up in his home town before Augustus' death. He may have embarked on his career as a tax collector in the Alps very soon after the areas named were subdued in 16-15 BC; he may even have had the difficult task of imposing the new system on the Alpine tribes. The Vindalicians lived in the area south-west of present-day Augsburg, and the Raetians gave their name to a new province, still under a legate (EJ 241) but later to pass into the hands of an equestrian prefect (EJ 244); and the Vallis Poenina was the Valais, including the Great St Bernard Pass. Perhaps as early as 12 BC, if he held his posts without interruption, Sagitta passed to the Iberian peninsula. How much of it concerned him is not clear from the document; in any case the boundaries of provinces did not always coincide with the limits of a procurator's activities: perhaps the entirety, perhaps only one or both of the imperial provinces. In his last post, in Syria, Sagitta would have been in control of revenue, of the Emperor's property and of supplying the legions in a province of first-class importance.

The following document, which belongs to a much later period, the reign of Trajan, shows how an equestrian official might pass from one kind of function to another, each of increasing responsibility.

15. Smallwood, *Nerva-Hadrian*, 277; from Reate in Italy

To [Publius] Prifernius Paetus Memmius Apollinaris, son of Publius, of the Quirina Tribe; member of the quinquennial board of four with jurisdiction; master of the youth; prefect of the Third Cohort of Breucians; military tribune of the Tenth Legion, Gemina; prefect of the First Squadron of Asturians; awarded the Untipped Lance, Banner and Mural Crown by the Emperor Trajan on the Dacian campaign; procurator of the province of Sicily; procurator of the province of Lusitania; procurator of the five per cent inheritance tax; procurator of the province of Thrace; procurator of the province of Noricum; set up by Publius Memmius Apollinaris, son of Publius, of the Quirina Tribe, to his devoted father.

The distinction of Prifernius' service in Trajan's first Dacian War of 102 speeded up his later career. As procurator in Sicily he was in charge of the Emperor's estates, in Lusitania of state revenues as well; after another year spent supervising the collection of the tax that fed the military Treasury (74), Prifernius became governor of Thrace; as such he will also have been in charge of the collection of revenues, so his previous experience will not have gone to waste. But this difficult province was handed over to a senatorial legate in 106, after the final victory over the Dacians, and Prifernius proceeded as governor to the peaceful and well established province of Noricum (cf. 11).

So much for the penetration of Roman governmental personnel into the fabric of the Empire. It did not go far; and Rome obviously needed a vast infrastructure of loyal communities and individuals to work her will for her; Prifernius, like Minucius Italus (79), was part of that too, as member of the 'board of four' in his municipality (they consist of two aediles and the duovirs: Mackie 1983, 33, n.11).

Areas deep in the Empire as well as at the periphery that were difficult to control, or not likely to yield much in the way of taxation, or both, were often left in the hands of dependent rulers, who could be deposed or moved about as Rome wished, a practice that had developed out of Rome's high-handed treatment of Greek states and barbarian tribes in the period of her great expansion outside Italy, from the mid-third century to the end of the Republic. These rulers had no redress but depended on the goodwill, originally of the senate and those members of it who were their patrons, under the Principate of the ruling dynasty. They owed their appointment to known loyalty to Rome; estimated efficiency in keeping their subjects under control; friendship with the Emperor or his close kin; and bribes offered his servants.

16. Suetonius, *Deified Augustus*, 48

As to kingdoms that came into his possession by right of conquest, except for a few he either returned them to those from whom he had taken them or conferred them on other rulers. Allied kings too he united one with another by ties of kinship: he was very ready to bring about and foster individual ties of marriage and friendship, while he cared for them as a whole as integral parts of the Empire: he used to appoint guardians to those who were under age or of unsound mind until they came to maturity or recovered their reason; and the children of very many of them he educated and brought up alongside his own.

Augustus could not allow Cleopatra's Egypt to survive, but the important dependencies of Galatia and Cappadocia were continued until the deaths of their rulers Amyntas and Archelaus (25 BC and AD 17); Herod of Judaea was helped by his enmity to Cleopatra and in 4 BC was succeeded in part of his kingdom by his son (another Archelaus), who proved unsatisfactory; Juba II, son of a king of Numidia deposed by Julius Caesar, was given Mauretania in 25 BC; each region had its problems (**53**). Marriage alliances linked Archelaus to Herod and Juba, and among others educated at Rome the future King Agrippa I (see **13n.**) was brought up with Tiberius' grandson Drusus Caesar. The Emperors were creating an interrelated network of potential rulers who would be available when necessary and thoroughly loyal to the Caesars. (The reference to client kings out of their minds is presumably to Archelaus of Cappadocia, Cassius Dio, *Roman History*, 57, 17, 3f.; he led a stormy life and was on trial at Rome when he died.)

On the conditions that made it advantageous to grant an area to a dependent king Strabo is informative.

17. Strabo, *Geography* 14, 5, 6, p. 671

The region (Rough Cilicia) was made by nature for brigandage and piracy. . . , and with a view to all that it was thought that the district should be under kings rather than subject to Roman governors who were sent out to administer justice, who were not going to be everywhere at once, nor with an armed force. And so Archelaus in addition to Cappadocia took Rough Cilicia.

Some dependencies were tiny enclaves within provinces, kept on out of inertia or because they provided an opportunity of dispensing patronage. The position of all client dynasts was precarious in every sense; many had turbulent pasts to live down.

18. Strabo, *Geography* 12, 8, 8f., p. 574f.

The outlying areas of Olympus, then, are well populated, but the heights are covered with prodigious thickets and defensible positions well adapted to sheltering brigands. Petty chieftains often set themselves up there, too, who can subsist for a good length of time, such as Cleon, the brigand chief of our own day. (9) This man came from Gordiucome, a place which he later built up, turned into a city, and called by the name of Juliopolis. But for his robber camp and base of operations he originally used the strongest of these positions, which was called Callydion. He proved useful to Antony, descending on the men who were collecting money for Labienus during the time when he was in control of Asia Minor, and hindering their operations. In the Actium campaign, however, he abandoned Antony and went over to Caesar's commanders. The price he got was higher than he deserved: he added what he received from Caesar to what he had already been given by Antony, so that instead of being a brigand he set himself up in the guise of a dynast. He became priest of the Mysian deity of Zeus Abrettenos, but also held as subject a part of Morene, which is another district of Mysia, and finally he also took over the priesthood of Comana in

Pontus. He arrived there and came to the end of his life within the space of a month (p. 575): an acute disease carried him off, whether it simply happened to strike him down as a result of over-eating or whether, as the inhabitants of the temple land said, it was due to divine anger. The temple precinct is where the priest and priestess have their dwelling: apart from other forms of ritual purity the precinct is most distinctly kept from being defiled by the consumption of pig meat. This goes for the whole city, and no pig is as much as brought into it. But Cleon gave a prime demonstration of his brigand mentality as soon as he first entered the place by infringing this custom. It was as if he came to profane the rites, not to be their minister.

Temple states evidently required special treatment. Cleon's successes over Labienus belonged to the years 40-38 BC, when the latter overran Asia Minor in the Republican cause (but with the help of the Parthians).

There was work for dependent dynasts in the west as well.

19. EJ 166; on the arch of Susa near the summit of the Cénis Pass

To Imperator Caesar Augustus, son of the deified Caesar, Supreme Pontiff, in his fifteenth year of tribunician power, hailed imperator for the thirteenth time: dedicated by Marcus Julius Cottius, son of King Donnus, prefect of the communities listed below (the name of 14 Alpine tribes follow) and by the communities that were in his charge as prefect.

The command of Julius Cottius along the cols of Mont Genèvre and Mont Cénis was designed to keep lines of communication in one pair of hands after Augustus' conquest of the Alps (C.M. Wells, *The German Policy of Augustus* (Oxford, 1972), 71). For Cottius and his son Donnus (13-44) the former kingship was converted into a prefecture like that of Baebius Atticus (**11**). The tribes under Cottius had mostly accepted Roman rule and so were favourably treated (Pliny, *Natural History*, 3, 138), but six of those on this roster of 9-8 BC are also included in a contemporary list of tribes conquered by Augustus (EJ 40). The energy shown by King Donnus in building roads over the Alps was still remembered in the fourth century (Ammianus Marcellinus, *History*, 15, 10). Claudius restored the title of king to Donnus' son Cottius II (44-63) and his realm was enlarged (Cassius Dio, *Roman History* 60, 24, 4). The achievements of the dynasty made it possible for Nero on Cottius' death to take over the kingdom as a procuratorial province, the Cottian Alps (Suetonius, *Nero* 18): successful dependent kingdoms were self-defeating. (For posterity of client rulers, see **215**.)

In Britain the most successful ruler was Tiberius Claudius Cogidubnus; but it is no longer to be believed that Cogidubnus was granted the senatorial title of legate.

20. Smallwood, *Gaius-Nero* 197, with J.E. Bogaers, Britannia 10 (1979), 243ff. and Pl. 9ff.; Noviomagus, Britain

The temple was dedicated to Neptune and Minerva for the welfare of the Divine House on the authority of Tiberius Claudius Cogidubnus, High King of Britain, by the guild of smiths and its members out of their own resources, [- - -]ens the son of Pudentinus providing the site from his own purse.

Tacitus, *Agricola* 14, 2, notices the long loyalty of Cogidubnus to his Roman masters, but the beginning and end of his reign, the extent of his kingdom, his function in the province and the meaning of his title remain matters of discussion. He may have been a member of the ruling family of the Atrebates of Berkshire and Hampshire whose king Verica had been driven by encroachments of the Catuvellauni to flee to Rome and so provided Claudius with a pretext for invading in 43. The restoration of the kingdom, its capital at Noviomagus, with a palace for the ruler at Fishbourne, gave proof of Roman good faith. Cogidubnus may have claimed the more grandiloquent title on being given charge of additional tribes (after the revolt of 48 or of 60? Or for supporting Vespasian's bid for power in 69? Barrett, *Britannia* 10 (1979), 227ff. surveys the possibilities).

Some areas were explicitly styled free of direct rule. The Lycian federation of cities was allowed its freedom until 43 (**149**) and again for a brief period later; Nero freed Achaea, and it too was reduced to provincial status once again by Vespasian (Suetonius, *Deified Vespasian* 8, 4).

21. Strabo, *Geography* 14, 3, 2f., p. 664f.

But the Lycians continued to show such political skill and discretion in their way of life that while the Cilicians won successes that gave them control of the sea as far as Italy, they still remained unmoved by the prospect of any ill-gotten gains but kept within the established administrative confines of the Lycian federation. (3) There are twenty-three cities with a vote. They assemble from each city at a common council centre, choosing whatever city suits them. The largest of the cities each commands three votes, the middle-sized two, and the rest one. (p. 665) They pay contributions and perform other financial services in the same proportion. . . . In the council the Lyciarch is chosen first, then the other authorities of the federation. Common courts are also appointed, and there was a time when they used to deliberate on peace, war and alliances. It is no longer to be expected that this should be so; these things are of necessity in the hands of the Romans, unless they have made an exception, or if it is in their interest. Jurymen and magistrates likewise are chosen in the same way from each city in proportion to the number of votes they have. And so their excellent form of government has brought them continued freedom under the Romans, and they enjoy the privileges of their forefathers.

Freedom was a privilege allowed intermittently since Republican times to individual cities (**4**; see **119**). For them even less than for areas like Achaea and Lycia did it mean independence, as Dr Mackie points out. Sometimes it was guaranteed by a treaty — which the Romans could tear up.

22. Suetonius, *Deified Augustus* 47, 2

Certain cities which enjoyed treaty rights but which abused their autonomy to the point of imminent disaster he deprived of their freedom.

Freedom allowed the cities jurisdiction over Roman citizens and it was the deaths of such that sometimes occasioned its loss, as with Lycia in 43 (**149**). At best free cities were exempt from direct taxation, but unless they had been given special additional privileges they had to perform the financial offices expected by Rome of her friends (see R. Bernhardt, *Historia* 29 (1980), 190ff.). The Lycian federation thought it worthwhile to set up a cult of the members of the imperial family before it lost its freedom (*IGR* 3, 474). The status of cities was important to them for other than financial reasons: they carried on their relations with the suzerain on the dignified basis of diplomacy (see, e.g., **115**); for Rome what mattered was the running of the Empire, by local authorities of whatever status.

So important were the cities in tax-collecting, maintenance of law and order and the upkeep of roads that, like the Emperor, they appear in every section of this book. Here it is enough to illustrate the encouragement Rome's rulers gave to city development; other relevant passages are to be found elsewhere, because the spread of city life in areas new to Roman rule had other purposes: those of reconciling their inhabitants to the suzerain and of fostering a form of government that the Romans knew from Greece and from their own experience (see **40**, **147** and **153**).

The second century sophist Aelius Aristides, intent on telling the Romans what they wanted to hear, informed them in his *Oration* 26, the *Panegyric on Rome*, 94, that the whole world was full of cities, founded, developed and improved by them. The policy may still be seen being pursued perhaps as much as a century and a half after that speech in a letter from unidentified Emperors to a governor.

23. *ILS* 6090; from Tymandus in Pisidia

[- - -] thoroughly [- - -] to the people of Tymandus likewise [- - -] to our knowledge [- - -] your [- - -] has brought, we have observed the exceptional earnestness, the intense enthusiasm shown by the people of Tymandus, dearest Lepidus, in their aspiration to attain at our instance the rights and status of a city. And so, since it is inherent in our nature to increase the standing and number of cities throughout our entire world, and since we see that their desire to receive the title and enhanced dignity of a city is exceptional (the said people giving the most serious undertaking that the supply of city councillors from among them will prove to be adequate), we have thought it proper to consent.

Consequently we wish you to see that you urge the said people of Tymandus, now they have attained their earnest desire, to strive alongside all our other cities faithfully to fulfil those duties which it is incumbent upon them to acknowledge, now that they have obtained the rights of a city.

However, in order that, along with other cities which have the right of assembling in council, formulating a decision and performing all the other actions which have been made their legal right, that same city too may be able to act in accordance with our grant, they will have to elect magistrates too and aediles likewise, as well as quaestors, and take any other actions that may be necessary. It will be appropriate for this same constitutional procedure to be maintained in perpetuity, provided that the city deserves it. In the meantime, however, it will be your duty to enrol members of the city council to the number of fifty. The immortal gods will grant in their benevolence that their resources increase and that a more numerous supply of councillors may be secured.

In the mid-second century the Tymandeni had been organised as a village, although by then it had not the normal village elders, but its own magistrates, the 'generals' (*strategi*, *IGR*, 3, 311). The Emperors' grant now raised Tymandus to the status of a real Greek city, with council and magistrates of the standard type (the Emperors use Latin equivalents: for the actual terms in use see, e.g., **42**), though with no additional rights or exemptions in relation to the central government. In spite of the Emperors' evident fears (cf. **217ff.**), Tymandus kept its status and appears as a city in the sixth-century list of Hierocles.

The variety of communities that might exist side by side is shown by a passage dealing with Narbonensian Gaul.

24. Strabo, *Geography* 4, 1, 11f. p. 186f.

There was a time when the Allobroges used to put many tens of thousands of troops into the field, but now they farm the plains and

Alpine valleys. Some of them live in villages, but those who have most to show for themselves live in Vienna (i.e. Vienne). It used to be a village but was called the tribal capital all the same, and they have turned it into a city. Vienna is situated on the Rhône . . . (12) As to the territory that belongs to the other (i.e. western) bank of the river, Volcae called Arecomici occupy most of it. Narbo is spoken of as their port, but it would be more accurate to call it that of the rest of Gaul too, so far is it ahead of the rest in the number of those who use the trading station there. The Volcae border on the Rhône, with the Sallyes stretching parallel to them on the other side, and the Cavari too. It is the name of the Cavari that prevails, and that is used to denote all the barbarians in this region. Not that they are barbarians still: for the most part they have gone over to Roman ways in language and habits, and some of them in form of government as well. There are other tribes, small and insignificant, which march with the Arecomici as far as the Pyrenees. The capital of the Arecomici is Nemausus, which falls far short of Narbo in the numbers of foreigners and merchants in its population but outstrips it in native-born citizens: it has twenty-four villages belonging to it which are outstanding for the numbers of related tribesmen that they support. It also possesses what is known as Latin Right (p. 187), which means that those who have been deemed worthy of holding the offices of aedile or quaestor in Nemausus become Roman citizens. For this reason the tribe is also exempt from the jurisdiction of the governors of praetorian rank who come from Rome.

These Gauls were among those whose example of urbanisation the Britons were so eagerly to follow a century later (**147**), and they were of related stock (but for the pull of the tribe see **158**). Narbo had been a Roman colony since 118 BC, with veterans added in 45 BC. Vienna and Nemausus reached the status of Latin colonies (and consequent full Roman citizenship for their magistrates, as Strabo says) at the end of the Republic, when veterans settled in them; Vienna reached full Roman rights by a grant of Gaius Caligula. Strabo overestimates the informal independence that Latin status brought Nemausus: a Latin community simply seemed more reliable to the Romans (see Mackie 1983, 102). Both cities had been provided with town walls by Augustus in 16-15 BC, and both covered more than 200 ha, more than twice the area of Narbo.

Villages subject to neighbouring cities are found elsewhere in Narbonensis, as well as further afield (for another arrangement, see **142**).

25. *ILS* 6761; Nicaea, Narbonensis

To Gaius Memmius Macrinus, quaestor and duovir at Massilia; quinquennial duovir and prefect representing the quinquennial duovir;

agonothete; superintendant of the people of Nicaea; from his friends.

Nicaea was founded by the Greek city of Massilia and, as Strabo remarks (*Geography* 4, 1, 9, p. 184), remained under Massiliote control under the Empire. Macrinus held the regular offices at Massilia, which enjoyed the privilege of treaty rights with Rome: the financial post of the quaestorship and that of the supreme magistracy there, the duovirate modelled on the two-man Roman consulship; in its five-yearly form, that of the quinquennial duovirate, it was particularly honourable and carried with it the task of keeping the roll of councillors up to date, as well as the list of citizens (like the Roman censors). Macrinus both held this office and acted as representative of an absentee holder. The agonothete, or presenter of Greek games, is a rarity in the west, and due to the influence of Massilia. Also Greek is Macrinus' title of 'superintendant' of the Nicaeans (the word gives us the English 'bishop').

The municipal offices found at Massilia, or posts closely related to them, have occurred in earlier documents, held by equestrian officials (**11f.**, **14f.**; see also **86**). The tenure of these posts by men involved in Roman administration reveals one form of link between the two levels of government.

Further, the standardisation (cf. also **23** and **153**) shows Rome and the cities of Italy imitated in the provinces. Only in her colonies did some impose a constitutional blueprint; municipalities raised from townships or conglomerations of villages to that rank in recognition of standing, achievements, loyalty or the presence of a high proportion of Roman citizens among their inhabitants could all the same organise themselves along well-established lines, obtaining a charter from the Roman government which may not have been adequate as a detailed guide to constitutional procedure but was a symbol of their privileged status (Mackie 1983, 101 and 220ff.). From Spain we already possess part of the charters of the triumviral colony of Urso (*ILS* 6087) and of two Flavian municipalities. Malaca and Salpensa (MW 453) attained their status as part of a general grant of Latin rights (see **24n.**) made in Spain by Vespasian; the charters, which derive from a single Roman model, date from 82-4 (Domitian is not yet styled 'Germanicus').

26. MW 454 (51-63); bronze tablet from Malaca, Baetica

[- - -? Nomination of candidates.

51. If up to the day on which declarations of candidature] ought to be made, declaration has been made in the name of no-one, or in the name of fewer persons than are due to be elected, or if, out of the persons in whose name declaration has been made there are fewer eligible to stand at the elections under this law than are due to be elected, then that

person whose duty it is to hold the election is to post up in such a way that they may properly be read from ground level the same number of names of persons who are entitled to seek the relevant office under this law as are lacking to complete the total due to be elected under this law. Those whose names have been posted up in this way are, if they wish, to nominate in the presence of the person who is to hold the election one person each who is likewise qualified and they likewise who have then been nominated by those persons may, if they wish, nominate in the presence of the magistrate one person each, likewise qualified. And the magistrate before whom that nomination has been made is to post up the names of all those persons in such a way that they may properly be read from ground level; and he is to hold the election from among all of them likewise, just as if declaration had been made on their own account with a view to seeking election for office in accordance with this law by the day appointed and as if they had undertaken to seek office of their own accord without desisting from that purpose.

Holding of elections.

52. Of the duovirs currently in office and likewise of those who henceforth are duovirs in the municipality, it shall be whichever of the two is senior in age, or, if any cause shall intervene to make it impossible for him to hold the elections, then the other of the pair who under this law is to hold assemblies for the election of duovirs, likewise of aediles and quaestors and for the election of substitutes. And as the votes ought to be cast according to the arrangement of voting units provided for above, so he is to have the votes cast by ballot. And the persons who are elected by this method are to hold the office that they have obtained at the polls for one year or, if they have been elected in place of another, during the remaining part of that year.

Voting unit in which resident aliens are to cast their votes.

53. Whoever in that municipality shall hold assemblies for the election of duovirs, likewise of aediles and quaestors, is to draw one of the voting units by lot, in which resident aliens who possess Roman or Latin citizenship may cast their vote, and they are to have the opportunity to cast their votes in that voting unit.

Persons eligible to stand for election.

54. The person whose duty it is to hold elections is to see to it first that duovirs who are to preside with jurisdiction are elected from that class of freeborn persons stipulated and included in the terms of this law, then next in succession aediles and likewise quaestors from that class (etc.); provided that he does not take account at elections of the candidacy of any person seeking the duovirate who is less than 25 years of age, or who has held that office less than five years previously; likewise of any person standing for the aedileship or quaestorship who is less than 25 years of age or who is subject to any of those disabilities which, if he were a Roman citizen, would disqualify him from inclusion

in the body of councillors and those enrolled among them.

Conduct of voting.

55. The person holding the elections in accordance with this law is to summon the citizens of the municipality to give their votes in their voting units, in such a way that he summons all the units to the vote simultaneously, and that they give their vote by ballot each in its separate voting enclosure. He is to ensure likewise that at the ballot box of each voting unit there are three citizens of the municipality who are not members of that voting unit, who are to guard the votes and sort them, and he is to make sure before they do that they each swear that he will show good faith in counting and reporting the votes. Nor is he to prevent the candidates from stationing their own guards, one each at each ballot box. And those guards stationed by the person who holds the elections and likewise by the candidates are each to give his vote in that voting unit at whose ballot box he has been stationed as a guard, and their votes are to be equally valid and effective as if each of them had cast his vote in his own voting unit.

Case of candidates who obtain an equal number of votes.

56. As each man obtains a greater number of votes than his competitors in each voting unit, so the person holding those elections is to declare him ahead of the others as the successful elected candidate for that voting unit, until the required number has been completed. In a unit in which two or more candidates have the same number of votes he is to prefer and declare first elected a married man or one who counts as such to an unmarried man without children, if he does not count as married; a man with children to one without; one with more children to one with fewer; provided that two children lost after they have been given their name or one son lost after puberty, or daughter of marriageable age, are counted as one surviving. If two or more candidates have the same number of votes and are of the same condition, he is to cast their names into an urn and as each man's is drawn so he is to declare him elected ahead of the others.

Drawing of lots amongst the voting units; candidates who carry an equal number of voting units.

57. When the list of results of all the voting units has been reported, the person holding the elections under this law is to place the names of the voting units into an urn and draw the names of the several units from it, and as the name of each unit is drawn he is to order the men elected by it to be announced; and as each candidate in turn carries the majority of the total number of voting units, he is to declare him, as soon as he has taken oath according to this law and guaranteed public funds, a successfully elected candidate until there are as many magistrates as are due to be elected under this law. If two or more candidates carry the same number of voting units, he is to act in the same way as is provided for above for those who are equal in the number of votes cast for them,

and he is to declare each candidate elected first on the same principle.

Prevention of obstructions to the holding of elections.

58. No-one is to intervene or to do anything else to prevent the holding and completion of elections in the municipality under this law. Anyone who knowingly and wilfully acts otherwise to prevent them is to be liable for each offence to pay a fine of ten thousand sesterces to the citizens of the Flavian municipality of Malaca, and the right of bringing an action for that sum or concerning it, claiming it and suing for it is to be available to any citizen of the municipality who wishes and who is entitled to do so under this law.

Swearing in of candidates who have secured the majority of the total number of voting units.

59. As each of the candidates seeking election to the duovirate, aedileship or quaestorship wins the majority of the total number of voting units, before the person holding the elections declares that man a successfully elected candidate he is to cause him in public at an assembly to take an oath by Jupiter, the Deified Augustus, Claudius, and Vespasian Augustus and Titus Augustus and by the Genius of Imperator Domitian Augustus and by the gods of the household that he will perform those things which are incumbent upon him in accordance with this law, and that he neither has done nor knowingly and wilfully will do anything against this law.

Guarantee for the public funds of the citizens of the municipality by candidates for duovirate or quaestorship.

60. On the day on which the elections are held, before the voting takes place, at the discretion of the person holding those elections, each of the persons who seek election to the duovirate or the quaestorship in the municipality, and each of those besides who are brought by nomination into the same condition because declarations of candidature have been made in the name of fewer persons than are required, so that they are also to be voted on in accordance with this law, is to provide sureties to the public funds of the citizens of the municipality that the public monies of those citizens which they will be handling during their term of office shall be secured for them. If it appears that the guarantee afforded by those sureties is inadequate in that respect, the candidate is to pledge property in real estate at the discretion of the same person. And he is to receive sureties and property from these candidates in good faith, until a proper guarantee has been secured which he is satisfied to be a proper one. As to any of those persons on whom voting is due to take place at elections to the duovirate or quaestorship, if he is responsible for preventing proper guarantee being secured, the person holding the elections is not to take account of his candidature.

Co-optation of a patron.

61. No-one is to co-opt a patron for the citizens of the Flavian municipality of Malaca on behalf of the municipality or offer the position

to anyone without the authority of a decree passed by the majority of the city council, which decree shall be passed when not less than two thirds are present and give their vote by ballot on oath. Anyone who co-opts a patron for the citizens of the Flavian municipality of Malaca on behalf of the municipality by another method contrary to these provisions, or offers the position to anyone, is to be liable to pay the sum of ten thousand sesterces to the public treasury of the citizens of the Flavian municipality of Malaca, and a man co-opted patron or offered the position contrary to this law is not on that account to be a patron of the citizens of the Flavian municipality of Malaca.

Prohibition against demolition of buildings by any person who does not intend to replace them.

62. No-one in the town centre of the Flavian municipality of Malaca or in the built-up areas adjoining that centre is to unroof, pull down or procure the demolition of a building which he is not going to restore within the subsequent year, without a resolution of the councillors and those on the roll of the council taken when the majority of them are present. Any person who acts contrary to these provisions is to be liable to pay the citizens of the Flavian municipality of Malaca a sum equivalent to the value of the property, and the right of bringing an action for that sum or concerning it, claiming it and suing for it is to be available to any citizen of the municipality who wishes and who is entitled to do so under this law.

Public contracts, publication of the terms that govern them and registration in the municipal records.

63. Whoever presides as duovir with jurisidiction is to farm out local taxes, not only indirect but direct, or any other contract that it is required to lease out in the common name of the citizens of the municipality. He is to make sure that any contracts he makes, terms he specifies, sum paid for the contract, sureties accepted, properties offered in guarantee, pledged or mortgaged and persons accepted as assessors of the value of the property, are registered in the public records of the citizens of the municipality, and he is to have them publicly displayed for the entire remaining period of his year of office in such a way that they may properly be read from ground level, in whatever place the councillors and those enrolled on the council deem that they are to be posted.

The first surviving clauses (51-60) lay down electoral procedure modelled on that which prevailed at Rome until in 14 the populace were reduced to electing men pre-selected by the senate (Tacitus, *Annals* 1, 15, 1f.): the candidates are voted on by a number of voting units, whose results are declared in an order determined by lot. As each candidate carries a majority of the units he is declared elected to office. The order in which the choice of the voting units is declared is determined by lot, so that although it is not known how membership of the units was determined, wealth, residence and other considerations should have no consistent effect on election results. (At Rome it was not lot that determined the order in all elections.) The conditions used to break tied votes are based on the rules laid down in the Papian-Poppaean Law on marriage of 9 (see Tacitus, *Annals* 2, 51, 2). The voting units are also named after divisions of the Roman people (*curiae*), but divisions which had long since lost practical significance.

For the rights of resident aliens (53), see Mackie 1983, 44ff.; their contribution to a community may be seen from **153**.

The charter envisages the possibility that there will be too few candidates for the posts available (51 and 60); but that does not mean that it was thought likely (cf. **217ff.**); the legislator had to take all contingencies into account; equally the emphasis on the accountability of officials and concern with public funds (60, 64-9) is not to be taken as an indication of widespread dishonesty (cf. **70, 188f.**).

For the patron (61), who had no duties but was expected generally to look after the interests of the community, see Mackie 1983, 87 and 144 n.6, and **143ff**. The patron would be a man of standing, very often a senator, ex-governor of the province. The regulation is designed to prevent collusion between a corrupt patron and groups within the city (**172**); another precaution, attested at Urso, clause 130f., and imposed in 11 (Cassius Dio, *Roman History* 56, 25, 6) forbade appointment until six months after the governor had left office.

For the prohibition against demolishing buildings (62) see P. Garnsey in *Studies in Roman Property*, ed. M.I. Finley (Cambridge, 1976), 133ff.

Lastly in this structural survey comes an element intermediate between the city or other community and the Roman provincial administration: leagues of cities in the East, councils of leading men of the tribal communities in the West. Many of the former dated back to the Republic (**21, 119**), and developed as a means of coping with Hellenistic monarchies; whether or not some of the latter were developments of rudimentary assemblies already in existence and encouraged by the Romans (**121**), others wholly new creations (**120, 122f.**), they were equally instruments of empire. These councils, sometimes drawing representatives from a whole province, or from several, sometimes covering only part of a province, played no part in government, it is agreed: they had no legislative or executive power. But they affected government by making known the views of the leading men of the provinces (**159**), by disseminating decisions of general application made at Rome, by instituting proceedings against officials (**59f.**, cf. **172f.**) and by mediating between cities (**57**).

3

Force

Tranquillity for Italy, peaceful conditions in the provinces, the security of the Empire: these are listed by Julius Caesar as the basic achievements for a statesman (*Civil War* 3, 57, 4). The prime means of attaining them was the army, and the military tone of Roman power from the Emperor down to equestrian prefects is clear from the documents cited in the previous chapter, especially **2**, **3** and **17**. Whatever else a governor achieved in his term of office it was success in maintaining peace in his province (Pliny, *Letters* 10, 117), sometimes in advancing Roman power beyond it, that was recorded on monuments set up in his honour and that won him the insignia of a Triumph (the ceremony of the full Triumph had soon come to be reserved for the Emperor and his kinsmen).

27. Smallwood, *Gaius-Nero* 228 (MW 261); from Tibur near Rome

To Tiberius Plautius Silvanus Aelianus, son of Marcus, of the Aniensian Tribe; pontiff, priest of Augustus; member of the board of three for minting bronze, silver and gold; quaestor of Tiberius Caesar; legate of the Fifth Legion in Germany; urban praetor; legate on the personal staff of Claudius Caesar in Britain; consul; proconsul of Asia; praetorian legate of Moesia, into which he brought over more than a hundred thousand of the peoples from across the Danube to pay tribute, along with their wives, children and chieftains or kings; he put down an incipient movement of the Sarmatians, although he had sent a considerable portion of his army to take part in the invasion of Armenia; kings hitherto unknown or hostile to the Roman people he brought over to the river bank under his protection to pay homage to the Roman standards; to the kings of the Bastarnae and Roxolani he returned their sons, to the king of the Dacians his brothers, captured or carried off from the enemy; from some of them he received hostages; by which ?achievements he both assured the peaceful condition of the province and advanced? it, having removed the king of the Scyths from his siege of Chersonesus beyond the Dnieper. He was the first to support the grain supplies of the Roman people by means of a substantial measure of wheat from the province. When he had been recalled from his mission as governor of Spain in order to take up the prefecture of the City, and was holding the prefecture, the Senate honoured him with the award of triumphal honours on the motion of Imperator Caesar Augustus Vespasian, whose speech included the following words:

'His governorship of Moesia was such that the award of his triumphal honours ought not to have been left to me; but the fact is that his tenure of the Prefecture of the City during the delay has enhanced his claim to distinction.'

Imperator Caesar Augustus Vespasian made him consul for the second time while he held that same prefecture.

The monument, discussed most recently by P. Conde and R.D. Milns, *Historia* 32 (1983), 185ff., was found near the mausoleum of Silvanus' family, which produced the general who led Claudius' invasion of Britain in 43. Silvanus was consul in 45 and governor of Moesia *c.* 57 or 60 to 67. His method of bringing tribes on to Roman territory was well tried on the Rhine (Tacitus, *Germania* 28, 5) and Danube (Strabo, *Geography* 7, 3, 10, p. 303). The wheat he sent to Rome, perhaps after the fire of 64 (see Conde and Milns, ibid., 191), may have been grown by them, unless it came from the Chersonese and S. Russia. For the tribal movements that caused the problems dealt with by Silvanus, see Carroll and Milns. The Sarmatians were nomads from beyond the Don settled in two branches, Roxolani and Iazyges, respectively at the mouth of the Danube and between Pannonia and Dacia. This success against them fits 58 or 62, when legions were moved east; after losing the Fifth, Macedonian, in 62 Silvanus had only the Seventh, Claudian, and the Eighth, Augustan. The Bastarnae were a tribe of Germans who also lived at the Danube mouth, and the Scyths were nomads pushed west and into the Crimea by the Sarmatians; the help given Chersonesus was a measure of gun-boat diplomacy, connected perhaps with plans that Nero entertained for an expedition to the Caucasus (Pliny, *Natural History* 6, 40; Tacitus, *Histories* 1, 6; Suetonius, *Nero* 19, 2); certainly Rome was determined to control the Black Sea shores and the routes across it (cf. **35**).

Silvanus' claims were neglected by Tacitus, as they had been by Nero; they hinge on the phrase about the peaceful condition of the province, and what he 'advanced'. What was expected of a governor is clear enough, and it is worth remembering how it might look to the resistance: 'They make a desert and call it peace' (Calgacus rallying his men against the Roman advance into Scotland, Tacitus, *Agricola* 30, 6).

The probable numbers of the Roman armed forces of the Principate have been given in Chapter 1. Each legion had a paper strength of 5,120 men; non-citizen 'auxiliary' troops were in their own units of infantry, cavalry, or combined forces, each unit being of about 500 or 1,000: see Breeze and Dobson 1978, 148ff.

The most important commands might provide a governor with three or four legions; some equestrian provinces contained only auxiliary units, others were reinforced by detachments of legionaries; some provinces as we have seen were regarded as 'unarmed' (**4f.**).

Without going into details, Tacitus gives an account of the numbers of legions in each province in 23 (his figures allow for the temporary removal of one Pannonian legion to Africa).

28. Tacitus, *Annals* 4, 4, 4–5, 6

Next the old scheme of a trip to the provinces, which had often been used as a cover, was taken up again. The Emperor explained the reasons: the number of soldiers requiring discharge and the need to replenish the armies by holding levies. Volunteers for the army were hard to come by, he said, and those that did come forward were not reaching normal standards of courage and discipline, because it was for the most part penniless vagabonds who were taking to military service of their own accord. (5) He went on to give a brief review of the strength of the legions and the provinces under their protection. (6) I think that I too should give the same recital, and show the military resources of Rome in those days, the allied kings, and how much more restricted in size the Empire was.

(5, 1) Italy was in the care of two fleets stationed one on each of the seas on either side, at Misenum and Ravenna, and the neighbouring coast of Gaul in that of warships that Augustus had captured when he won the battle of Actium and sent to the town of Forum Iulii with a strong force of oarsmen. (2) Our main strength, however, was along the Rhine, where eight legions were stationed as a recourse against Germans and Gauls alike. The provinces of Spain, of which the conquest had recently been completed, were occupied by three.

(3) The peoples of Mauretania King Juba had received as the gift of the Roman People. (4) The rest of Africa was kept under control by two legions, and Egypt by the same number; then a vast sweep of country from Syria to the Euphrates by four legions; as neighbours they had Hiberian, Albanian and other kings, who are protected by our might from encroachments from outside. (5) Rhoemetalces and the children of Cotys held Thrace, and the legions the banks of the Danube, two in Pannonia, two in Moesia. The same number were stationed in Dalmatia, in positions to the rear of the others from which they could be summoned to their aid from no great distance, or to Italy if it suddenly needed help, though the city had a garrison of its own: three urban and nine praetorian cohorts raised for the most part in Etruria and Umbria or from the old Latin territory or colonies of ancient Roman foundation. (6) At strategic points in the provinces, however, were placed allied ships, squadrons of cavalry and auxiliary cohorts, more or less equivalent

to the legions in strength. But it has proved a tricky task to trace them: they were moved about from one place to another as occasion demanded, were sometimes increased in size and sometimes diminished.

In the following passage the forces are given as they were in 5, with notes on changes that had taken place between then and the writer's own day.

29. Cassius Dio, *Roman History* 55, 23, 2-24, 8; Greek

At that time twenty-three legions of citizen soldiers (or, on other accounts, twenty-five) were maintained. At the present time only nineteen of them remain: the Second, Augustan, quartered in Upper Britain; three legions numbered the Third, the Gallic, stationed in Phoenicia, the Cyrenaican, stationed in Arabia; the Augustan, in Numidia; (3) the Fourth, Scythian, in Syria; the Fifth, Macedonian, in Dacia; two legions numbered the Sixth, of which one, the Victrix, is stationed in Lower Britain, the other, Ferrata, in Judaea; the Seventh, usually named Claudian, in Upper Moesia; the Eighth, Augustan, which is in Upper Germany; (4) and the two Legions, numbered the Tenth, one, the Gemina, in Upper Pannonia, the other in Judaea; the Eleventh in Lower Moesia, the Claudian (two legions are so called from the Emperor Claudius, because they did not rise against him in the rebellion of Camillus); (5) the Twelfth, Fulminata, in Cappadocia; the Thirteenth, Gemina, in Dacia; the Fourteenth, Gemina, in Upper Pannonia; the Fifteenth, Apollinaris, in Cappadocia; (6) the Twentieth, which bears the titles Valeria Victrix and is stationed in Upper Britain. These last are troops which in my opinion Augustus took over and kept in being, along with those that are called the Twenty-second Legion and are quartered in Upper Germany, even though they were not by any means universally known by the name Valeria and do not use this title any more. (7) These are the surviving Augustan legions. As to the rest, some have been disbanded altogether, while some have been merged with other legions by Augustus himself or by other Emperors, which is how they have come to bear the name Gemina.

(24, 1) Seeing that I have been led into giving an account of the legions, I shall now tell of the others as well, those of the present day, roughly how they were enrolled by subsequent emperors, so that it will all be written out in one section and easily available to anyone who wants any information about them. (2) It was Nero who organised the First Legion, the one called Italica, which has quarters in Lower Moesia, Galba the First, Adiutrix, which is in Lower Pannonia, (3) and the Seventh, Gemina, in Spain; Vespasian the Second, Adiutrix, in Lower Pannonia, and the Fourth, Flavian, in Upper Moesia and the Sixteenth, Flavian, in Syria; Domitian the First, Minervian, in Lower Germany,

Trajan the Second, Egyptian, and the Third, Germanica, (4) both of which he also called after himself; Marcus Aurelius the Second in Noricum and the Third in Raetia, both of which are called Italian; Severus the legions called Parthian, the First and the Third in Mesopotamia and the intervening Second in Italy.

(5) That is the present number of legions of troops on the regular lists apart from urban troops and the praetorian guard, but at that time, under Augustus, there were being maintained those I have mentioned (whether they totalled twenty-three or twenty-five) along with allied troops, infantry, cavalry and sailors, whatever the total was (I am unable to give the exact figure). (6) There were also the bodyguard, consisting of ten thousand men and organised in ten sections, (7) and picked horsemen from abroad bearing the name Batavians after the island in the Rhine, because the Batavians are first class horsemen. (8) I am unable, however, to give their exact number, any more than I can that of the veterans recalled to the colours. (These are the men that Augustus began to deploy from the time when he recalled to the colours against Antony the men who had served with his father and kept them on; even now they are a separate corps and carry batons, like centurions.)

The names of the legions and their origins are discussed by Webster 1974, 109ff. For veterans and men recalled to the colours after service, see, e.g., **10** and **13**.

The monument below gives a list of legions as they were in the reigns of Marcus Aurelius-Septimius Severus, arranged, with the exception of the latest additions, in geographical order from west to east.

30. *ILS* 2288; on two columns, one preserved in the Vatican Museum

Names of the Legions

*Second Augustan	Second, Adiutrix	*Fourth, Scythian
Sixth, Victrix	Fourth, Flavian	Sixteenth, Flavian
*Twentieth, Victrix	*Seventh, Claudian	*Sixth, Ferrata
Eighth, Augustan	First, Italian	*Tenth, Fretensis
*Twenty-second, Primigenia	Fifth, Macedonian	*Third, Cyrenaican
First, Minervian	*Eleventh, Claudian	Second, Trajanic
Thirtieth, Ulpian	*Thirteenth, Gemina	*Third, Augustan
First, Adiutrix	*Twelfth, Fulminata	Seventh, Gemina
Tenth, Gemina	Fifteenth, Apollinaris	Second, Italian
Fourteenth, Gemina	Third, Gallic	Third, Italian
First, Parthian	Second, Parthian	Third, Parthian

The distribution is three legions in Britain; two in Upper Germany,

two in Lower; three in Upper Pannonia, one in Lower; two in Upper
Moesia, three in Lower; one in Dacia; two in Cappadocia; three in
Syria; two in Judaea; one each in Arabia, Egypt, Numidia and Spain.
For Marcus Aurelius' two 'Italian' legions and the 'Parthian' of
Septimius Severus, added out of geographical order, see **29**.

Legions still in the same area (e.g. Germany, eastern frontier) if not
in the same province, as they were at the end of Nero's reign are marked
with an asterisk. Considering that of the legions on the list 13 were
raised after Nero's reign, there seems to be a considerable degree of
stability.

Comparison with Tacitus' list for 23 (**28**) shows that the German
armies had lost four legions, Spain two, Syria and Egypt one each. Of
armed provinces not yet in existence in 23, Britain still claimed a
startling three legions (cf. **1**). Judaea after its revolts had reached a total
of two, the same as Septimius Severus' own newly organised province of
Mesopotamia. But the most startling change is the concatenation of
legions along the Danubian provinces: it is clear where Rome was feeling
the pressure; and in the East the two legions in Cappadocia, stationed
there by Vespasian, illustrate the increased importance attached to N.
Asia Minor, partly as a continuation of the Danubian defences.

The lists give no idea of the mobility of legions within their allotted
sphere of operations even after the wide-ranging movement of legions
under Augustus had slowed down under his immediate successor (the
Ninth, Hispana, was temporarily transferred to Africa from Pannonia,
20-3), not to be resumed except in years of crisis and revolution such as
68-70. Even when legions were permanently stationed in stone-built
fortresses, as they came to be on the Rhine from Claudius' time
onwards, their function in the early Principate was that of a mobile
striking force, and so effective at a distance (Luttwak 1976, 1ff.). If this
was a virtue, as Luttwak stresses, it was imposed by necessity: the
striking power of each legion had to be made the most of because Rome
could not afford to support more (cf. **74**); note the complaint of Silvanus
that his achievements were won with depleted resources (**27**), and
Tiberius' difficulty over recruiting (**28**).

Legions were not always deployed as complete units: detachments
were increasingly used in the second century.

31. *ILS* 1111; from the temple of Aesculapius, Lambaesis, Numidia

[Aulus] Julius Pompilius Piso Titus Vib[ius ?Varus Laevillus] Bereni-
cianus, son of Aulus, of the Cornelian Tribe; member of the judicial
board of ten; [military] tri[bune of the Thirteenth Legion, Gemina],
and likewise of the Fifteenth, Apollinaris; urban quaestor; raised [to the
rank of ex-tribune of the people; praetor] supported for election by the
Emperors; legionary legate of the Thirteenth Legion, [Gemina, and

likewise of the Fourth, Flavian]; placed in charge of the First Legion, Italian, and the Fourth [Flavian, with all their] auxiliary [forces] and full capital disciplinary powers; [praetorian legate] of the Emperors [of the Third Legion, Augustan]; designated to the consulship.

Pompilius served at Apulum and in Cappadocia as military tribune, and reached the praetorship before 169. He returned to the Thirteenth as its commander and then took on the Fourth, which was stationed at Singidunum in Upper Moesia. Then, with the powers of a governor, he commanded combined detachments of that legion and the First, which was stationed at Novae in Lower Moesia, perhaps to take part in hostilities in Dacia a little after 170, perhaps to administer newly occupied Sarmatian territory (A. Birley, *Marcus Aurelius* (London, 1966), 242). As legate of the Third he was in control of the military zone in Africa, 176-7, probably remaining there until his consulship in 180.

Junior officers who were professional soldiers were kept on the move even when the legions had settled down into permanent fortresses; it was good for discipline.

32. Smallwood, *Nerva-Hadrian* 294; from Rome

Dedicated to Tiberius Claudius Vitalis, son of Tiberius, of the Galerian Tribe; he gave up his rank of Roman knight and accepted a centurionate in the Fifth Legion, [Macedonian]; was advanced from the Fifth Legion, Macedonian, to the [First] Legion, Italian; was awarded the Twisted Necklet, Armbands, Chestpiece, and Rampart Crown in the Dacian War; was advanced from the First Legion, Italian, to the First, Minervian; was again awarded the Twisted Necklet (etc.), in the Dacian War; was advanced from the First Legion, Minervian, to the Twentieth, Victrix; was likewise promoted in the same legion; and further advanced from the Twentieth Legion, Victrix, to the Ninth Legion, Hispana; was advanced from the Ninth Legion, Hispana, to the Seventh Legion, Claudian, Devoted and Faithful; was further advanced in the same legion; served in the second cohort as the fourth-ranking centurion for eleven years; lived to the age of forty-one.

For the advancement of centurions through the six positions in each of the ten cohorts of a legion, see Parker 1958, 277ff., with diagram, and Webster 1974, 117ff.

Vitalis' first two postings were with legions in Lower Moesia; and the First, Minervian, with which he held his third, left Lower Germany for the Danube in 101-2 and took part in the conquest of Dacia. Next, Vitalis served with two British legions, returning to Upper Moesia for his last posting. His rapid promotion through his first offices was due to good social standing as well as to gallantry. The next subject must have begun service as a common soldier; he had to be more patient.

33. *ILS* 2653; from Lambaesis; the monument shows the bust of a man holding a book

To the shades of Titus Flavius Virilis; centurion of the Second Legion, Augustan; the Twentieth, Valeria Victrix; then Sixth, Victrix; the Twentieth, Valeria Victrix; the Third, Augustan; the Third, Parthian Severan, as the sixth-ranking centurion of the ninth cohort. He lived seventy years, served forty-five seasons. Lollia Bodicca his wife and Flavius Victor and Flavius Victorinus his sons, who were his heirs, had the monument erected at a cost of 1,200 sesterces.

Virilis had risen only to the second lowest cohort in the legion after forty-five years' service. He served in all the British legions (and must have met his wife in Britain, to judge by her name); then he was posted to Numidia and transferred from the Third, Augustan, to the newly created Third, Parthian.

The auxiliary troops that the literary sources found so hard to trace (**28f.**) must have been almost equally elusive to the inhabitants of the provinces that they were protecting, so discreet was their presence in the countryside (Aelius Aristides, *Oration* 26, *Panegyric on Rome* 67a); but they were very widespread (cf. **152**) and of incomparable value in performing work that the legionary heavy infantry were unsuited to, as cavalry, archers, slingers, foot-patrols and scouts: Breeze and Dobson 1978, 151ff. There is no missing them on Hadrian's Wall.

34. Smallwood, *Nerva-Hadrian* 323(a); from Magna

Dedicated to the Augustan Good Fortune, for the welfare of Lucius Aelius Caesar at the prompting of a vision: Titus Flavius Secundus, prefect of the first cohort of Hamian Archers, discharged his vow gladly and deservedly.

The date is 136-7, and the Hamian Archers, who had been raised in Syria and continued as specialists to be recruited from there, were garrisoning the fort at Carvoran, to which they returned under Marcus Aurelius after an interval at Bar Hill during the reign of Antoninus Pius.

The cohort, though nominally of five hundred, was probably made up of six 'centuries' of 80 men, like the legionary cohort (**32f.**); it was one of a dozen such on the Wall in Hadrian's time, alongside seven cohorts nominally a thousand strong and three cavalry units (many of the cohorts had cavalry attached to them: see **85**); nearly 15,000 men in all.

These troops not only garrisoned the Wall: they had built it, and officers and men are found engaged in the planning and construction of military or primarily military works throughout the Roman Empire (**94ff.**).

The Roman navy was a junior service; its duties were mainly those of policing the seas and repressing piracy, escort work, occasionally of transporting troops up-river in Germany or across the Channel. Besides the fleets at Ravenna, Misenum and Forum Iulii (**38**), there were forces on the Channel, on the Rhine and Danube, near Antioch, at Alexandria and in the Black Sea.

35. EJ 227; Greek, from Ilium

The council and people honoured Titus Valerius Proculus, procurator of Drusus Caesar, who destroyed the pirate vessels in the Hellespont and kept the city in every respect free of burdens.

Proculus performed these services to Ilium during the years 17-20, when the Emperor's son Drusus was in overall control of the Balkans.

The peaceful condition of the provinces was not to be achieved only by dealing with military threats from outside. It was part of the army's function, and the greater part of most governors' function, to police areas already provincialised.

36. Ulpian, Duty of the Proconsul, Book 7, in *Digest* 1, 18, 13, Introduction

It is appropriate for a good governor who takes his duties seriously to see that the province under his control is kept quiet and peaceful. He will secure this without difficulty if he takes conscientious measures to make sure that the province is free from malefactors and that he hunts them out: he ought besides hunting out temple robbers, highway robbers, kidnappers and thieves, to inflict on each of them the penalty that he deserves and to punish people harbouring them; without them a robber cannot hide for very long.

The distinction between the criminals specified here and the religious fanatics, freedom fighters and so on who appear in Chapter 11 might sometimes be hard to draw. Certainly the position of the legions in the early Principate, especially of those in Syria, Spain and Egypt, shows that maintaining internal order was part of their work (see also **28** on the Rhine legions and **17** on client kings).

For very minor work such as the supervision of traffic through small cities, a single officer sufficed, with a few other ranks.

37. Pliny, *Letters* 10, 77

Gaius Pliny to the Emperor Trajan.

You have acted with the greatest foresight, my Lord, in instructing the distinguished senator Calpurnius Macer to send a legionary centurion to Byzantium. (2) Consider whether in your view the interests of the people of Juliopolis should be looked after in the same way. Although their city is extremely small, it has very heavy burdens to bear, and its comparative weakness means that damage inflicted on it is proportionately serious. (3) But the whole province will benefit from any help you give the people of Juliopolis: they stand at the head of the road leading into Bithynia and provide travel facilities for the vast numbers who pass through the city.

Juliopolis is the former Gordiucome (**18**), and Calpurnius Macer governor of the armed province of Moesia. Both Juliopolis and Byzantium were suffering from the transit of the military (cf. Tacitus, *Annals* 12, 62f., for an earlier complaint from Byzantium, and see below, **54** and **91**). Trajan refused Pliny's suggestion: it would form a precedent. Indeed, in the later Principate, officers were placed at staging posts of the imperial transport service (**69ff.**), especially, but not exclusively, in the eastern provinces.

38. *ILS* 9073; pedestal found at Rusicade, Numidia

To Jupiter Best and Greatest, I have fulfilled my vow, to the Genius of Imperator Caesar Marcus Aurelius Claudius Augustus, Unconquered, Pious, and Fortunate: Aelius Dubitatus, soldier in the ninth praetorian cohort, in the century of Etrius; for nine years I have run the staging post at Veneria Rusicade, my fellow soldiers being safe and happy [- - -].

The dedication belongs to 268-70. Rusicade was a colony in the confederation of four under the leadership of Cirta (**142n.**) and a significant port, terminus of a road built from Cirta by Hadrian which brought down grain from the district for export to Italy. It is no surprise that it needed policing.

As Aelius Aristides has to admit, *Oration* 26, *Panegyric on Rome* 67a, real urban unrest was always a possibility, especially in large cities that had once been the capitals of Hellenistic monarchies, such as Antioch and Alexandria (**120, 204**); but there was racial friction in Caesarea also (which had not come down in the world), and there the disadvantages of using troops raised in the same area became evident.

39. Josephus, *Jewish War* 2, 266-9; Greek

Another disturbance arose at Caesarea, involving the Jews who formed part of the population in a quarrel with the Syrians there. The Jews claimed that the city belonged to them, their argument being that its founder, who was King Herod, had been a Jew. The other party conceded that it was a Jew who had sent settlers there, but said that the city itself belonged to the Greeks all the same, as he would not have established statues and temples in it if he had built it for Jews. (267) These were the points at issue between the two sides; their wrangling proceeded to armed violence and every day the more reckless members of the two sides would dash out to fight, for the Jewish elders were unable to restrain their own partisans, while the Greeks thought it a disgrace to be put down by Jews. (268) Although the latter had the advantage of wealth and strength of numbers, the Greek element had that of being supported by the troops; the greater part of the force the Romans had there had been levied in Syria and as kinsmen to the Greeks were ready to lend their assistance. (269) Of course the authorities were anxious to check the disorder and were continually arresting those who were particularly aggressive and punishing them by having them flogged or put in chains. Not that what those who were arrested went through caused the rest any hesitation or fear: they were simply stimulated to riot still more.

These disorders took place in 59-60, and ended with the procurator of Judaea, Felix, letting his auxiliary troops loose on the victorious Jews and then sending two deputations to Nero to plead the case. But it was the city authorities who were primarily responsible for order, and would be held so by the Romans if they failed to keep it, as the city clerk of Ephesus was aware (*Acts of the Apostles* 19, 40).

Some cities, the Roman colonies that were settlements of veterans, were well placed to maintain order in the district in which they were located. That, with satisfying the discharged legionary's hunger for land of his own and providing new recruits in the next generation, was the main function of the colonies, so that even after legionaries were finally discharged, they could continue to police the provinces — but in fixed garrisons (cf. **60**, **64**). Roman veteran colonies of about 3,000 men, wives and children added, kept the *esprit de corps* of the legions, for many of the men had already served together. The colonies might be planted in areas where land had been taken from natives known to be hostile or too weak to resist. In the long run a colony could do more harm than good: so with Camulodunum in Britain, founded as Colonia Claudia Victricensis in 50. The grievances that provoked Boudicca's rebellion ten years later were many, but hatred of the ex-solders was particularly acute.

40. Tacitus, *Annals* 14, 31, 5-32, 2

They had recently been established in the colony at Camulodunum and were driving the 'prisoners and slaves' from their homes, expropriating their farms. The soldiers encouraged the lawlessness of their former comrades: they lived the same kind of life and hoped to be given the same free rein. Besides, the temple set up in honour of Claudius was seen as a citadel of a tyranny that was to have no end, and the men who had been chosen to serve as priests were squandering whole fortunes, ostensibly on the cult. The extirpation of the colony seemed an easy task, too: it had no fortifications to protect it. Our officers had paid too little attention to that: they thought of comfort, not practicality. (32, 1) Meanwhile the statue of Victory at Camulodunum collapsed without apparent cause, and turned its back as if it were fleeing before the enemy. (2) Women too were whipping themselves into a frenzy, and prophesying imminent destruction, and in their council chamber the members heard the inarticulate grumbling of the barbarians; howling echoed in the theatre and a vision was seen in the Thames estuary of the colony in ruins. More: the Ocean looked as if it was made of blood and when the tide went out it left behind it things shaped like human bodies, encouraging the Britons as much as it terrified the veterans.

Not all the colonies were founded with such brutality, or loathed by the tribes on whose territory they were placed. At about the same time as Camulodunum was founded the Ubii brought over the Rhine by Marcus Agrippa had received some veterans in their midst, being given the title Colonia Claudia Ara Agrippensium; they remained steadfastly loyal to Rome throughout the German and Gallic revolt of 70 (Tacitus, *Germania* 28, 5; *Histories* 4, 28). The old-style colony did not survive the first century: Tacitus, *Annals* 14, 27, 4, speaks of it as a thing of the past in 60; see **64**.

The military colonies were paramount among the cities for the maintenance of peace by physical force or the threat of it, but small unprivileged communities could play an important role on occasion, as the Volubilis monuments prove (**153**), not only in the original subjugation but also against later revolts, witness the help given by Gallic cities against rebels in the revolts of 21 and 68-70 (**196**). The Romans may have flattered themselves that the cities needed no militia of their own (Aelius Aristides, *Oration* 26, *Panegyric on Rome* 76; cf. **175**), but the governor was often far away and the cities had to rely on self-help, even against incursions from outside the Empire.

41. Pausanias, *Guide to Greece* 10, 34, 5; Greek

But Elatea was a place reached by the Costobocian raid that overran Greece in my time. A man named Mnesibulus gathered a troop of men round him, slaughtered a large number of the barbarians, and fell in the battle. This Mnesibulus, besides other victories on the running track carried off at the 235th Olympics the single-lap race, and the double-lap race carrying a shield.

The invaders came from Poland or Russia some time after 161, when the 235th Games were held. Mnesibulus' background as an athlete is worth noting: the gymnasium and its associations would have provided his recruits; and the original military function of athletics is shown by one of the very races that Mnesibulus won (over a distance of about 357 m (1171 ft)).

The raid was an emergency, foreshadowing the raid of the Heruli in the following century (Millar 1969 (12), 26ff.). Maintaining everyday law and order was a permanent problem. In the second century a new official is found in the Greek cities of Thessaly, Thrace, Asia Minor and Syria, and in Egypt: the irenarch. That suggests that brigandage in the countryside was becoming serious; so does the way he was chosen: a list of ten leading men was submitted to the governor by the city concerned, and he made the choice (Aelius Aristides, *Oration* 50, *Sacred Tales*, 4, 72). The irenarch was equipped with a force of mounted police called *diogmitae*, 'pursuers'.

42. G. Mihailov, *Inscriptiones graecae in Bulgaria repertae* 4 (Sofia, 1966), 1953; Greek, on a funerary monument from Serdica, Thrace

Good [Fortune]! Bassus Moca [- - -, who became] priest and first [archon and i]renarch and si [tarch] in his own [city, constructed the] funerary monument and the [altar] for himself during his lifetime, in the second [consulship] of Bellicius Torqu[atus Tebani]anus and [- - -]

The inscription illustrates some of the other offices held in a Greek city. First archon is the leading magistrate; the irenarchy and sitarchy (which made Bassus responsible for purchasing grain for his city) were particularly onerous and strenuous positions, the latter potentially costly as well.

The document belongs to the second century, perhaps in 124, 143 or 148, when consuls called Bellicius Torquatus are attested; but Mihailov considers the lettering to favour the second half of the century.

We may see the irenarch in action with his forces at Smyrna before the martyrdom of Polycarp.

43. Musurillo, *Christian Acts* 1, 6, 1-7, 2

And as his pursuers kept on his trail he moved to another little estate. His pursuers were on the spot at once, and when they did not find Polycarp they arrested two slaves, one of whom talked under torture. (6, 2) It was out of the question for Polycarp to hide when he had those who gave him away in his own household. And the irenarch, whose destiny it was to be called by the same name as Herod, was eager to bring Polycarp into the stadium: that was how Polycarp was to fulfil the lot that was his, by becoming a sharer in Christ, while those who betrayed him might undergo the punishment of Judas himself. (7, 1) Taking the slave with them, then, the mounted police and horsemen set out with their regulation weapons at about dinner time on the day before the Passover Sabbath, 'coming out against a thief'. They made a concerted rush on the house late in the evening and found him lying down in a bedroom upstairs. He could have left there and gone away to another place but refused. 'The will of the Lord be done'; he said. (7, 2) Hearing that they had arrived, then, he went downstairs and talked to them. Those who witnessed it were surprised at his age and his calmness, and at there being so much anxiety to arrest an old man like that.

Polycarp was appointed Bishop of Smyrna by St John, according to Tertullian, *Objection against Heretics* 32, and he was executed there at the age of 86 (section 9 of the document above), some time in the third quarter of the second century. (An additional touch of verisimilitude is given the story by the mention of the stadium: there is no record of an amphitheatre, the conventional setting for martyrdom, in the city.) The irenarch cannot of course bring Polycarp into the stadium on his own responsibility: the proconsul appears in section 9. The point is made by the mid-third century martyr Pionius (10, 15), who asks other local officials why they are taking over the proconsul's functions. A general ruling on the powers of the irenarch was given by Antoninus Pius when he was governor of Asia.

44. Marcianus, The Public Courts, Book 2, in Digest 48, 3, 6, Introduction and 1

The deified Hadrian replied in these terms to Julius Secundus and the reply has been given on other occasions that credence is not necessarily to be given to the letters of those who send allegedly convicted men to a governor. The same instruction has been issued with regard to irenarchs, because it has been discovered that they do not always write their reports in good faith.

(1) But there also survives a section of the instructions which the deified Antoninus Pius published in his edict when he governed the province of Asia: that when irenarchs arrested brigands they should interrogate them about their accomplices and those who harboured them; that they should enclose accounts of these interrogations in their letters and send them under seal to the judicial enquiry to be conducted by the magistrate. Consequently those who are sent along with the written statement are to be given a fresh trial even if they have been despatched with the letters or even accompanied by the irenarchs. Both Antoninus Pius and other Emperors have replied in the same spirit, that even men who have been put on record as wanted are to be tried not as

if they were as good as convicted but as if the matter were coming up for the first time, if there is someone to make a case against the irenarch. And therefore whenever someone conducts a preliminary examination it is proper for the irenarch to be ordered to attend and expound what he has written. If he does so carefully and accurately, he is to be commended; if he has not paid sufficient attention to his work and his evidence is not detailed enough, the governor should simply record that the irenarch's report was inadequate; if however the governor discovers that his report shows unfavourable bias or that he has reported things as said which were not said, let him make an example of him, so that he does not try anything else of the same sort again.

Antoninus Pius was proconsul of Asia in the mid-thirties of the second century, Julius Secundus perhaps of Africa a year or two earlier (*JRS* 52 (1962), 222).

For the 'instructions' issued to governors at the beginning of their term of office, see **6**. The 'reply' or 'rescript' (**45**) is a written answer given by an Emperor to any application made to him, whether by a humble petition (libellus) (**47**) returned with the response given at the foot or by a letter to which he replied in the same way (Sherwin-White 1966 (1), 559; Millar, 1977 (1), 213ff.).

The encroachments of irenarchs on the judicial sphere are more readily understood when the latitude allowed Roman magistrates in criminal cases is remembered: executive and judicial functions are sometimes hard to distinguish. (For similar encroachments, see **53**, and for the abuse of power in general, see Chapter 10.)

4

Law

The settlement of disputes in an institutionalised and peaceful way, so as to inhibit further dissension, and only another way of securing order: this definition of 'law', put forward by A. Watson in *The Nature of Law* (Edinburgh, 1977), does not mean that we have to deny the Romans concern for justice and equity (see **58**, **63**, **184**); but that concern is superfluous to this chapter.

The process might involve individuals of the same or differing status, Roman or non-citizen, local communities or officials, Roman officials, or any combination. No matter, either, that all manner of processes jostle each other: in trial by jury in the provinces or at Rome on charges established by statute; inquiries into conduct alleged by informers to be criminal; civil cases brought by litigants; arbitration between communities and decisions rather administrative than legal; police action: the end is order.

Much business was left to the jurisdiction of local authorities (**26** and **144f.**), some fell to the Emperor or senate (e.g. **72**, **120**, **142**, **221**), with the Emperor entertaining appeals against the jurisdiction of governors (cf. **6** and **113**), but a very large number of the more serious provincial cases were taken to their conclusion by governors and their legates (**17**, **44**), who spent much of the year on circuit to cities designated as assize centres (**7**; in second-century Asia apparently fourteen in number: Habicht 1975 (2)).

The principles on which a province was to be run were sometimes laid down in the 'provincial law' drawn up by the men who created the provinces (**150**), but as each governor entered office he issued an edict setting out the basis of his own administration (**44**).

45. Ulpian and Venuleius on the Duty of the Proconsul, in *Digest* 1, 16, 4, 3f.; 6; 10f.

. . . The same author (Ulpian) in *The Duty of the Proconsul*, Book 1 . . .: (4, 3) But before the proconsul has entered the confines of the province decreed to him he ought to send an edict concerning his arrival including some means of introducing himself, such as any friendly relations or connection he has with its inhabitants, and in particular

46

excusing anyone from coming to meet him either as the representative of a community or on his own account, on the ground that it is proper that each individual should greet him in his home territory.

(4, 4) He will be acting in due and proper form if he sends the edict to his predecessor and indicates on what day he means to enter the confines of the province. Very often when these matters are left uncertain and are not known beforehand they upset the provincials and hamper the administration(4, 5) . . . (4, 6) It is after this, when he has entered the province, that he ought to delegate jurisdiction to his legate, not do it before he has entered the province . . . But if he does do it beforehand and remains of the same mind when he has entered the province, the correct opinion is that the legate's possession of jurisdiction seems to begin, not from the moment it was delegated, but from when the proconsul has entered the province.

(10) The same author (Ulpian) in *The Duty of the Proconsul*, Book 10: it will behove him to remember that a proconsul ought to go on dealing with all business until the arrival of his successor, since the proconsulship is indivisible, and the welfare of the province demands that there should be someone to make it possible for the provincials to transact their business: for that reason he will be duty-bound to administer justice until his successor's arrival. (10, 1) He is warned not to send away his legate out of the province before he leaves himself both by the Julian Law against misconduct by governors and by a reply given by the deified Hadrian to Calpurnius Rufus, proconsul of Achaea.

(11) Venuleius Saturninus, *The Duty of the Proconsul*: if there is anything that demands a particularly serious punishment, the legate ought to refer it back to the proconsul, for he has no right to inflict capital punishment nor to administer summary punishment nor to inflict severe corporal punishment.

The provisions of 4, 4-10 were designed to smooth relations between outgoing and incoming proconsuls (the former had to leave within thirty days of the arrival of his successor). The provision in 4, 6, results from the rule that a proconsul's power could be exercised only within his province (*Digest* 1, 16, 1): it would be anomalous for the legate to exercise jurisdiction before the proconsul acquired it.

For the capital jurisdiction of governors see **184**n.

Under the Principate the conduct of governors continued to be regulated by a comprehensive and severe measure of more than a hundred clauses, the Julian law passed by Julius Caesar in his first consulship of 59 BC (*Digest* 48, 11).

The following documents, first and fourth in a series of edicts which were issued by Augustus in the years 7-6 and 4 BC (see also **58, 84**), show a jury system in use and abuse in the province.

46. EJ 311; Greek, on a stele in the market place, Cyrene

1

Edict of Imperator Caesar Augustus, Supreme Pontiff, in his seventeenth year of tribunician power, hailed Imperator for the fourteenth
time: whereas I find that the Roman citizens of all age groups in the
province of Cyrene who possess a census qualification of 2,500 *denarii* or
more, from whom the juries are selected, number 215 all told; and
whereas the embassies from the cities of the province have complained
that there are certain conspiracies amongst those same men which are
taking a severe toll of the Greeks in capital cases, the same persons
taking turns to bring accusations and to bear witness for each other's
benefit; and I myself have discovered that certain innocent parties have
been completely overborne by this method and brought to pay the
supreme penalty; it seems to me that until the senate takes counsel about
this matter or I myself find some better remedy, those who are in charge
of the province of Crete and Cyrene will act well and properly if they put
forward the same number of Greek jurymen from the highest census
ratings in the province of Cyrene as of Roman citizens. No-one, Greek
or Roman, is to be less than twenty-five years of age, nor is he to have a
census rating and property worth less than 7,500 *denarii*, provided that
there is a sufficient number of such men: but if the number of jurymen
who have to be put forward cannot be reached by that means, they are
to put forward those who possess not less than half this census as
jurymen in capital cases involving Greeks.

If a Greek who is brought to trial and is given the option, one day
before the prosecution opens its case, of having all the jurymen in his
case Roman citizens or half of them Greeks, chooses the latter, then
when the lots have been weighed and the names written on them, the
names of the Roman citizens are to be drawn from one urn, those of the
Greeks from the other, until the total of twenty-five names from each
group is reached. Of these the prosecution may reject one of each, if he
wishes, the accused three from all, provided that he does not reject all
Romans or all Greeks. Then all the remainder are to be free to proceed
with the voting and the Roman citizens are to cast their votes separately
into one basket, the Greeks into another. Then, when the votes of each
group have been counted separately, the governor is to declare clearly
what the verdict of the overall majority is.

And since the kinsmen of the victims do not usually allow unlawful
killings to go unavenged and it is likely that there will be no lack of
Greek prosecutors to bring cases against those responsible on behalf of
victims who were their kinsmen or fellow-citizens, future governors of
Crete and Cyrene will act correctly and fittingly in my opinion if they do
not accept a Roman citizen as prosecutor in a case involving the killing
of a Greek of either sex, unless someone who has received the

distinction of Roman citizenship should wish to bring a case in consequence of the murder of one of his kinsmen or fellow-citizens.

4

Edict of Imperator Caesar Augustus, Supreme Pontiff, in his seventeenth year of tribunician power: with regard to whatever disputes arise between Greeks in the province of Cyrene, with the exception of those involving capital penalties, which whoever is in charge of the province ought either to determine and settle himself or provide a panel of jurors for them; for all remaining cases it is my pleasure that Greek jurors should be provided, unless a man who is defending the case or the accused person wishes to have Roman citizens as the jury. For cases arising between them from the time this edict of mine was issued and for which Greek jurors are provided, it is not my pleasure that anyone should be selected from the same city as that from which the plaintiff or accuser comes or the person who is defending the case or the accused person.

The jury courts of Cyrenaica were based on the courts at Rome, and were probably introduced into the province when it was taken over in about 74 BC, only seven years after Sulla had systematised the Roman jury courts; they do not supersede the authority of the governor to settle cases himself (see below).

The first edict is concerned with capital cases. Roman citizens had been exploiting their monopoly of the jury panels to make away with their enemies, either for purely political reasons or to get their property as well. Those without Roman citizenship are referred to as Greeks because they were members of Greek cities and spoke that language; the term excludes tribal natives of the province and immigrants without rights in the cities, such as Jews (**10** and cf. **120**). Judicial murders (conceivably following riots in which fatalities had occurred — for later sedition and discord at Cyrene, see **174**) — had evidently been allowed to pass by governors (cf. **183**), and the Greek cities had made representations to Augustus himself. The paucity of Romans with substantial property, like the fatalities and faction, may reflect a continuing depression after the end of the civil wars in 30 BC: Cyrene had supported Antony.

In the fourth edict there is doubt as to precisely which cases are to have all-Greek juries. Some scholars, taking their cue from the last sentence, have suggested that only cases involving litigants from different cities are in question. That is against the run of the edict, which up to the last sentence seems to be dealing with all cases between Greeks; the provision of the last sentence is a restrictive afterthought. De Visscher 1965, 126, believed that the cases in question are those specifically referred to the governor as intractable, which he then remits to the jury; there is little to support this in the text. These suggestions were prompted by the difficulty of believing that the governor had to cope with every case, however petty. The difficulty might be resolved by regarding all non-capital cases as already being handled by the cities, perhaps, as Dr Mackie suggests, on a centralised system. In the wake of the first edict they seek to rid themselves of an effective domination of their jury courts by Roman citizens; the governor is brought in only in passing as controlling capital cases.

In Sicily under the late Republic the provincial law provided that disputes between fellow-citizens should be settled by their own courts, between those of different cities by juries drawn by lot; in Cilicia it was at the governor's discretion whether cities should use their own laws or not (Cicero, *Verrines* 2, 2, 32; *Letters to Atticus* 6, 1, 15).

Even after Caracalla enfranchised the free population of the Empire local custom was respected: see also **157n**.

47. *Codex of Justinian* 6, 32, 2

Imperator Valerian Augustus and Imperator Gallienus Augustus to Alexander. Since you assert that the text of his will was given to you by your father for the particular purpose of publishing it in his native land, you may publish it there so that it be made known according to the local laws and customs, on the understanding that in the absence of witnesses you take care first to approach the governor of the province whether in person before his tribunal or by petition and with his permission ensure the attendance of men of good repute to be present when the will is opened and to seal it up again. Posted in public, 27 October in the consulships of Maximus (for the second time) and Glabrio.

The year is 256.

A jury system was in use in Bithynia-Pontus, and perhaps in Asia (Sherwin-White 1966 (1), 640, on Pliny, *Letters* 10, 58f.), but cases that fell under the public laws of Rome, like the homicides of **46** (1), were in the minority. Normally the governor took cognisance *ad hoc*, on his own authority; although he kept to the principles enunciated in his edict his power was enormous, even monarchical. The following account of a late second-century *cognitio* (inquiry) against Christians in Africa shows the procedure in practice and may be compared with Pliny's famous inquiry in Bithynia seventy years before, *Letters* 10, 96f.

48. Musurillo, *Christian Acts* 6

Martyrdom of the Scillitan Saints.

During the consulships of Praesens (for the second time) and Claudianus, 17 July, at Carthage, in the council chamber: Speratus,

Nartzalus and Cittinus, and Donata, Secunda and Vestia were brought in, and the proconsul Saturninus said: 'You can win the clemency of our Lord the Emperor if you return to a sound state of mind.'

(2) Speratus: We have never done any harm, we have given no aid to an act of iniquity; we have never cursed anyone but, misunderstood as we are, we have given thanks, because we give due honour to our own Emperor.

(3) The proconsul Saturninus: We too are religious, our religion is a simple one, and we swear by the guiding spirit of our Lord the Emperor and offer prayers for his welfare, which is what you too ought to do.

(4) Speratus: If you give me a quiet hearing I shall tell you the mystery that lies in simplicity.

(5) Saturninus: If you start abusing our rites I shall not give you a hearing; no, take an oath by the guiding spirit of our Lord the Emperor instead.

(6) Speratus: I do not recognise the Empire of this world but rather serve that God whom no man has seen nor can see with mortal eyes. I have not committed theft; if I buy anything I duly pay the tax on it because I recognise my Lord, the Emperor of kings and all peoples.

(7) The proconsul Saturninus (to the others): Give up clinging to this fancy.

Speratus: It is an evil fancy to commit murder, to bear false witness.

(8) Saturninus: Have nothing to do with this madness.

Cittinus: We have no other fear than the Lord our God who is in Heaven.

(9) Donata: Honour to Caesar as Caesar; but fear is for God.

Vestia: I am a Christian.

Secunda: What I am is what I want to be.

(10) The proconsul Saturninus (to Speratus): Do you insist on being a Christian?

Speratus: I am a Christian.

And they all agreed with him.

(11) The proconsul Saturninus: Don't you wish to have time to think about it again?

Speratus: In a cause as just as ours there is no point in second thoughts.

(12) The proconsul Saturninus: What have you got in your case?

Speratus: Books and letters of Paul, a just man.

(13) The proconsul Saturninus: take a stay of execution for thirty days; you are to think about it.

Speratus again: I am a Christian.

And they all agreed with him.

(14) The proconsul Saturninus read out his decision from a tablet: 'It is my pleasure that Speratus . . . and the rest, who have admitted that they live by the Christian rite, since they have obstinately persisted when

the chance of returning to Roman ways was offered them, should be executed by the sword'.

(15) Speratus: We thank God . . .

(16) The proconsul Saturninus ordered a herald to make the announcement: 'Speratus (etc.) have been ordered to be led out to execution.'

(17) As one man they all said 'Thanks be to God', and were immediately beheaded for the name of Christ. Amen.

Gaius Bruttius Praesens and Sextus Quintilius Condianus were consuls in 180, and the full name of the proconsul, who is seen in his capital at Carthage, was Publius Vigellius Saturninus. In spite of the slip in the name of the second consul and the addition of six names not in the original indictment to the list of those executed, these details, like the resemblance to the proceedings before Pliny, give verisimilitude.

No accuser appears: the governor himself takes the initiative on the basis of denunciations, one of those to Pliny being anonymous (*Letters* 10, 96, 5; Trajan disapproved). This is not the place to discuss the charge: (see Barnes 1968 (10)), but the passage illustrates (14) Christian 'apostasy' from the Roman way of life, which in the third century may have been felt to endanger the Empire (**55, 228**), the contumaciousness (cf. **50**) which appears in Pliny (96, 3), as a secondary reason for punishing them, and (17) their execution 'for the name of Christ'. Pliny is uncertain (96, 2) whether the 'name' of Christian is what is liable for punishment or the criminal acts that go with it. It may be that especially after their association with the Great Fire of Rome in 64 Christians were assumed actually or potentially guilty of multifarious crimes, arson the worst. Such acts could rarely be proved, and the governors' main concern was peace in his province, so that recantation was offered as a way out.

It was not only at assize centres that a governor had to offer jurisdiction: he might be tackled at home.

Corinth, capital of Achaea, is the scene of a second-century drama, the unmasking of a wholesale poisoner by one of her victims.

49. Apuleius, *The Golden Ass*, 10, 28

The doctor's wife had an inkling straightaway of what the matter was when the havoc wrought by the appalling potion wound its destructive way through her lungs. Soon her laboured breathing made her certain sure, and she rushed to the actual living quarters of the governor, shrieking loudly and calling on him for the help he was duty-bound to give. Her claim that she was going to reveal the most monstrous crimes brought a noisy crowd together, and made sure that the governor accorded her instant admission and an instant audience. Then when she had delivered herself of a precise account from the very beginning of every atrocious act perpetrated by the supremely cruel woman, without warning she became wildly incoherent, clamped her mouth tight shut — it had been gaping open until then — and after a long drawn out grinding of the teeth collapsed lifeless at the very feet of the governor. He was a man of considerable experience and did not allow slackness or delay to let the trail of that poisonous viper's multifarious crimes grow cold. He immediately had the woman's personal servants brought before him and forcibly extracted the truth from them by torture. As to the woman, he contented himself with sentencing her to be thrown to the wild beasts, which was milder than she deserved, but no other suitable torment could be devised.

Not only senatorial but equestrian governors possessed capital jurisdiction; the most famous trial in the ancient world took place before one, that of Jesus before Pilate (*Matthew* 27; *Mark* 15; *John* 18).

Violence and political trials predominate in the literature, but documentary evidence tells more of the painstaking and humdrum efforts of governors — senatorial and equestrian — to resolve disputes, especially those concerning property and boundaries. Not surprisingly: the successful party would want the decision recorded in a permanent and conspicuous form. Decisions made could not always be enforced, as the history behind this decree of a proconsul of Sardinia demonstrates.

50. Smallwood, *Gaius-Nero* 392 (MW 455); bronze tablet from Esterzili, Sardinia

Copied and checked in the consulship of Imperator Otho Caesar Augustus, on 18 March, from the file of the proconsul Lucius Helvius Agrippa, which was produced by the quaestor's clerk Gnaeus Egnatius Fuscus, and in which was written that which is written out below (table 5, sections 8-10):

13 March. Lucius Helvius Agrippa, proconsul, after hearing the case gave his decision: Since it is to the advantage of the state that judicial decisions, once taken, should be adhered to; and since Marcus Juventius Rixa, the distinguished imperial procurator, has given judgement more than once on the case of the Patulcenses to the effect that the boundaries of the Patulcenses were to be maintained as they had been regulated in the bronze tablet by Marcus Metellus, and has on the most recent occasion given judgement that he had been inclined to punish the Galillenses who were repeatedly bringing up the dispute and failing to adhere to his decree, but out of respect for the forbearance of the best and greatest of Emperors had been content to admonish them in his edict that they should refrain from causing trouble, abide by judicial decisions, and by the following 1 October withdraw from the properties

of the Patulcenses and return them to vacant possession; while if they persisted in their obstinate refusal to obey he would take severe measures against the leaders of the disturbance; and since the distinguished senator Caecilius Simplex was subsequently approached on the same issue by the Galillenses, who claimed that they could produce from the imperial archives the document relevant to the subject, and gave judgement to the effect that it was only humane that a postponement should be granted to allow for the production of evidence, and granted an adjournment of three months until 1 December, by which time the map had to be produced or he would follow the map in the province; and since I too, having been approached by the Galillenses, who offered reasons for their failure as yet to produce the map, granted an adjournment until 1 February last, and am fully aware that the delay was convenient to the persons in possession: let the Galillenses depart by 1 April next from the territories of the Patulcenses Campani which they had taken over by violence; while if they do not act in accordance with this judgement, let them know they will be liable to punishment for their disobedience, which has been prolonged and by now frequently condemned.

Members of the governor's advisory board: Marcus Iulius Romulus, praetorian legate; Titus Atilius Sabinus, praetorian quaestor; Marcus Stertinius Rufus the son; Sextus Aelius Modestus; Publius Lucretius Clemens; Marcus Domitius Vitalis; Marcus Lusius Fidus; Marcus Stertinius Rufus. Witnessed and sealed by: Gnaeus Pompeius Ferox; Aurelius Gallus; Marcus Blossius Nepos; Gaius Cordus Felix; Lucius Vigellius Crispinus; Lucius Valerius Faustus; Marcus Lutatius Sabinus; Lucius Cocceius Genialis; Lucius Plotius Verus; Decimus Veturius Felix; Lucius Valerius Peplus.

The decree belongs to 69 and the dispute had lasted since 114 BC, when the proconsul Marcus Metellus had established the boundaries in dispute between the two peoples. The decision of Metellus was reiterated by Rixa, procurator 66-7 (Sardinia, which was often turbulent, had passed to imperial control under an equestrian governor in 15 and remained imperial until 67, when Caecilius became the first of a new series of senatorial governors). The document the Galillenses sought time to obtain was the original adjudication of Metellus, which was in the imperial archive at Rome; governors had been relying on the version kept in the province, and so did Helvius Agrippa when he issued this decree, six weeks after the time allowed them for production of the original had finally expired. Five days after it was issued, his quaestor's clerk provided an authenticated copy which the Patulcenses used as a basis for the present document to provide public evidence of their title to the land.

The decisions seem to have been taken by the various governors on their own responsibility, but it is clear from the words of Rixa that the Emperor Nero had been approached, presumably by the claimants on both sides; he had not altered the judgement but enjoined forbearance in carrying it out (the Galillenses had enjoyed very lengthy tenure of the land). The seals were affixed to the document to authenticate the copy.

Not only procurators governing provinces but those charged with the collection of taxes and the management of imperial estates are found helping to resolve disputes.

51. Smallwood, *Gaius-Nero* 387; Greek, on three stones at Düver, about 8 km (5 miles) south-west of Lake Burdur, central Asia Minor

In accordance with a letter of the deified Augustus Germanicus Caesar, Quintus Petronius Umber, legate of Nero Claudius Caesar Augustus Germanicus, and Lucius Pupius Praesens, procurator of Nero Claudius Caesar Augustus Germanicus, fixed the boundaries, the territory on the right to belong to the people of Sagalassus, that on the left to the village of the people of Tymbrianassus, the property of Nero Claudius Caesar Augustus Germanicus, in which the people of Sagalassus have an interest of one fifth.

This stream on which the three stones were originally planted, and which eventually runs into Lake Burdur, was the disputed boundary between an imperial estate containing the village of Tymbrianassus (Örenler, a little north of Düver) and the territory of the leading city of this part of Pisidia, Sagalassus, which lay in the mountain range about 45 km (28 miles) to the north-east: see G.E. Bean, *Anatolian Studies* 9 (1959), 84ff.

Claudius had written to the governor and procurator giving his decision on this boundary but had died before it could be executed. It was natural for the imperial procurator to be involved, seeing that one of the interested parties was the Emperor himself, owner of the estate on which Tymbrianassus stood. But a senatorial resolution of 53 had also extended the jurisdiction of procurators whose business was in theory only the management of the Emperor's private estates (Tacitus, *Annals* 12, 60), so that eventually this grade of procurator could give judgement, usually of course on matters concerning the estates under his management. The rights of procurators in this respect were hedged about with restrictions (which they did not always observe) but the principle is clearly recognised.

52. Ulpian, The Duty of the Proconsul, Book 9, in the section on the Fabian Law, quoted in the *Comparison of Mosaic and Roman Law*, 14 (On Kidnappers), 3, 1f.

Proceedings under the Fabian law are also frequent before the tribunals of governors, although certain procurators of Caesar have also performed this function in the provinces as well as at Rome . . . (2) . . . In a province it is the function of the provincial governor and it does not otherwise fall to the procurator to proceed on this count unless he is performing the functions of governor in the province. (3) Clearly after the opinion given on the Fabian law the duties of a procurator do involve him in this process. However, although a procurator who is not the governor of any province does not normally take cognisance of capital cases either, the Emperor Antoninus (Caracalla) has decided that he may take cognisance of cases under the Fabian law. The same official by a decision of the Emperor Antoninus has received jurisdiction under the Julian law on the repression of adultery.

Ulpian, writing in the reign of Caracalla, notes that only procurators governing provinces may take cognisance of capital cases; the exception, which they have previously usurped, was expressly made by Caracalla: kidnapping, false imprisonment and trading of Roman citizens, and the enticement, concealment or trading of another man's slave. The Fabian law (of uncertain date but earlier than 63 BC) originally had a pecuniary penalty; under the Principate the low class offender was sent to the mines or crucified, the more respectable lost half his property and was relegated for life. The adultery law (18 BC) was not capital: it involved a fine and relegation. That Caracalla's concession lasted is doubted by Brunt 1966, 469.

53. *Codex of Justinian* 3, 26, 1-4

Imperator Severus Augustus and Imperator Antoninus Augustus to Dioscurus.

(1) Who does not know that an enquiry into an undefended murder case cannot be held before our procurator? And that property cannot be claimed for the imperial Treasury otherwise than if the charge has been dealt with before the magistrate empowered to impose the penalty on the persons convicted? Of course on the death of persons charged with murder it is perfectly reasonable for the case to be heard also by procurators. Posted in public, 9 May in the consulship of Lateranus and Rufinus (197).

(2) The same Augusti to Arista. We do not perceive why you wish to bring a case that belongs to the office of our procurators to the notice of the proconsul. For although it is the object of the enquiry to establish

whether your father killed himself from fear of punishment, and whether his property ought to be claimed for the imperial Treasury for that reason, the question to be enquired into now is not that of the charge or the penalty to be paid by a dead man, but that of his property. 20 September in the consulships of Aper and Maximus (207).

(3) The Emperor Antoninus (Caracalla) Augustus to Heliodorus. My procurator, who is not discharging the functions of governor of a province, while he is empowered to enforce the penalty for abandoning a prosecution, equally is not empowered to give judgement to the effect that it should be inflicted in virtue of a decision pronounced by him. 23 August, in the consulship of Laetus and Cerealis (215).

(4) The Emperor Alexander (Severus) Augustus to Maxima. Since you say that you bought estates from my procurator when he offered them for sale, you are necessarily obliged to pay the price for them. Since you say that you have also handed over these same estates to the persons on whose instructions you purchased them, my procurator, if you bring an action and seek a hearing from him, will take cognisance, so that you may obtain the money which is owed to you under the head of the price and the interest which has to be paid to the imperial Treasury. Posted in public, 12 October in the consulships of Maximus and Paternus (233).

The Emperors' decisions in (1) and (2) show the procurator unable to take capital criminal cases, but able, after they have been decided by the competent magistrate or have lapsed with the defendant's death, to adjudicate on confiscation of the property: if the defendant could be shown to have killed himself to avoid a judicial penalty, his property was forfeit (*Digest* 48, 21, 3; 49, 14, 45, 2). The task of the procurator is to execute pecuniary penalties, which as Brunt remarks (1966, 473) may involve jurisdiction, but not to determine whether they should be imposed (3). The procurator is prefectly competent (4) to hear a case involving money owed to the imperial Treasury for estates sold from the imperial property to private individuals.

The jurisdiction exercised by procurators within imperial domains (both those that probably began as the private property of members of the imperial family and those that may have come, as mines might, into the possession of the Emperor in virtue of his official position) is shown in the next document, in the rules governing management of mines in Spain (**73**), and in the appeal of the tenants of an estate in Lydia (**221**).

54. W.H.C. Frend, *JRS* 46 (1956), 46ff.; Greek, with official rubrics in Latin; from Sulmenli (?Eulandra), Asia

[In the consulships of - - - and - - -], 30 May, at Anossa. Panas of the Anosseni said: 'Those who have to work the road [- - -] (or, draught oxen ought to [- - -] the road) from Amorium. We take over also from Philomelium and from Mirus [- - -] up to the rest house'. The procurator Threptus said: 'These roads which you say you (the stone reads 'we') serve [- - -] how far do they stretch and where are ?teams of oxen ?produced?' Panas: 'For this road we produce [- - -; to those] coming from Synnada we provide from the fifth milestone, and from Amorium [- - -], and from Mirus towards Camaxus four miles are imposed on us.' [Alexander of Antimach]eia: 'And we [?are responsible for] everything that comes from Amorium and from Ancyra ?although we are poor.' Threptus to the Anosseni: 'What is your village's tax contribution?' Panas: '[- - -] thousand, four hundred *denarii*.' The procurator Threptus: 'And how many *denarii* that of the Antimacheni?' Alexander: 'Two thousand, seven hundred and fifty.' Threptus: [the procurator]: 'This sum has been exacted under a number of procurators already and it has suited you and you have been satisfied with it. You ought [- - -] then to provide services [in the same ratio] as your tax rating.' Panas: 'We shall use an advocate [?to appeal to D]ocimium.' The procurator Threptus: 'What is the point of saying more than you already have? ?You ought then [- - -] to contribute in the same ratio as your tax rating and that of the Antimacheia.' [(Another section of the record) - - - the procurator Threptus]: 'Seeing that stores are said to have been given to the people of Antimacheia and in turn [- - -] to you, you will undertake half, the people of Antimacheia half. Symphorus the under-centurion [will take care of this ?as I have awarded it] so that you do not have any ground for complaint in the future, ?nor the people of Antimacheia on] its account, so that each of the two villages may know that this is how it must be.' [Panas: - - -] 'But if we are to deliver transport facilities to Antimacheia, how will it be?' Threptus [the procurator: '- - -] up to the point where the relief takes over you shall serve half and half.'

Aurelius Sym[phorus] sends greetings to [the Anosseni and Anti]macheni, villagers and elders. Since you have appealed to my [?excellent and - - -] Lord Procurator Aurelius Threptus concerning the transport facilities which were remitted you [- - - S]ynnada, his Excellency has thought it proper to determine and to make [- - - clear] to you how each of you ought to take up half the provision of transport facilities from [- - -] village. He has instructed me as to the manner in which I am to give my attention to this matter. I enjoin [you in accordance with the decisions taken by my Lord the Procurator] Aurelius Threptus that if anyone shall set himself against what has been determined by the Lord Procurator he shall come to know the danger to himself.

[Aurelius Symphorus sends greetings to ?the elders of An]timacheia. In accordance with the dispositions made in his memorandum by the [excellent - - -] procurator Aurelius Threptus, you are to take care in accordance with the task laid upon you to [?take on - - -] the provision of transport facilities, while if you are remiss, you shall give account of it.

[In the consulships of the Emperor Antoninus (Caracalla) (for the third time) and Caelius B]albinus, 11 October, at Prymnessus. The procurator Philocurius: '[- - -] to the decisions they are in a state of civil disobedience; those who are in a state of civil disobedience [shall be punished in accordance with] the decisions'. Valens: 'The Anosseni request that they should be allocated a soldier on police duty.' [Philocurius the procurator: 'To ?guarantee] the decisions I shall provide a soldier.'

In the consulships of Marius Perpet[uus and Mummius Cornelianus]. 10 October, at Synnada. The procurator Novellius: 'The demarcation [handed down by Threptus] can not be cancelled and for that reason they shall [see that they conform to] its terms.' (Another section of the record.)

The procurator Novellius: 'Agathon [?the under-centurion - - - in accordance with] the terms previously laid down by Threptus shall make sure of this [- - - If] he catches any persons [failing to obey] he shall bring it to my attention and I shall give a decision and [- - - he shall ?provide service] to the registrar in accordance with the award [?arranged] by Threptus [- - -] the decisions. But if the Anosseni fail to obey, [- - -] of the payment [- - -].'

The two villages in dispute formed part of a large imperial estate and were subject to the jurisdiction of the procurator who was responsible for the management of these estates in the Asian Province. The subject of the dispute is the contribution each is to make towards animals, carts and fodder for transport and carriage of officials and others using the local roads, which in the Caystrus valley were numerous and busy: for the system see **89, 91ff.** In our document it and the contributions both go by the originally Persian name of *angareia* (in the Persian Empire an *angareios* was a mounted royal courier: Herodotus, *Histories* 3, 126); the system survived a further 800 years, as Frend points out.

The first hearing, which Frend suggests took place about 200, takes place at the village that brought the case. Anossa has been responsible for supplying short stretches of road coming from Amorium, 27 km (17 miles) to the N.E., Mirus, 32 km (20 miles) to the N.W. and Philomelium, 34 km (21½ miles) to the S.E. (these roads converged at a staging post or rest house near the village) and from Synnada, 16 km (10 miles) to the S.W. The opposing village is responsible only for the main route leading from Ancyra and Amorium, Ancyra being 228 km (143 miles) distant to the N.E., and Frend suggests that it was overlapping obligations on this route that gave rise to the dispute. The Antimacheian spokesman's plea of poverty leads the procurator Threptus to enquire about the respective tax assessments, and his first solution is that they should contribute to the travel facilities in the same proportion. But in a part of the hearing not recorded he learns that the villages exchange stores and ordains an equal contribution from each. Having soldiers at his disposal he orders an under-centurion, Symphorus, to see that his decision is implemented. This man's two letters to the villages, extremely respectful to his superior, peremptory to them, are included in the record; the first is addressed impartially to both, the second to the offending Antimacheni.

Next come excerpts from a second hearing, of 213, held at Prymnessus, 6 km (4 miles) E. of Eulandra. The Anosseni, once more the plaintiffs, may have been claiming harassment by the Antimacheni, or by officials using the service (cf. **91ff.**); for soldiers on police duty, see **36f.**

The third hearing takes place nearly a quarter of a century later in 237, at Synnada, before yet another procurator, who upholds Threptus' final decision and sends a subordinate to enforce it. The involvement of the registrar, a financial officer who sometimes acted as a public notary, suggests that there may have been pecuniary penalties for failure to comply.

The editor remarks on the outspokenness of the villagers before the authorities; it may be enhanced by abbreviation in the transcript; but they clearly fought with determination for their rights.

Within the territories of cities their magistrates had petty jurisdiction.

55. *Acts of the Apostles* **16, 16; 18-24; 35-39; Greek**

(16) While we were on our way to prayer a young woman possessed of prophetic power happened to fall in with us. She was providing a good living for her master by divining . . . (18) But Paul was disturbed, and turned and said to the spirit, 'I command you in the name of Jesus Christ to come out of her'. And it did so, the same hour. (19) When her masters saw that their prospects of a livelihood had gone they laid hold of Paul and Silas and dragged them to the authorities in the market place. (20) They brought them before the magistrates and said, 'These men, who are Jews, are turning our city upside down, (21) and they are proclaiming a way of life that is out of the question for us to accept or practise, when we are Romans.' (22) And the crowd joined in the attack on them and the magistrates tore off their clothes and ordered them to be flogged. (23) When they had inflicted many strokes on them they threw them into prison, instructing the warder to keep a safe watch on them. (24) On receiving these instructions he thrust them into the inner part of the prison and secured their feet in the stocks . . . (35) Next day the magistrates sent lictors with instructions to 'free those men'. (36) The warder reported those words to Paul. 'The magistrates have sent word

that you are to be freed: so come out now, and go your way in peace.'
(37) But Paul said to them, 'They have flogged us in public without trial,
Roman citizens as we are, and thrown us into prison. Are they now
going to go on to expel us in secret? No, let them come themselves
instead and bring us out.' (38) The lictors reported these words to the
magistrates; when they heard that they were Roman citizens they took
fright and (39) came in person to mollify them, took them out and asked
them to leave the city.

This episode of the early years of Nero's reign takes place in a Roman
colony, Philippi on the Egnatian road in Macedonia. The writer gives the
colony the 'generals' common as magistrates in Greek cities not the
regular colonial duovirs. But he correctly shows them exercising their
right to inflict flogging (though not on Roman citizens), even without
trial, in the interests of law and order, and to imprison vagrants: their
two attendant lictors are 'rod-holders' in the Greek text (cf. **86**). For
effective limits on their powers against the wealthy, see **108**.

The accusation made against Paul and Silas was of a kind likely to win
a hearing at any time in a community self-consciously alien to its
environment, as a Roman colony was (Sherwin-White 1963, 82), and the
insistence that Paul and Silas were Jews played on that fact and made the
magistrates more likely to listen: large-scale disturbances involving Jews
had taken place at Alexandria in 41 (**120**), the Jews had been expelled
from Rome in 46 (Suetonius, *Deified Claudius* 25, 4), and there had
been troubles in Judaea; for the charge that Christians repudiated the
Roman way of life, see **48**.

Provision for formal procedure before the duovirs with jurisdiction
(for whom see also **26**) is made in the charter of Urso in Spain, which
was modelled on a blueprint for all colonies.

56. *ILS* 6087; from the fourth column of the third of four bronze tablets found at Urso in Baetica

102. A duovir who holds a judicial enquiry under this law or who
exercises jurisdiction, which jurisdiction is not obliged under this law to
be exercised in the course of one day, is not to hold his enquiry or
exercise his jurisdiction before the first hour of the day or after the
eleventh. And that duovir is to allow each set of plaintiffs, to the
initiator of the case four hours to put the case for the plaintiff, to his supporting speaker two. If any plaintiff gives part of his own allotted time to
another, the duovir is to increase the time allowed for speaking to each
of the men to whom the concession has been made by the same amount
of the first speaker's time as he has given up to him; the duovir is to
decrease the time available to anyone who has given up part of it to
another by the amount he has given up to each man. Whatever total

number of hours is appropriately to be made available to all the plaintiffs for each hearing, the duovir is to make available the same number of hours and as many again to the defendant for each hearing or to whoever speaks on his behalf.

The charter was engraved in the Flavian period, but Dr Mackie points out that some of its provisions seem to represent conditions at the end of the Republic; local magistrates' powers were restricted later on (Mackie 1983 (2), 99ff., 163ff.). The cases in section 102 might not all be civil suits: Dr Mackie cites the elaborate system of assessors provided in sections 95f. and 125f.; and the allowance of a certain number of hours to each party resembles provisions made in Roman laws, notably the Julian law against misconduct in the provinces (**59**); the impression of jury trial makes it look as if the sums of money at stake, or the penalties, were too great for the duovir to be allowed to decide on his own.

It was not for provincial councils to legislate nor did their officials exercise jurisdiction, but they were involved in legal processes in two important ways: first, disputes between member cities might be referred to them for arbitration.

57. EJ 321, Greek, from Cierium, Thessaly

[- - - the cities] are in dispute with each other [- - -] it is requested that secretly and under oath [- - - the people of Met]ropolis acting as judges, under the presidency of [- - -], being obliged to [- - -] to you, in accordance with which the judgement [- - -] votes were taken under oath, [298 in favour of the people of Cierium, [31 in favour of] the people of Metro]polis, 5 invalid [- - -].

[To Gaius Popp]aeus Sabinus, legate of Tiberius Caesar, [- - -, secretary] of the members of the council, sends heartiest greetings. You wrote [to us] about the legal dispute which [the people of Cierium and those of Met]ropolis had over boundaries, [that you required those members of the council] to decide it whom you were indicating to me when we met at Aede[psus. You are informed that I] returned [home immediately] and laid the case before the [current] council [of the Thessalians in session at La]rissa and sitting in the month of Thyos. And you are to know that [when both parties presented themselves for the] hearing and speeches had been made on both sides, [the votes were taken secretly under] oath, 29[8] for the people of Cierium, [3]1 for those of Metropolis, 5 invalid. We considered it appropriate [to write informing you] of this. [Farewell.]

To Gaius Pop]paeus Sabinus, legate of Tiberius Caesar, [- - -], general of the Thessalians, sends greetings. You wrote both to me and to the [members of the council] that [the council] had referred the decision about the legal dispute which the people of Cierium and those of

Metropolis had over boundaries. You are to know then that [the members of the council sitting in the] month [of Thyos were cited] and gave [their votes] under oath and in secret, 298 [for the people of Cierium], 31 for those of Metr[opolis, 5 invalid.] We thought it appropriate then [to write informing you of] this, [so that - - -] the decision may obtain your confirmation with a view to [- - -],

Achaea and Macedonia were under Sabinus 15-35. The governor referred back the boundary dispute to the council of Thessaly, an ancient political assembly; but their vote evidently had to be confirmed by him if it was to remain unchallenged.

Clearly the number of votes cities had varied, presumably according to their size (so too in **21** and **173**).

Another and more significant legal role played by provincial councils was that of organising joint prosecutions of governors and other Roman officials who had committed offences during their term of office, a procedure which was open to individual cities and even persons but which the Romans themselves admitted presented difficulties. From 4 BC a new procedure was open to them.

58. EJ 311; Greek, stele from the market-place, Cyrene

5.

Edict of Imperator Caesar Augustus, Supreme Pontiff, in the nineteenth year of his tribunician power: the decree of the senate passed in the consulships of Caius Calvisius and Lucius Passienus while I was present and taking part in the drafting, which is pertinent to the welfare of the allies of the Roman People, I have determined to send to the provinces, and I annex it to my edict, so that it may become known to all who are in our care; it will make it clear to all who live in the provinces how much thought the senate and I give to preventing any of our subjects being submitted to unfair treatment or exactions of money.

Decree of the senate

Whereas the consuls Gaius Calvisius and Lucius Passienus Rufus spoke on 'matters pertinent to the welfare of the allies of the Roman People which Imperator Caesar Augustus, our leading citizen, desired in accordance with a resolution of the board of advisers which he has drawn by lot from the senate to be referred by us to the senate', the pleasure of the senate was as follows: Our ancestors provided by law for the establishment of courts for the restitution of property, so that our allies might be able more easily to sue for wrongs done them and to obtain property taken from them. Legal proceedings of this kind, however, sometimes prove extremely burdensome and disagreeable to the very persons on whose account the law was enacted, when witnesses have to be drawn from distant provinces who are persons of slender means, some of them infirm from disease or old age.

Accordingly the senate's pleasure is that if after the passing of this decree of the senate any of the allies wish to sue for restitution of property whether exacted from them as communities or as individuals (provided that the person who took it is not subject to a capital charge) and appear in connection with this property before one of the magistrates who are responsible for summoning the senate, the magistrate is to bring them before the senate as soon as possible and to grant them as advocate to speak on their behalf in the senate whomsoever they request. No one who is allowed exemption from performing this duty by the laws is to act as advocate if he is unwilling.

?(In order that there may be judges) for those who bring complaints in the senate, let them be heard, so that the magistrate who grants them access to the senate may the same day, in the presence of the senate with not less than two hundred members attending, draw lots from all the ex-consuls who are either in Rome itself or within twenty miles of the city, to the number of four; likewise from all the ex-praetors in Rome itself or within twenty miles of the city, to the number of three; likewise from all the rest of the senators or those who are entitled to give their opinion in the senate, who are at that moment either in Rome or within twenty miles of the city, two. He is to draw the name of no person who is seventy years old or more or who is assigned either to a magistracy or to some other function, or who is president of a court or in charge of grain distributions, or who is prevented by disease from performing this duty and has openly taken oath in presence of the senate to that effect and has offered three members of the senate to swear to the truth of it, or who is connected to the defendant by blood or marriage in such a way as to be exempt under the Julian law on jury courts if he is unwilling from giving evidence against him, or anyone who the defendant swears in the presence of the senate is a personal enemy of his; but he is not to take oath against more than three.

From the nine persons chosen by lot in this way, the magistrate who draws the lots is to ensure that within two days the parties seeking restitution of their property and the person from whom they seek it make rejections alternately, until five are left. If any of these jurymen dies before the case has been judged, or if any other cause prevents him from giving judgement and his reason is acceptable to five members of the senate on oath, then the magistrate in the presence of the jurymen and those who seek restitution and of the person from whom restitution is sought is to draw further lots among the men who are of the same rank and who have held the same offices as the man whose place is being reallotted, provided that he does not draw a man whom the senate is not permitted by this decree to include in the allotment to try the defendant (or perhaps the stonecutter meant to write, whom it is not permitted by this decree of the senate, etc.).

The jurymen selected are to hear evidence and give judgement on those sums only that the defendant is alleged to have exacted from communities and individuals, and they are to order him to return the total sum of money that the plaintiffs demonstrate has been carried off from them as individuals or communities, provided that the jury gives its verdict within thirty days. Persons under an obligation to determine these matters and declare a verdict are to be released from all public service, apart from the public rites of religion, until they have come to a decision and declared their verdict.

It is the pleasure of the senate that the magistrate who has drawn lots for the jurymen or, if he is unable, the senior consul, should preside over these proceedings and grant facilities to summon witnesses who are in Italy, provided that he does not permit the person seeking private restitution to summon more than five, those acting for a community more than ten.

Likewise it pleases the senate that the jurymen who are drawn in accordance with this decree should declare their several opinions openly, and concede the verdict given by the majority.

Several measures for the protection of the property and personal safety of provincials against senatorial officials had been passed since 149 BC culminating in the Julian law of 59, which had more than a hundred clauses (Cicero, *Letters to his Friends*, 8, 8, 3), imposed a multiple indemnity on the culprit, and even allowed for a penalty when violence had been used against the victims. The procedure was slow and cumbersome; 120 witnesses might be subpoenaed (Valerius Maximus 8, 1, 10) and a year allowed for the collection of evidence (Tacitus, *Annals*, 13, 43, 2). Now a short procedure is introduced for cases where there is no question of violence and the victims seek only the return of their property, and the case is to go before the senatorial board of five instead of being heard by one of the large courts of mixed panels of senators and knights. Convenient the limitation on witnesses might be, but it surely lessened the chances of securing a conviction.

The first attested case of prosecution of a governor by a provincial organisation under the Principate is that of Gaius Silanus, the proconsul of Asia convicted in 22 (Tacitus, *Annals* 3, 66ff.). The short procedure was not used: his offence was aggravated by physical violence and he was attacked in the senate not only by senatorial prosecutors but by the greatest orators of the entire Asian province. Not only senatorial governors but equestrian procurators might become the target (Tacitus, *Annals* 4, 15, 3ff.).

The course of a prosecution in the senate may be illustrated from the younger Pliny's report of the trial of Julius Bassus, governor of Bithynia-Pontus.

59. Pliny, *Letters* 4, 9, 1-10; 12-22

Gaius Pliny sends greetings to his friend Cornelius Ursus. Over the last few days Julius Bassus defended his case. He is a man who has led a troubled life and is well known for his misfortunes. He was put on trial under Vespasian by two private individuals; he was referred to the senate, was long kept in suspense and was eventually acquitted with flying colours. (2) Being a friend of Domitian, he was afraid of Titus, but it was Domitian who sent him into honourable exile. He was brought back by Nerva and was allocated Bithynia, from which he returned as an accused man, facing a prosecution that was as fiercely conducted as his defence was loyal. The verdicts given on his case were various, but the majority were almost charitable, if I may put it that way.

(3) Pomponius Rufus, an alert and energetic person, took the case against him and was backed up by Theophanes, one of the provincial envoys, who initiated the case and sparked it off. (4) On the other side there was myself: for Bassus had imposed on me the task of laying the foundation of his entire defence, of speaking of his distinction (which both his family's renown and the very vicissitudes he had undergone made considerable), (5) of telling of the conspiratorial activities of the accusers that the opposition had in their pay, of describing the grounds for hostility that he had given to all the worst troublemakers, such as Theophanes himself.

Bassus had wanted me likewise to meet the charge that was proving most damaging to him. As far as the others were concerned, they may have sounded more serious, but he was entitled not merely to an acquittal but to a vote of thanks as well. (6) What was bringing him down was the fact that, being an ingenuous and unsuspecting person, he had taken things from the provincials on the basis of his friendship with them (he had been quaestor in Bithynia too). This the prosecution called thefts and robberies: his own name for them was gifts.

But the law does forbid the acceptance even of gifts. (7) What was I to do at this point? What line of defence should I try? Denial? I was apprehensive that what I was afraid to admit would look like outright theft. Besides, denying a known fact would have aggravated his offence, not diminished it, especially when the defendant himself had left counsel not a leg to stand on: he had told numbers of people, even including the Emperor, that he had taken only the smallest presents, and those only on his birthday or at the Saturnalia — and had sent them to a large number of people as well. (8) Was I then to ask for clemency? I would have been cutting the defendant's throat by admitting that his offences were such as to mean that he could only be saved by an act of clemency. Was I to defend his behaviour as correct? Instead of doing him any good, I should have shown up my own lack of respect for the court. (9) I decided to keep to a kind of mid-way course through the problem; and I seem to have succeeded.

Night interrupted my speech, as it does battles. I had been in action three and a half hours and had an hour and a half left. (The prosecution had received the six hours allowed by the law, the defence nine, and the accused had divided his time between me and the man who was to speak after me on the basis that I was to have five hours at my disposal and he the rest.) (10). The success of my speech was counselling me to silence and an end of speaking; it is reckless not to be satisfied when things are going well. Besides, I was apprehensive in case my bodily strength should desert me when I took up the task again: it is more difficult to resume than to continue . . . (12) But Bassus implored me, repeatedly entreating me and practically in tears, to use up my allotted time. I gave way and put his welfare before my own. It came off: I found the senate so attentive, so fresh, that they seemed rather to have been stimulated than satiated by my previous speech.

(13) Lucceius Albinus followed me, with such deftness that our speeches are regarded as having combined the diversity of two speeches with the unity of thought of one . . . (14) Herennius Pollio spoke in reply, pressing us hard and effectively; then came Theophanes again. He showed the same extreme lack of respect at this point as he did elsewhere, by claiming time for his own speech (extra time at that) after two polished speakers of consular rank. He went on till dusk and actually after dark when lights had been brought in. (15) On the following day Homullus and Fronto did wonders with their speeches for Bassus; the fourth day was taken up with hearing the evidence.

(16) The verdict of Baebius Macer, the consul designate, was that Bassus was liable to the full rigour of the law on the recovery of property, that of Caepio Hispo that the board of assessors should fix the amount to be paid without prejudice to Bassus' status. Both were right. (17) 'How can that be' you ask, 'when they gave such different verdicts?' Well, because one had to agree with Macer, who had the law in mind, that he was right to condemn the man who had taken gifts contrary to the law, and Caepio's view that the senate may both relax and intensify legal penalties, as indeed it may, justifies his overlooking behaviour that is certainly forbidden but not infrequently practised.

(18) Caepio's view prevailed; in fact when he rose to give it he was cheered, something that usually happens when a senator sits down again . . . (19) All the same, opinions were divided two ways among the public as they were in the senate: those who approved of Caepio's proposal criticize that of Macer as inflexible and harsh; those who approved of Macer's call the other ill-founded and even self-contradictory: they argue that it is inconsistent to keep a man in the senate when you have sent him before the assessors.

(20) There was a third proposal too. Valerius Paulinus agreed with Caepio and put forward the further view that a motion should be put to the senate about Theophanes when he had given an account of his

mission. He was being accused of having acted in the course of his prosecution in a way that made him liable under the very same law he was invoking against Bassus. (21) But although this proposal won extraordinary approval from the overwhelming majority of the senate, the consuls did not follow it through. (22) Paulinus however won a reputation for his sense of justice as well as for standing his ground. The senate was adjourned and Bassus was greeted by a large crowd of people cheering loudly and highly delighted. The well known story of his earlier vicissitudes had been brought to mind, his name was known to people from the danger he had been in, and, though a man of fine physique, he was old, unkempt and downcast; that had won people over to him.

Early 103. Julius Bassus had been governor of Bithynia-Pontus a year or two earlier, and may be the governor whose criminal acts were listed by Dio of Prusa (**172**). The sentences of exile and resultant deaths mentioned by Dio would give ground for a more serious charge than that of taking money, but it was not entertained by the senate at Bassus' trial. Sherwin-White cites Ulpian in *Digest* 1, 16, 6, 3, Marcian at 48, 11, 1, 1, and Venuleius, ibid., 6, 2, for the gradual introduction of a distinction between small gifts and large, with 100 *aurei* as the final limit overall.

The two proposals of (16) differ in that Baebius Macer sought Bassus' expulsion from the senate. Flexibility in procedure and penalties (17) allowed the senate to show leniency, at least when the rights of provincials were in question. But it emerges from Pliny, *Letters*, 10, 56, 4, that Bassus' acts as proconsul were rescinded and his judicial decisions were made subject to a rehearing if the case were brought within two years. That would be surprising if Bassus' offences had been merely technical (16).

What Valerius Paulinus was proposing in (20) was that Theophanes should be charged with taking money for organising the prosecution (cf. (5)); Sherwin-White cites Venuleius in *Digest* 48, 11, 6, 2, for the offence. (The polished consular advocates who precede him in (14) are his fellow prosecutors Rufus and Pollio, not Pliny and Lucceius!)

5

Financing

The Roman Empire had to pay (**1**): not only had the costs of conquest and organisation to be met, but groups and individuals for whose benefit it had been developed must take a profit, legitimate or otherwise: senators, knights and people, from booty, land, business and the exercise of power. This continued under the Principate, but there were changes. Not only were victories, many won in Germany and the Balkans, less enriching (although Trajan's conquest of Dacia, completed in 106, did bring in quantities of gold), but what senatorial commanders retained was relatively meagre. The equestrian companies lost their hold on direct taxes; instead, individuals accepted salaried posts as imperial procurators and supervised the collection of dues by local officials (**13ff.**); senatorial governors likewise received salaries (Cassius Dio, *Roman History* 52, 23, 1; 25, 2; 53, 15, 4). The position of soldiers and the people of Rome, on the other hand, improved under the Principate: pay, booty and land continued to come the way of the soldiers, and the people could look on the distribution of free grain as a right (**104**), with money distributions as an occasional supplement. The people profited from booty, whoever won it: the prizes of victory were traditionally devoted in part to construction, and that meant employment (Brunt, *JRS* 70 (1980), 81ff.). Army and people were well placed to put pressure on the one individual who, partly because of their support (**2**), was best able to command the resources of the state.

In the Emperor we find both the greatest of the senators on the make, and the man who had effectively assumed responsibility for state financing: in him private profit and the needs of the state merged. We can leave aside the perpetual but incalculable factor of private opportunism and move to the overall balance sheet, starting with income and going on to disbursements. Since control was now concentrated in the hands of the Emperor it is not relevant to ponder whether the revenues at his disposal were theoretically those of the state (see Brunt 1966), 'crown' property (Crawford 1976) or personal acquisitions (**209**).

It is useful (with Hopkins 1980, 101), to divide the provinces into an outer ring in which armies were stationed and an inner ring of relatively rich tax-exporting areas. The question is how much the costs of the former left from the revenues of the latter for the support of Italy: then there are the finances of local communities to consider.

Whether the rate of taxation imposed by Rome was 'low' or 'high' is a matter for discussion (see Hopkins 1980, 105; Brunt 1981). The prerequisite for its successful extraction was an accurate assessment of wealth.

Augustus had left Judaea under Herod the Great, but Herod's successor had made himself unpopular and after ten years he was deposed; Sulpicius Quirinius, consul 12 BC, was sent to govern Syria and reduce Judaea to provincial status in AD 6. The census he immediately took is mentioned by Josephus, *Jewish Antiquities* 18, 1ff., and by *Luke* 2, 2, as well as the following document. Roman haste led here (as elsewhere, cf. **196**) to the unrest described by Josephus, and that ultimately to the nationalist uprising of **199**.

60. EJ 231; in Venice since the seventeenth century

Quintus Aemilius Secundus, son of Quintus, of the Palatina Tribe, serving in the camp of the deified Augustus under Publius Sulpicius Quirinius, Caesar's legate in Syria, won military honours as prefect of the First, Augustan, Cohort and of the Second, Naval, Cohort. On the orders of Quirinius I was also the person who conducted the census of the city of Apamea; 117 thousand citizens of both sexes. I was also despatched by Quirinius against the Ituraeans in Mount Lebanon and captured one of their strongholds; and prior to military service I was prefect of engineers on the accredited staff of the consuls, and quaestor, twice aedile, twice duovir, and pontiff in the colony. On this spot were laid to rest Quintus Aemilius Secundus, son of Quintus, of the Palatina Tribe, my son, and Aemilia Chia my freedwoman. This tomb will not pass further to the heir.

Secundus was a native of the colony of Berytus, founded **c**. 15 BC, and his post as 'engineer' was now equivalent to that of an *aide de camp*. For disturbances in Mount Lebanon, see Strabo, *Geography* 16, 2, 18, p. 755; the colony had been founded to deter them (cf. **40**).

When a community's population was known, and the value of their property declared, they could be made responsible for the payment of a lump sum (**70**).

Uniformity is not to be expected over an area as diverse as the entire Roman Empire: type of produce, economic development and degree of monetarisation, all varied (**114**); and the Romans found diverse schemes of taxation operating in the provinces they created.

61. [Hyginus,] The Establishment of Boundaries, 205L

Lands subject to tax have many systems. In some provinces they provide a fixed proportion of their produce, some a fifth, some a seventh, others provide money, doing this on the basis of a valuation of the ground. Fixed rates of payment have been established for land; in Pannonia, for instance, there is first and second class arable, meadows, mast-bearing woods, common woodland and pasturage. On all these types of land tax has been fixed by their productivity per *iugerum*. In the valuation of these lands care must be taken over the measurements to prevent habitual usage prevailing after false declarations have been made.

The quota on produce as opposed to tax based on the capital value of property is less equitable than it appears, at least in years of dearth, as Brunt points out (1981, 170): the big landowner could sell his remaining produce at a raised price, while the subsistence farmer might have to buy seed on the market. A whole decade of bad harvests might tend, as Dr Nash suggests, to favour large estates.

The surveying of the territory of Pessinus on the orders of Caracalla is attested.

62. J. Devreker, Latomus 30 (1971), 352ff.; boundary stone from Pessinus, Phrygia; Greek

Good Fortune! Imperator Caesar Marcus Aurelius Antoninus, Unconquered, Pious and Fortunate, Augustus, Supreme Pontiff, Greatest Parthicus, Greatest Britannicus, Greatest Germanicus, holder of tribunician power, 19 times consul, 4 times proconsul (*sic*), Father of his Country, ordered the lands on the entire territory of the distinguished city of Pessinus to be measured up with the sacred ?measuring rod, under the supervision of Caesius Felicissimus, leading centurion, in the consulships of Catius Sabinus (for the second time) and Cornelius Anullinus.

The stone was cut in 216, and the lapicide should have written 'in his 19th year of tribunician power, 4 times consul, proconsul'.

Devreker argues that the territory was measured by the sacred, i.e. imperial, '*gramme*' (the lapicide has bungled the Latin *groma*, an instrument illustrated by J. Dilke, *The Roman Land Surveyors* (Newton Abbot, 1979), 50) to facilitate exaction of taxes for Caracalla's forthcoming Parthian war (cf. **75**). It is, however, conceivable that the action was taken in the interests of the great temple city itself, to restore income lost through illicit occupation of public or temple land; the measures taken by Hadrian for the temple of Zeus at Aezani (Smallwood, *Nerva-Hadrian* 454; discussion forthcoming in *MAMA* 9) would be a partial parallel, with, as Devreker points out, a leading centurion supervising the action.

Details of registration are given by Ulpian in his extended work on censuses (the surviving evidence for censuses is collected by Brunt 1981, 171f.); he seems to imply that they took place every ten years.

63. Ulpian, Censuses, Book 3, in *Digest* 50, 15, 4

The census regulations provide that landed properties are to be registered for census purposes in the following manner: name of each estate; in what city territory and parish it is; two nearest neighbours; acreage of the arable land sown within the previous ten years; number of vines the vineyard has; olives, acreage and number of trees; acreage of meadowland mown within the previous ten years; pasture-lands, estimated acreage; likewise woodland for felling. The person registering is to make all the estimates himself.

(1) The registrar ought to make due allowance for the claims of equity: this would mean that it would be consistent with his duty for a man who has a quantity of land entered in the public records and is unable to make use of it for reasons stipulated to be given tax-relief. On the same principle too if he has lost part of his land because of a landslide he will be entitled to be given relief by the registrar. If vines have died or his trees are stricken with drought it is inequitable that that quantity should be entered in the census return; whereas if he has cut down trees or vines he is none the less required to declare the former total at the time of the census, unless he offers the registrar convincing reasons for cutting them down.

(2) A man who possesses land in another city territory has to declare it in the city where the land is, for tax raised on land should lighten the burdens of the city in whose territory the land is in ownership.

(3) Although grants of immunity from taxation made to certain individuals are extinguished with the death of the individual, nevertheless immunity attached without specific restrictions to districts or cities is thought to be given on such terms as to make it heritable.

(4) If I declared an estate when I was in possession of it, while the plaintiff who was suing for it did not, it has been decided that his action still stands.

(5) In registering slaves one must take care that their nationalities, ages, functions and skills are individually registered. (6) The owner is also obliged to register for census purposes fish ponds and harbours. (7) Salt pans, if there are any on the property, are also to be registered as such for the census. (8) If anyone fails to declare any immigrant or tenant farmer he is liable to the penalty of chaining for misdemeanours connected with the census. (9) Any births taking place after the census figures have been handed in or acquisitions made afterwards can be handed in by declarations made before the work is finally completed. (10) In the case of a man who has made a request for a special concession involving permission to alter his census return and then discovers after his request has been granted that he ought not to have made it because there was no call for an alteration, he will not put himself at a legal disadvantage for having requested permission to alter his return: there have been repeated written replies to this effect.

Although Italy had been exempt from direct tax since 167 BC, Roman citizens with property in the provinces were normally liable, unless they were members of cities which by a fiction were treated as part of the peninsula. The benefits of the 'Italian right' were not only fiscal: holders also enjoyed a privileged form of land tenure.

64. Ulpian, Censuses, Book 1, in *Digest* 50, 15, 1

One should be aware that there are certain colonies that possess the Italian right. One of these is the most splendid colony of the people of Tyre in Syria Phoenice, of which I am a native: it was notable for its territorial possessions; the passage of centuries had given it extreme antiquity; it was mighty in war; and it was very determined to keep the treaty it made with the Romans; for the deified Severus and our present Emperor have granted it the Italian right for its outstandingly distinguished loyalty to the state and the Roman Empire. (1) But the colony of Berytus too in the same province is one that the favours shown it by Augustus have made influential and (as the deified Hadrian calls it in a speech) 'Augustan'; and it has the Italian right. There is also the colony of Heliopolis, which received the constitution of an 'Italic' colony from the deified Severus as an outcome of the civil war. (3) There is also the colony of Laodiciea in Coele Syria, which the deified Severus granted the Italian right for services in the civil war. For the colony of Ptolemais, which is situated between Phoenice and Palestine, has nothing but the title of colony. (4) But the city of Emesa in Phoenice our present Emperor has given the status of a colony and put it in possession of the Italian right. (5) There is also the city of Palmyra in the province of Phoenice, situated close to uncivilised tribes and people. (6) In Palestine there have been two colonies, Caesarea and Capitolina, but neither has the Italian right. (7) It was the deified Severus also who founded a colony in the city of Sebaste. (8) In Dacia too the colony of the Zernenses, founded by the deified Trajan, has the Italian right; (9) Sarmizegethusa also is in possession of the same right; likewise Colonia Napocensis, Colonia Apulensis and the village of the Patavissenses, which secured colonial status from the deified Severus. (10) In Bithynia there is also the colony of Apamea and in Pontus that of Sinope. (11) In Cilicia there are also Selinus and Trajanopolis.

Other colonies in possession of the right are listed in the same chapter of the *Digest*; they are in Spain, Gaul and Germany as well as the East. What Sherwin-White 1973(a), 276, calls a 'somewhat barbarous list' shows that one criterion for the grant was loyalty to the successful claimant in a civil war, in this case that of 193 between Severus and Pescennius Niger: the tribulations of an outpost of empire like Palmyra make a more reputable claim. Sherwin-White, 316, convincingly sees the origin of the grant under Caesar and Augustus as a concession to expatriate Italians, especially those in far-flung parts of the Empire, where the distinction between settlers and natives had to be maintained. It was not necessarily confined to colonies (Selinus was not one); and individuals could possess comparable rights, as Sherwin-White, 317, points out (**154**). Communities could also possess immunity without having the Italian right proper: see **153**.

There was considerable diversity in the indirect taxes levied in provinces and dependencies: note the sales tax casually implied for Africa in **48**.

While collection of direct taxes passed from equestrian companies to the cities (**63, 67ff.**), supervised by Roman officials (**14**), indirect taxes such as customs dues remained largely in the hands of private contractors who did the work and made their profit by extracting more from the provincials than they had undertaken to produce for the state (see Brunt in Jones 1974 (6), 180ff.). Not surprisingly there were complaints about the 'publicans' of *Matthew* 9, 10; see Tacitus, *Annals* 13, 50f., where Nero's response was to suggest abolishing indirect taxation; in the event he ordered only that the rules governing each impost should be made known.

65. *AE* 1923, 22; from Thuburbo Maius, Africa

Consecrated to the Augustan Venus. Titus Carfanius Barbarus, son of Titus, of the Pollian Tribe, and Tiberius Claudius Timonianus, son of Spurius, of the Papirian Tribe, acting directors of the company dealing with the four public taxes of Africa, made the dedication. Venustus, manager, at his own expense, reconstructed the chapel from its foundations.

The taxes in question were all being collected by a single company. They were, in the view of De Laet 1949, 247ff., the customs dues, normally levied at $2\frac{1}{2}$ per cent, sometimes at 5 per cent or even 12 per cent; a 5 per cent tax on the freeing and a 4 per cent tax on the selling of slaves; and a 1 per cent tax on inheritances; these are found in combination elsewhere. The name of the company shows that it was organised before Numidia and Mauretania came into existence as separate provinces.

Customs posts manned by the company's agents are naturally found in the coastal towns of north Africa; this inland station would have been responsible for collecting dues at a crossing of the Meliana river.

The pivotal role of the cities in maintaining the Empire is illustrated by the part they played in collecting imperial taxes. The jurists show them appointing men (not always councillors) for the purpose, and a committee of ten (or twenty) leading men guaranteeing revenue.

66. Paulus, Monograph on Judicial Inquiries, in *Digest* 49, 18, 5

The deified Antoninus the Great (Caracalla) wrote a reply with his father to the effect that discharged soldiers were exempted from the duty of contributing to the construction of ships. (1) But they also enjoy immunity from exacting tribute; that is, they are not to be appointed tax collectors. (2) But discharged soldiers who have agreed to be enrolled in city councils are compelled to perform civic functions.

67. Papinian, Answers to Queries, Book 1, in *Digest* 50, 1, 17, 7

The function of exacting tribute is not classified as degrading and for that reason is also entrusted to members of city councils.

68. Ulpian, Opinions, Book 2, in *Digest* 50, 4, 3, 10f.

It was formerly acceptable for men to be elected to the board of ten leading men before the age of twenty-five (but not if they were on military service), because this is a burden that seems rather to fall on a man's estate. (11) The task of exacting tribute payments is agreed to be a burden on a man's estate.

69. Arcadius Charisius Monograph of the Financial Obligations of Citizens, in *Digest* 50, 4, 18, 26

The functions of the boards of ten or twenty leading men are of a hybrid nature, as Herennius Modestinus determined on excellent grounds, both in commentary and in discussion: for members of the boards when they exact tribute payments are both performing a personal service and making up for losses to the imperial Treasury by paying in the names of deceased persons. So that this function ought properly to be counted in the hybrid group.

Ulpian's emphasis on the job as one that imposes a burden on a man's estate (as opposed to one that costs only time and work) leads Dr Mackie to suggest that the 'ten leading men' could simply pay someone else to do the actual work.

How a state coped with the tax assessment imposed on it by Rome, and the interest shown in the process by Roman officials, are shown in an elaborate document from the Peloponnese.

70. *IG* 5, 1, 1432f., with A. Wilhelm, Jahresh. d. österr. arch. Inst. 17 (1914), 1ff.; Greek, from Messene in Achaea

In the [priesthood] of Agathos, [in the sixth month]. Decrees.

(1) [Aristocles], secretary [of the councillors], introduced the assessment of the 8 obol tax into the council, with an account of the [revenues accruing from] it and how each has been spent on the purposes ordained, showed that he had used it for nothing [other than these purposes], and made his statement of the sums of money still owing from the tax in the theatre before non-members of the council and in the presence of Vibius the praetorian legate, taking into account how as far as possible the sums owing might be collected for the city, having regard to the view of all the councillors themselves as to the carrying out of the impost, without these contributions involving either taking out a loan or incurring a deficit. In this connection also the councillors approved his care and integrity and with Vibius the praetorian legate were eager to do him the honour of a bronze statue, while Vibius the praetorian legate personally gave him in the presence of all the citizens the right to wear a gold ring, and the councillors themselves accorded [him] the same honour along with the statue, and a number made their view clear by acclaiming the acceptance of the honours by Aristocles the secretary of the councillors. Upon his acceptance the councillors passed the following resolution:

To congratulate Aristocles for the care and integrity with which he conducts himself in connection with the public interests of the city in his administration of business on behalf of the city both currently and on all other occasions; and that the honours that have been given him by the councillors and praetorian legate are to be permanently his; and that he is to be permitted to set up the statue in front of the city hall and to inscribe on the pedestal: 'The city, to Aristocles son of Callicrates, secretary of the councillors, for his merits and the unfailing loyalty he shows to it'; but that the costs of the statue and its pedestal are to be paid from the revenues of the city and he is himself to supervise the setting up of the statue and pedestal.

(2) Whereas Aristocles the son of Callicrates on succeeding to the office entrusted to him by the magistrates and councillors took prompt care for the proper protection both of the city and of its inhabitants, as far as it lay within his power; first of all he gave his attention to the clear daily writing up on the wall of all the financial transactions of the city by those responsible for handling any business of the city, setting a beneficial example to worthy men of integrity and justice in the conduct of office, while he himself, desiring to be free of any taint of suspicion whatsoever in the entire citizen body as to the integrity of his dealings, has engaged in no financial transaction either on his own account or covertly through the agency of others; instead he has appointed men of sound character as collectors for each civic duty and financial transaction, and secures the city a completely sound state of affairs at a time when imposts have been laid upon it involving many large sums. He has achieved many important advantages to the benefit of the city at the

hands of the governors, some here in the city, some as an envoy. Further, in entertaining governors and numerous other Romans too he devotes the expenditure of his own money to the advantage of the city. And he has paid attention to the just and equitable administration of all the other affairs of its inhabitants, proving worthy of the offices that it had previously put into his charge; on account of his excellent conduct in those offices too he was given the honour of statues by the city. And on account of the merits inscribed above, Memmius the proconsul and Vibius the praetorian legate have each in recognition of his conduct given him the right to wear the gold ring, as has the council also, while all with one accord declared that it was right that Aristocles should be given honours worthy of him for all the merits inscribed above, and all the citizens have been eager to accord him the honour of a statue and two carved portraits; and it is fitting that good patriotic men whose concern is entirely disinterested should be congratulated and honoured with the appropriate forms of distinction.

Accordingly the council and people have decreed as follows: To congratulate Aristocles the son of Callicrates, on his care in matters of public interest and for his integrity and his disinterestedness [and benevolence toward the] citizens, [likewise] too for the many substantial [achievements which are bringing advantage to the city - - -].

(1433). (In this document 70 drachmas make a mina.)

(Assessment of)	Talents	*Minae*	Staters	Drachmas	Obols	*Chalci*
[Cresphon]tis (tribe):	122	30	1		8½	
[Daiphonti]s (tribe):	106	56	5		8	
Ar[istom]achis (tribe):	249	4	20		10	
Hyllis (tribe):	149		15		1	
Cleodaea (tribe):	261	50	1		4	10
Aliens, with Romans assessed in the tribe:						
	129	11	22	1		
Totals:	1,018	32	1(!32)		8(!1½)	10

Artisans (those not included in the tribes), for whom the sum total of property is reckoned at:

	31	49	15		10	
Also Olympic victors:	4	15	13		9	

Also the Romans not assessed under Damon, and those under protection of treaty relations, without the adjustment, since it is still pending ?audit:

	118	21	22		7	

Value of the adjustment to the assessment adjudged after audit or registered by those concerned, apart from those liable to tax whose position is not yet determined, up to the tenth month:

	73	25	12		11	

Also those who have not submitted an assessment but are liable to pay the contributions, coming to a total of:

	7	50	25			
Totals:	1,256(!1,254)	5(!14)	16(!21)		10(!9)	10

From this is to be subtracted the assessment of those who were assessed under Damon at the same rate:

| | 2 | 34 | |

The valuation of Hippica and Callista, estates of Thalon, with adjustment:

| | 8 | 37 | 21 | | 8 |

The Automeia estate of Nemerius assessed by Damon:

| | 2 | 50 | |

| Totals: | 14 | 1 | 21 | | 8 |

Remainder, on which the 8 obol tax is to be levied:

| | 1,242 | 4(!3) | 30 | | 2 | 10 |

On this, tax at 8 obols: 99,365 *denarii*, 2 obols.

Of this there has come in, by the thirteenth day of the seventh month, as inscribed on the wall by the collectors:

83,574 *denarii*, 3 *chalci*

Remainder, still to come in: 15,797 (!15,791) *denarii*, 5 (!1) obols, 9 *chalci*

(This includes tax due from)	Denarii	Minae	Staters	Drachmas	Obols	Chalci
Men on active service:	411					6
Estates of free persons deceased:	487					6
Manual workers on public service:	89				2	6
Slave oarsmen:	82				5	
Arrears:						
Cresphontis:	1,870				4	
Daiphontis:	1,158				3	6
Aristomachis:	2,202				5	
Hyllis:	2,177				4	6
Cleodaea:	1,480				5	6
Aliens:	3,752					
Unassessed:	97				2	

Romans and persons from cities in treaty relations:
1,424

Exempt from tax, and Olympic victors:
1,349

For a date of 35-44 for this inscription, see A. Giovannini, *Rome et la circulation monétaire en Grèce* (Basel, 1978), 115ff., and Hopkins 1980, 121 n.59. It seems that a sum of 100,000 *denarii*, the target of the calculations (cf. the figure of 99,365 *denarii*, 2 obols) was imposed on Messene as its tax contribution. The honorand divided up the burden in the form of a tax of 8 Attic obols in the *mina*, 6 to the *denarius* (1.9 per cent).

The stone first gives the value of property owned by Messenians and aliens, subtracts the assessments of those exempt or already taken into account, and arrives at a total of taxable property: the total sum to be realised by imposing the 8 obol tax on this capital follows, then the amount already raised, and finally the arrears.

In spite of his honours Aristocles has not got his sums quite correct, or the stonecutter has let him down (! indicates each fresh error, with corrected figure following).

Note the exclusion of some artisans and manual workers in the mines from the tribes (cf. **186**).

The resources at the disposal of the Emperor did not come only from taxation: enormous sums accrued by inheritance (cf. Tacitus, *Agricola* 43, 4), confiscation (**72**), and booty (cf. Pliny, *Natural History* 12, 111ff.). The balsam gardens that Pliny mentions illustrate the diversity of the sources of imperial revenue.

71. *IGR* 4, 131; from Miletopolis, Mysia

Memorial of Alexander, which he constructed for himself during his lifetime and for his wife and for his children. If any person inserts anyone else, he shall pay 501 *denarii* to the imperial Treasury and 501 to the city.

It was very common in the eastern provinces to protect a tomb from unauthorised use by setting a fine for violators; by making the fine payable to the imperial Treasury, even in senatorial provinces like Asia, the owners tried to make the fine a real deterrent: the imperial agents were thought to be keen collectors. Alexander made doubly sure by giving his city an interest in protecting his tomb as well.

It was largely by confiscation that the Emperors came to control the all-important gold, silver and copper mines of the Empire. The passage that follows gives an early example.

72. Tacitus, *Annals* 6, 19, 1

After the downfall of these people, Sextus Marius, the richest man in the Spanish provinces, was accused of incestuous relations with his daughter and thrown from the Tarpeian Rock. And in case there should be any doubt of its being the size of his fortune that caused his ruin, Tiberius sequestered for his own use his gold and copper mines, although they had been confiscated to the state.

This is an event of the year 33. Tacitus implies that the mines entered the private possession of the Emperor; but the justification for transferring the mines (near Corduba in Baetica) to his control would have been the heavy expense to the imperial Treasury of running the imperial Spanish provinces.

73. Smallwood, *Nerva-Hadrian* 439; Vipasca, Lusitania, on the last of a series of bronze tablets

[- - - sends] greetings to his friend Ulpius Aelianus.

(1) [- - -] is to pay [? the] imperial [procurator] forthwith. If anyone does not do so and is convicted of having smelted ore before paying the price as prescribed above, the share of the occupant is forfeit and the procurator of the mines is to sell the entire mine. The person who has proved that the tenant has smelted ore before paying for the half share belonging to the imperial Treasury is to receive one quarter.

(2) Silver mines must be worked in accordance with the prescription embodied in this law. Prices for them will be maintained on the generous terms of the most sacred Emperor Hadrian Augustus: ownership of the share that belongs to the imperial Treasury is to pass to the person who first pays the fees for the shaft and delivers 4,000 sesterces to the imperial Treasury.

(3) Anyone who, out of a total of five mines, strikes ore in one, is to carry on work in the rest without interruption, as is laid down above; if he fails to do so, another is to have the power to take over occupancy.

(4) If anyone begins operations immediately after the expiry of the twenty-five days granted for the accumulation of funds but afterwards ceases them over a period of ten successive days, another is to have the right to take over occupancy.

(5) When a mine has been sold by the imperial Treasury and has been left unworked over a period of six successive months, another is to have the right to take over occupancy, on the basis that when ore is produced from it one half is to be reserved for the imperial Treasury in the usual way.

(6) The occupant of the mine is to be permitted to have the partners he wishes, on the basis that each partner is to contribute expenses in the same proportion as his interest in the partnership. If anyone fails to do so, then the man who has incurred the expenses is to have an account of the expenses incurred by him posted up for three days in succession in the most frequented part of the market place and is to give notice by crier to each of his partners that he is to contribute his share of the expenses. Any partner who does not do so, or who acts in any way wilfully to avoid contributing or to deceive any one or more of his partners, is not to have a share in that mine, and that share is to belong to the partner or partners who incurred the expenses.

(7) That person or those tenants who have incurred expense in connection with a mine in which there were several partners are to have the right of recovering from their partners what has manifestly been spent in good faith.

(8) Tenants are to be permitted to sell to one another at the best price they can obtain also those shares of mines which they have bought from

the imperial Treasury and for which they have paid the full price. Anyone who wishes to sell his share or to buy one is to make a declaration before the procurator who is in charge of the mines; buying and selling by other methods are not to be permitted. The owner who is in debt to the imperial Treasury is not to be permitted to dispose of his share by way of gift.

(9) Ore which has been produced and is lying at the mines shall be conveyed to the workshops between sunrise and sunset by those to whom it belongs. Anyone who is convicted of having taken ore from the mines after sunset or at night is to have to pay 1,000 sesterces to the imperial Treasury.

(10) Anyone who steals ore, if he is a slave, the procurator is to have him flogged and sold on the understanding that he is to be kept in chains in perpetuity and is not to be kept in any mines or territories belonging to them; the price fetched by the slave is to belong to the master. If the thief is a free man the procurator is to seize his property and banish him from the confines of the mines in perpetuity.

(11) All mines are to be carefully propped and made stable, and the tenant of each is to replace rotten wood with props of fresh and adequate material.

(12) It is not permissible to touch or interfere with piers or props left behind as supports nor to do anything wilfully to render those props and piers less secure or to make them less easy to pass.

(13) As to anyone who is convicted of having damaged a mine, caused it to collapse, interfered with the installations at its head, or of having done anything wilfully to render that mine less stable, if he is a slave he is to be flogged at the discretion of the procurator and sold by his master on the understanding that he is not to be kept in any mines, while the procurator is to confiscate the property of a free man to the imperial Treasury and banish him from the confines of the mines in perpetuity.

(14) Anyone who is working copper mines is to keep away from the channel that drains water off from the mines and he is to leave not less than fifteen feet clear on either side of it.

(15) It is not permissible to interfere with the channel. The procurator is to give permission to drive an exploratory shaft from the channel with the purpose of opening up new deposits, on the basis that the exploratory shaft is to have a width and height of not more than four feet.

(16) It is not permissible to explore or to work veins less than fifteen feet on either side of the channel.

(17) Anyone who is convicted of having acted otherwise in connection with exploratory shafts, if he is a slave he shall, after being flogged at the discretion of the procurator, be sold (by) his master on the understanding that he is not to be kept in any mines, while the procurator is to

confiscate the property of a free man to the imperial Treasury and to banish him from the confines of the mines in perpetuity.

(18) Anyone who [is working] silver mines is to keep away from the channel that drains water off from the mines and is to leave not less than sixty feet clear on either side of it, and he is to keep those mines that he has taken over or received as his allocation in operation as they are delimited. He is not to proceed further nor to collect slag in heaps nor to drive exploratory shafts beyond the confines of the mine allocated to him in such a way that [- - -]

The imperial administration did not work mines directly: private operators were supervised by a (freedman) procurator who also controlled the district round the mines (Smallwood, *Nerva-Hadrian* 440: both documents have been elucidated by Flach 1979). The document above is probably part of a letter sent to him by the provincial procurator of mines in the reign of Hadrian. If a prospector took on a copper or silver mine he received half free, while he had to buy the other half at a legally fixed price. The 'generosity' of Hadrian held the price for a copper mine at its old level and reduced that of a silver mine to 4,000 sesterces; prospectors had to give half their yield to the imperial Treasury.

As the Emperor secured control of an ever larger proportion of state revenue and his private wealth continued to play a vital part in state finances, the state Treasury proper became correspondingly weaker: we hear of subventions and economy commissions and by the end of the first century it was serving little more than the city of Rome itself.

More important is the question of the ability of the combined resources of state and imperial Treasuries to cope with the burdens placed on them. Army pay and, as the following passage shows, provision of bounties for discharged soldiers had caused serious problems from the beginning of the Principate. Here and in 52, 6, 1, but only obliquely in **85**, Dio brings out the importance of the army as the chief charge, running at at least 445,000 million sesterces a year (Hopkins 1980, 124f.). Tribute, says Ulpian in *Digest* 50, 16, 27, was what was attributed to the soldiers, and stipendiary communities paid their 'stipends' (see J. Richardson in *JRS* 66 (1976), 147ff., a reference I owe to Dr Mackie). The minting of coins was directly related to the military activity and the needs of the troops (Hopkins 1980, 110f.).

74. Cassius Dio, *Roman History* 55, 24, 9-25, 6

For these reasons, then, Augustus was in financial difficulties, and he brought a proposal before the senate that an adequate fund should be designated in perpetuity to ensure that the troops received from the taxes imposed both maintenance and bounties in generous measure without any inconvenience to any outside person . . . (25, 1) After this, in the consulships of Aemilius Lepidus and Lucius Arruntius, when no satisfactory source of funds was coming to light, but absolutely everyone was taking it amiss that it was being looked for, (2) Augustus contributed sums of money in his own name and in that of Tiberius to the treasury which he gave the name of the Military Treasury . . . (3) . . . , and he promised to do the same every year and accepted subscriptions from kings and certain communities; from private individuals he took nothing, although many of them would have been glad to contribute something, so they claimed. (4) But as these sources were minute in comparison with the size of the expenditure and what he needed was a source of supply that would not dry up, he instructed the senators each one independently to look for sources of funds, enter them in notebooks, and give them to him to examine; not that he had no sources of his own in mind but because that was the easiest way of persuading them to choose the one he preferred. (5) In short, when they had all made different proposals he gave his approval to none of them but instituted the 5% tax on inheritances and legacies that men might leave on their deaths, unless the beneficiaries were really close relations or the testators poor. He claimed to have found this tax drawn up in Caesar's memoranda. (6) It had been introduced once before, had subsequently been abolished, and was now introduced for the second time. This then was the way he increased the revenues.

The debates of 5-6 on discharge gratuities (not pay) ended in a result distasteful to the senate on two counts: the establishment of a new tax on their wealth and (implicitly) the hiving off of funds from the state treasury, making them unavailable for other purposes. Controversy continued (Cassius Dio, *Roman History* 56, 28, 4; Tacitus, *Annals* 1, 78, 2); even so, mutinies on the Rhine and in Pannonia in 14 showed that the new treasury was not a complete answer to the problem.

Unpopular emperors were accused of extravagance, sometimes rightly, but Caracalla's 'generosity' to the soldiers was a political necessity, for the security of the Empire as well as his own.

75. Cassius Dio, *Roman History*, Epitome of Book 78, 9, 1-7

Antoninus, then, this great admirer of Alexander, was fond of spending money on the soldiers, whom he used to keep about him in very large numbers, alleging in excuse one reason after another and one war after another: but as to all the rest of mankind he was working hard to strip, despoil, and wear them out, especially the senators. (2) Leave aside the gold crowns that he frequently demanded on the pretext of a never-ending series of victories over one enemy or another (I am referring not to the actual getting up of crowns, the cost of which is infinitesimal, but to the quantity of money given under that head with which the cities have always been used to 'crown' the Emperors). (3) Leave aside the supplies that we were having exacted from us in large quantities and from all sources, some of it as free gifts and some of it actually involving additional expenditure, all of which the man used to lavish on the soldiers or even used to sell off retail. Leave aside the presents he used to demand both from wealthy individuals and from communities, (4) and the taxes, new ones that he ordained as extras and especially the 10% tax that he created to take the place of the 5% tax on the freeing of slaves, inheritances to certain classes of people, and every form of legacy, doing away with succession rights and the exemptions from tax (5) allowed in the case of persons close kin to the deceased (that was why he designated as Roman citizens all the inhabitants of his Empire: the claim was that it was a privilege, but the real purpose was to increase his income from a measure of this kind: non-citizens did not pay most of those taxes). (6) Leave all these things quite aside: we were being forced at our private expense to build all kinds of houses for him whenever he set out from Rome and luxurious lodgings to break his journeys even the shortest. Not only did he never live in them but some of them he was destined never even to see. (7) Besides that we built theatres for wild beast hunts and racetracks all over the place, wherever he did spend the winter or even intended to, without getting any help from him. And they were all pulled down directly: I suppose the only object of all this activity was to ruin us.

Caracalla's measure of 212 (*P. Giessen* 40 in *FIRA* I², 88, with Sherwin-White 1973 (9), 392 n.3) gave citizenship to free inhabitants of the Empire. The doubling of taxes (see **74**) was reversed by Caracalla's successor (Cassius Dio 79, 12, 2).

Gold was offered by subjects to their rulers, or extorted from them, in the form of crowns, or to be made up into them. Caesar had received 'crown gold' from Italy in 47 BC; in 29 BC Octavian had remitted it for Italy (*Achievements* 21) but continued to accept it from the provinces, which had been accustomed to pay it to Roman commanders. Eventually offerings were expected on accession as well as after a victory (**209**).

It was naturally defence rather than the army's importance to the Emperor that was stressed when the need for taxes was explained to stipendiary and tribute-paying provincials (see **74**n.). Here is part of a speech put into the mouth of the Roman general Petillius Cerialis when the Treviri and Lingones were about to revolt in 70.

76. Tacitus, *Histories* 4, 74

'There was no end to independent kings and wars all over Gaul until you entrusted yourselves to our jurisdiction. The only burden we used our victory to impose on you, in spite of being provoked on innumerable occasions, was one that made it possible for us to maintain peace; for it is impossible to maintain quiet between tribes without the use of armed forces; these cannot be kept up without pay, nor pay without tribute. Everything else has been made accessible to all: you yourselves are very often in command of legions, you yourselves govern these and other provinces; there are no barriers, no locked doors. For all your distance, you have equal advantages from Emperors of good repute; it is their immediate neighbours who are the victims of those who lash out. Bear with the extravagance of your masters, or their greed, as you bear drought, excessive rainfall, or all the other natural disasters. There will be failings as long as the human race survives; they are not unrelieved, and there are good rulers who come between and make up for them. Surely you don't hope for a milder regime under the kingly rule of Classicus and Tutor, or that armies to stave off Germans and Britons will be equipped from a tribute lower than what you are paying now? If the Romans are expelled — which heaven forbid! — what will ensue but a state of universal tribal warfare? The structure that exists now has developed out of eighty years of success and civilisation. It cannot be uprooted without bringing disaster on those responsible. But the greatest danger will fall on you who have the gold and riches that above anything else lead to wars. Love and cherish peace, then, and the city which, whether we are victors or vanquished, we are equally entitled to call our own. You have the evidence constituted by both eventualities to warn you against preferring obstinate rebellion to obedience when one brings destruction and the other security.'

Julius Classicus and Julius Tutor, members of the Treveran tribe and the former at least from royal stock, led the Gallic revolt and the short-lived attempt to set up a 'Gallic Empire'. But, however well-justified, the increasing burden of supporting the army gave rise to fantasies (**210**).

Obligations to the population of Rome and to the inhabitants of the provinces must also be counted in the Emperor's financial responsibilities.

77. *Achievements of the Deified Agustus*, **Appendix (EJ p. 30f.)**

The total sum of money that he gave either to the state Treasury or to the common people of Rome or to discharged soldiers: 6,000,000,000 *denarii*. (2) New buildings he erected: temples of Mars, Jupiter Tonans and Feretrius, Apollo, the deified Julius, Quirinus, Minerva, Juno the Queen, Jupiter Freedom, the Lares, the Divine Penates, Youth, and the Great Mother; the Lupercal; the box at the Circus; the Senate House with the Chalcidicum; the Forum of Augustus; the Basilica Julia; the Theatre of Marcellus; the Portico of Octavia; the Grove of the Caesars across the Tiber. (3) He restored the Capitol and sacred buildings to the number of 82; the Theatre of Pompey; the aqueducts; the Flaminian Road. (4) The funds provided for theatrical shows, gladiatorial displays, athletic competitions, wild beast hunts, the naval battle, and the money conferred on colonies, municipalities and townships destroyed by earthquake or fire, or individually to friends and senators whose property qualification he made up are incalculable.

Gifts of money were voluntary; as a right the people demanded their free ration of corn, guaranteed under the Principate as far as such things could be by the Emperors, who were the targets of abuse (Tacitus, *Annals* 2, 87, 1; 4, 6, 6; 6, 13, 1) or even old crusts (**104**) if they failed to deliver it. Distributions of other kinds were intermittently added: oil under Septimius Severus (*Augustan History, Septimius Severus* 18, 3). Purchase of these supplies, when they were not produced on imperial estates or out of taxation, as well as their transport, were a charge on the imperial Treasury or the private funds of the Emperor (**104ff.**), along with construction and repair of trunk roads (**94ff.**) for which troops and captives were admittedly available as labour.

The practice of remitting tribute and disbursing sums for the restoration of cities damaged by fire or earthquake was continued.

78. EJ 49: Sestertius minted at Rome

Obverse: Legend (in centre): By Decree of the Senate; (round edge) Tiberius Caesar Augustus, son of the deified Augustus; Supreme Pontiff; in his twenty-fourth year of tribunician power.

Reverse: Legend: Restoration of the Cities of Asia. Tiberius, laureate, seated on chair of state, left, holding libation dish and sceptre.

The date of the coin is 22-3; help given to various cities is commemorated in a monument set up to Tiberius at Puteoli in 30 (EJ 50; and see Tacitus, *Annals* 2, 47).

79. MW 436; bilingual, from Megalopolis in Achaea

Imperator Caesar Domitian Augustus Germanicus, son of the deified Vespasian, Supreme Pontiff, in his thirteenth year of tribunician power, hailed Imperator for the twenty-second time, sixteen times consul, censor for life, Father of his Country, at his own expense completely restored the arcade for the people of Megalopolis after its destruction by fire.

The date is 93-4. Gratitude did not prevent the people of Megalopolis after Domitian's assassination from removing the names that identified him.

Domitian was a noted philhellene; so too was Hadrian who also gave help to the 'Great City', as the name means (*IG* 5, 2, 533); but it was a city largely in ruins that Pausanias described in his *Guide to Greece* 8, 33, 1, and moralised over.

This imperial generosity to provincial communities brings us to another point: Rome promoted city development and spent resources on it that might otherwise have gone to Italy (see especially **142**). That had not been the case under the Republic. Thus, while the inner ring of tax-exporting provinces continued to prosper, the taxes they exported were moving into the outer ring in support of the armies mainly, but also in the form of development grants: **134**. Thus the centre, Italy and Rome, the seat of the court and central government, did less well, and when the court left Italy for any length of time, as it did under Hadrian and continuously in the third century, it took its resources with it.

Further, the increasing profits to be made in developing areas did not now fall so much into the hands of Roman business-men (but for money-lending see **196**). They were increasingly available to the inhabitants of the provinces, who were closer to the great reliable markets that the armies provided and were able to supply demands for food, wine, oil, textiles, pottery and building materials that came from within the provinces themselves. Italians began to feel poor in relation to some other parts of the Empire, notably Gaul (Tacitus, *Annals* 11, 23, 5f.). But the considered, synoptic view of an Emperor, expressed during a debate on luxury, gives a more trustworthy picture than senatorial complaints, and it also singles out Italy as a country of consumers, not all of whom had earned the luxuries that they had come to expect from their position as rulers of an empire.

80. Tacitus, *Annals* 3, 53, 3-54, 9

'. . . The part I play is not that of an aedile, praetor or consul. (4) Something grander, more lofty, is expected of the leading man in the state; and although individuals are ready enough to take the credit for successes on themselves, failings that are widespread are blamed on one man. (5) What then am I to ban first or to prune back to its original state? The vast area covered by our country houses? The size and diverse origins of our slave establishments? The weight of gold and silver we own? The marvellous bronzes and paintings we possess? Our clothing, which makes no distinction between the sexes, and those peculiarly feminine foibles which result in the transfer to foreigners, our enemies, of our money in return for stones? . . . (54, 5) Why then did frugal habits once prevail among us? It was because individuals exercised self-control, because we were members of a single city; and the temptations were not the same even when we were masters only in Italy. Our victories abroad have taught us to squander other people's property, the civil wars our own. (6) How minor a matter it is on which the aediles offer their advice! How trivial if you take everything else into account! Nobody, I can assure you, brings forward any proposal concerned with Italy's dependence on resources from abroad or with the daily hazarding of the Roman people's means of life on the vagaries of sea and weather. (7) But the answer I suppose is that if the resources of the provinces do not come to the aid of masters, slaves and estates, our own hunting parks and country houses will see us through. (8) This is the responsibility that the leading man in the state has to bear, members of the senate; if that is neglected it will bring the whole state down. As to other failings, the remedy must be found in men's own resolution: (9) our own self-respect must make us senators change for the better, the poor the fact that they have no choice in the matter, and the wealthy their own satiety!

This letter of 22 shows the Princeps aware also of the drain of precious metal from Italy to areas outside the Empire (see M. Wheeler, *Rome beyond the Imperial Frontiers* (Lond, 1954), 137ff.); but he refuses to try to restrain the imperial people.

It was the increasing wealth of the provinces in relation to Italy that brought in its train the advance to power and honour of men of provincial origin (**158ff.**), until Cerialis' claim that there were no barriers (**76**) finally became the truth. The rulers were no longer the aristocracy of Rome and Italy who had engineered the conquest but the wealthy wherever they were.

But local authorities had long played a vital part in maintaining the Empire, not only by collecting taxes but by providing services and amenities that in a modern state might be the responsibility of central government. These had to be paid for out of local revenue, in direct taxes, rents on public property, admission fees for councillors, and more or less voluntary contributions from the well off.

81. MW 461; bronze tablet from Cañete, between Malaca and Hispalis

Imperator Caesar Vespasian Augustus, Supreme Pontiff, in the ninth year of his tribunician power, hailed Imperator for the eighteenth time, eight times consul, Father of his Country, sends greetings to the board of four and to the councillors of the Saborenses.

Since you indicate that you are in an unsatisfactory condition and labouring under many difficulties, I give you permission to construct a town centre, bearing my name as you wish, on level ground. The income from indirect taxes which you say were assigned to you by the deified Augustus I confirm; if you wish to add any new ones you will have to approach the proconsul about them: I can make no decision when there is no one to put the other side of the case.

I received your decree on 25 July and gave your envoys permission to retire on 29th. You have my good wishes.

The duovirs Gaius Cornelius Severus and Marcus Septimius Severus had the inscription cut on bronze at public expense.

Vespasian in 77 gave the people of Sabora, who now enjoyed Latin rights (see **24**, **26**) permission to remove their administrative centre and public buildings from a typical hilltop site to one in the plain under the name of Flavia Sabora; the difficulties they complained of were evidently caused by the inaccessibility of their original centre and its lack of space. Evidently too they were having difficulty in collecting local taxes; note that they were not permitted to raise new ones without permission: Rome was concerned for her own revenue.

For the 'board of four', see **15**.

Property and poll-tax, market dues and customs duties were obvious sources of revenue. Palmyra, which dominated the Syrian-Mesopotamian caravan route, concentrated on the last but needed its agricultural basis too (see J.F. Mathews, *JRS* 74 (1984), 157ff., a paper kindly put at my disposal before publication).

82. *Corpus Inscriptionum Semiticarum* **2, 3, 3913; Greek and Palmyrene; the stone is divided into four panels: 1 contains the decree of the council in both languages; 2, divided into three columns, contains the Palmyrene text; 3, cols. a-c and 4 a and b the Greek text (supplemented here from 2 without the gaps being indicated); across the top of 2 and 3 is the dating in Greek**

In the reign of Imperator Caesar Trajan Hadrian Augustus, son of the deified Trajan Parthicus, grandson of the deified Nerva, in his twenty-first year of tribunican power, hailed Imperator for the second time, three times consul, Father of his Country, in the consulships of Lucius Aelius Caesar (for the second time) and Publius Coelius Balbinus.

(Panel 1) In the year 448, on the 18th day of the month Xandicus: decree of the council.

In the presidency of Bonnes, son of Bonnes the son of Haerenus, with Alexander son of Alexander son of Philopator as secretary of council and people, in the magistracies of Malichus son of Olaees (Palmyrene: grandson of Mocimus) and Zebedas son of Nesa, when a regular meeting of the council was in session, the following decree was voted.

Whereas in former times very many of the items subject to tax were not included in the customs regulations but dues were collected as a matter of accepted practice (it was written into the contract with the lessees that the persons responsible for collecting the tax should exact dues in accordance with the regulations and with accepted practice), and disputes were very frequently arising between merchants and customs officers on this point; it has been decided that the present magistrates and the ten leading men should determine the items not included in the previous regulations and write them into the next contract and append the accepted dues to each category; and that as soon as the agreement with the lessee is formally concluded, they should be inscribed along with the original regulations on the stone plinth which stands opposite the shrine called after Rabaseire; and that the magistrates in office at any time, the ten leading men, and the public advocates should ensure that the lessee makes no illegitimate exactions.

(Palmyrene version of the preamble)

(Greek) For one cartload of every type of freight, dues on four camel-loads were exacted.

(Palmyrene version of this)

(Panel 2, over all three cols., Palmyrene heading, as follows) Customs regulations of the entrepôt of Hadriana Tadmor (local name of Palmyra) and of Aelius Caesar's springs. (The Palmyrene version of the regulations, revised as the decree required, then follows; it supplements the Greek.)

(Panel 3a, Greek) From those who import slaves into Palmyra or into its territory he shall exact, per person,	22 *denarii*
From one selling a slave within the city [and not] for export (or, [or] exported),	12 each
From one selling experienced slaves	10 each
And if the purchaser exports the slaves,	12 each
The said public tax collector shall exact for each camel-load of ?dried produce, imported	[?3]
Exported,	3
For each donkey-load, imported	[?2]
Exported,	[?2]
For each sheepskin of purple-dyed wool imported he shall exact	8 *asses*
Exported,	8
For each camel-load of scented oil in alabaster jars, imported he shall exact	25 *denarii*
and [for each] exported,	13
For a camel-load of scented oil in goatskin bags, imported he shall exact	13
Exported,	[?7]
For a donkey-load of scented oil in alabaster jars, imported he shall exact	13
Exported,	7
For a donkey-load of scented oil in goatskin bags, imported he shall exact	7
Exported,	4
For a load of olive oil in four goatskin bags on a camel, imported, he shall exact	13

Exported, 1[3]

For a load of olive oil in two goatskin bags on a camel, imported he shall exact [?7]

Exported, [?7]

For a load of fat in four goatskin bags on a camel, imported he shall exact 13

Exported, 13

For a load of fat in two goatskin bags on a camel, imported he shall exact 7

(Panel 3b) 7

Exported,

For a load of fat on a donkey, imported he shall exact [?7]

Exported, 7

For a load of salt fish on a camel, imported he shall exact 10

Exported, [-]

The said public tax collector shall exact from each of those who sell olive oil by [- - -]

[19 lines damaged]

The said public tax collector shall exact from each prostitute, from one who fetches a *denarius* or more, 1 *denarius* per woman

From one who fetches 8 *asses*, he shall exact 8 *asses* per woman

From one who fetches 6 *asses*, 6 *asses*

The said public tax collector shall exact from work-shops [- - -], bazaars, leather shops [- - -] according to the accepted practice, per month per workshop, 1 *denarius*

From those who import skins or offer them for sale, for each skin, 2 *asses*

Likewise itinerant clothes salesmen who sell in the city are to pay the public tax collector the appropriate due.

For use of the two springs (Palmyrene: which are in the city), per year, 800 *denarii*

The said collector shall exact for each camel-load of wheat, wine, chaff, or suchlike, for each journey 1 *denarius*

For a camel brought in unloaded he shall exact as was done by Cilix, Caesar's freedman, 1

(Panel 3c, containing the previous version of the regulations, opens with 22 lines destroyed; the heading would have corresponded to the Palmyrene heading from Panel 2)

Customs regulations of Tadmor and the Springs and the salt within the city and its territory, according to the contract fixed in the presence of Marinus the governor.

[- - -]

[- - -] For one camel-load, 4 *denarii*

Exported,	4
[- - -] sheep's wool, for each fleece imported,	4
Exported,	4

[Likewise] the said public tax collector shall exact for every kind of thing as provided above.

[- - -] for every *modius* of spice [- - -]	1 *as*

(Greek) Anyone who has salt at Palmyra or within its territories is to pay the public tax collector of the people

of Palmyra, per *modius*,	1 *as*
Whoever fails to do so is to pay	[2]

[- - -]

(The following provisions, incorporated in the regulations from an edict of a governor of Syria on the tax collector's powers to exact sureties, are found only in the Greek.)

From whomsoever the public tax collector [- - -] exacts sureties [- - -] let them be handed over [- - -].

[- - -]Let him take adequate surety of twice the amount for the public tax collector. With regard to this, the sum to be brought to the collector is to be double.

Sums claimed by the public tax collector from another person and from the public tax collector by another person are to be subject to the jurisdiction of the appointed official in Palmyra [- - -].

It is to be within the powers of the public tax collector to exact sureties from those who have not discharged their debts, either in person or through his agents, and if these sureties are not redeemed within [- - -] days, the collector is to be empowered to sell [- - -] in a public place without wilful fraud [- - -] was sold [?for more] than the tax due for payment, the public tax collector is to be empowered to act [as permitted by] the law.

Of the entrepôt of Palmyra and of the water sources of Caesar [- - -] to the lessee [- - -] to provide [- - -].

(Panel 4a) No-one else is to be empowered to exact, give, or take, [- - -] nor on any count [- - -], and if he does any of these things or [- - -] twofold is to be exacted.

[- - -]

(The fragmentary Greek and better preserved Palmyrene versions of the old regulations continue with another communication from a legate of Syria, Gai[us Licinius Muc]ianus, 68-9.)

Concerning the tariff of taxes between the people of Palmyra and [- - -] taxes, I have determined that [- - -] the tax should be exacted at the rate at which Alcimus leased it [- - -] and [- - -] regulations whatever he is going to share with them [- - -].

Whoever imports slaves into Palmyra or its territory

will have to pay the public tax collector	22 *denarii*
And he who exports them will pay him	12

And he who puts an experienced slave up for sale will pay [10]
and whoever [?exports him,   [-]
    And whoever imports [- - -]   10
    Or exports it,   12
He who exports an experienced slave [- - -] rate as has been laid
down in writing in the regulations.
    Anyone who offers [- - -] for sale shall pay   9
    And for export,   [-]
[- - -] was not written down because [- - -]

Anyone who imports wool [- - -] who also [- - -] into Palmyra is not
liable to pay dues on wools from Italy. When this is exported it is not
further liable for duty, as there was an agreement that the dues should
not be paid on these wools when they are exported.

For scented oil in goatskin bags the tax collector shall exact
according to the regulations, because on account of an error on the part
of the public tax collector [- - -] has been fixed in the regulations at 13
denarii.

The tax on animals for slaughter ought to be reckoned at a *denarius*;
it was none other than Germanicus Caesar who made clear in his letter
to Statilius that taxes ought to be reckoned by the Italian *as*. But dues of
less than one *denarius* the public tax collector by accepted practice shall
exact in small change. The tax shall not be owed on animals thrown out
to die. On edible stuffs I fix the tariff at one *denarius* per load, according
to the regulations, whenever they are brought in from outside the
boundaries or taken outside them; those being conveyed to the local
country districts or from them are to be free of dues, as was conceded to
them.

Pine cones and the like carried as merchandise it was thought should
be liable for dues at the same rate as that on the carriage of dried
produce, as is the case in other cities.

Camels, whether loaded or unloaded, when they are brought in from
outside the territory, incur dues at a *denarius* each, as the regulations lay
down and as the excellent Corbulo laid down in his letter to Barbarus.

(Panel 4b) With regard to camel skins, they have struck them out as
well: no dues are exacted; with regard to grasses and ?fallen leaves, the
decision is that they are liable, because they are sold on the open
market.

Dues on slave girls I have determined as stated in the regulations: the
public tax collector shall exact dues from prostitutes at the rate of one
denarius per woman for prostitutes who fetch a *denarius* or more, and if
one fetches less, he shall take the same as that.

For bronze images (statues), the decision is that the same is to be
exacted as for bronze, and a single statue is to pay half the tax due on its
value by weight, while two statues are to pay on the value by weight of
one.

With regard to salt, I have decided that it is right for it to be sold in the public square where the people assemble, and any Palmyrene who buys it for himself is to pay, as prescribed in the regulations, for every *modius*, one Italian *as*. And likewise dues on Palmyrene salt are to be exacted by the *as* as laid down in [?the regulations], and it is to be sold in Palmyra according to the accepted practice.

[- - -] dues on purple, because [- - -] 4½ [- - -] walking in the city [- - -] and tailors [- - -] dues to be exacted as written out above.

For one skin, imported,	2 *asses*
Exported,	[-]

For a load [- - -] as they also agreed.

A flock brought in from outside the territory, even if [- - -] it is brought in [- - -] is liable to dues, but if it is brought into the territory to be sheared tax is not due [- - -] and who [- - -] as they had agreed.

Tax is to be exacted at a rate of one *denarius* as prescribed in the regulations.

It has been agreed that grazing ought not to be liable for dues [?apart from the usual] taxes; but on animals brought into Palmyrene territory for grazing purposes it is due; the public tax collector is entitled to have the animals branded if he wishes.

The date of the decree ordering revision of the tariff is 18 April, 137; Palmyra had been visited by Hadrian seven years before, attained free status, and added his name to its own.

Panel 3a, 4a: experienced slaves are those who have served for a year in the city (*Digest* 39, 4, 16, 3).

Panel 3a: Dr Matthews points out that, given a *denarius* charged for the beast of burden, a camel-load rates twice as much as a donkey-load, and that the levy on unguent imported is twice as much as on exported.

Panel 3b, 4b: how often the prostitutes had to pay (monthly?) is not stated.

Panel 3b: The high water rate suggests to Dr Matthews that it was levied on the owners of private baths and commercial premises as well as on caravan-leaders for access to water for their animals, but not on ordinary inhabitants of the city.

Cilix the imperial freedman must have operated an imperial customs post, perhaps at Zeugma.

Panel 3c: the old version of the tariff is not only mutilated, but was written in abbreviated form (cf. 'as provided above'): some of its provisions already appeared on the stone in the revised form of the tariff.

Marinus is thought to have been an acting governor in the absence of or after the death of the legate of Syria proper: the possibilities canvassed by Dr Matthews (n.23) favour the reigns of Tiberius or Nero. Gnaeus Domitius Corbulo was legate *c*. 60-6, cited by Mucianus in 4a;

Germanicus Caesar, whom he also cites was in the East as heir to the Emperor in 18-19.

The official in Palmyra who is to adjudicate on disputes between the contractor and tax-payers could be a Palmyrene or, more probably, given the heavy Roman involvement in fixing the tariff, a Roman, and it is possible that this was the post held by Statilius and Barbarus, if they were not rather procurators in Syria.

Panel 4a: Alcimus will have been an earlier tax contractor whose terms had been approved by the legate of Syria.

The expenses of communities were met in part by disbursements from office holders and others.

83. Callistratus, Judicial Enquiries, Book 1, in *Digest* 50, 4, 14, Introduction and 1

Municipal office consists in the administration of public affairs which involves a particular status, whether it entails expenditure or comes free of outlay. (1) A duty may be public or to an individual. It is called a public duty that we undertake when we engage in the administration of public affairs which involve expenditure without conferring any claim to rank.

The author is distinguishing magistracies from the functions called in Greek cities 'liturgies'; in non-legal usage, significantly, the distinction is often lost sight of. Disadvantages of this method of meeting a community's expenses may be seen from **188ff.** and **217ff.**

Roman citizens tried to evade the burdens imposed by their communities of origin: that could not be allowed, whatever the rights and wrongs of their position.

84. EJ 311; Greek; stele from the market place, Cyrene

3

Edict of Imperator Caesar Augustus, Supreme Pontiff, in his seventeenth year of tribunician power: If any persons in the province of Cyrenaica have been honoured with the Roman citizenship I order them none the less to take their turn in performing liturgies as if they counted as Greeks, apart from those persons to whom, along with their citizenship, immunity from taxes has been granted by law or decree of the senate or by my father's or my own decision. And it is my pleasure that these same persons, to whom immunity from taxes has been given, are to enjoy exemption on property in their possession at the time of the grant; but they are to pay what becomes due on everything acquired later.

7-6 BC. There is an indispensable discussion of the text by Sherwin-

White, 1973 (9), 334ff.; the edict has given rise to various interpretations and to emendation, the words translated here 'as if they counted as Greeks' being taken as a reference to separate Greek communities, to a provincial council (of which it would be the earliest evidence) or as implying a distinction between personal and financial obligations.

The new Roman citizens who were trying to avoid local burdens had logic and history on their side; in Cicero's time it could still be claimed that a man could not be a citizen of two cities, owing services and duty to both (Cicero, *Speech for Balbus* 28, of 56 BC). That principle could not be maintained if the cities were to survive grants of citizenship to their leading men on any scale (see below, Chapter 9); And it would have been absurd to continue to maintain that Roman citizenship was comparable with that of any other city, however distinguished. Caesar the Dictator ('my father') had already written to the people of Mytilene affirming their right to tax Roman citizens (Sherk, *Docs.* 26b). Here Augustus argues, as Sherwin-White shows, calling it a 'sharp argument', that a grant of exemption from imperial taxes, which the new citizens lacked, would have included exemption from the performance of local public duties; in fact earlier documents, such as **154**, distinguish the two.

The importance that cities attached to keeping and adding to the number of persons able to make a substantial contribution to their civic chests is illustrated by a decree of Aquileia.

85. MW 336 (Smallwood, *Nerva-Hadrian* 268); statue base from Aquileia

To Gaius Minucius Italus, son of Gaius, of the Velina Tribe; member of the board of four with jurisdiction; prefect of the Fifth Cohort of Gauls (with cavalry attached); prefect of the First Cohort of Breucians with Roman citizenship (with cavalry attached); prefect of the Second Cohort of Varcians (with cavalry attached); military tribune of the Sixth Legion, Victrix; prefect of cavalry of the First Squadron of Elite Troops with Roman citizenship; decorated by the deified Vespasian with the Golden Crown and Untipped Lance; procurator of the province of the Hellespont; procurator of the province of Asia, which he was entrusted to govern by the Emperor in place of the deceased proconsul; procurator of the provinces of Lugdunum and Aquitania and likewise of Lactora; prefect in charge of the corn supply; prefect of Egypt; priest of the deified Claudius: by decree of the council.

(On the side) Publius Tullius Maximus [and three others], members of the board of four with jurisdiction, consulted the city senate on 30 May; the decree was witnessed by [- - -] Proculus, Gaius Appuleius Celer, Aulus Junius G[- - -], and Sextus Cossutius Secundus.

Whereas speeches were delivered in honour of [Gaius Minucius Italus], to the effect that, a man of the highest distinction, he has turned all the influence or [power] he has been able to win [as a holder of the highest offices] open to the equestrian ranks to [enhancing the magnitude and lustre] of his [native city]; and that he [believes that the tenure of an official post] gives him no greater happiness [than the opportunity] to work [on its behalf]; with regard to the action to be taken accordingly, they passed the following resolution:

Since Gaius Minucius [Italus - - -] this particular purpose of his merits [- - - ? that] he has enhanced its natural endowment by the addition of more districts, and above all other things it is universally known that it is at his request that the most sacred Emperor Trajan A[ugustus has decided] that the resident aliens who are normally accounted of our number [should perform] the duties of citizens [along with us]; and that it has come about [through him] that [we enjoy] in particularly full measure the favour of the greatest of Emperors: it is the pleasure of this council, and is deemed advantageous to the community, that a bronze statue together with a [marble base should be erected to him and that] our decree should be inscribed on the base, so that it [may be] more amply attested that [there is no] other method open to us of repaying [in a way commensurate with the services] and benefits conferred by this great man [than by making public] our pride [in him].

The motion was passed. In the second consulships of Tiberius Julius [Candidus and Gaius Ant]ius Quadratus.

This decree of 105 closely follows the form of a decree of the senate — a word that the council of Aquileia applies to itself.

Italus had held a series of military posts in Lower Germany (for the various types of auxiliary units he commanded see **34**); his acting-governorship of Asia after the execution of the proconsul in 88 is noticed by Suetonius, *Domitian* 10, 2. He passed immediately after holding the directorship of the corn supply at Rome to the prefecture of Egypt, holding it from 101-2 until mid-103: a man in a good position to secure a hearing from Trajan.

The duties mentioned are the liturgies of **84**: the provision of goods and services, such as oil for gymnasium or baths, games and public works, the undertaking of embassies were all expected of well-off citizens. At Aquileia, an important commercial centre, the contribution of resident aliens could make a substantial difference to city finances. As Dr Mackie points out, the inscription is taken to represent an early stage in the process whereby resident aliens became liable to public duties in their place of residence. She regards the description of them as 'normally accounted of our number' as an attempt to distinguish them from mere visitors (Mackie 1983 (2), 40).

86. Apuleius, *The Golden Ass* 10, 18

But the first thing is for me to tell you, however late in the day, what I ought to have done in the first place: who that man was that I have been talking about and where he came from. Thiasus — that was the name of my master — had Corinth for his native city, which is the capital of the whole province of Achaea. As his ancestry and status required, he had passed step by step through the other offices and had been put in the way of the post of quinquennial magistrate; and with the object of proving himself equal to the splendid task of holding the rods of authority he promised to give a gladiatorial show, the spectacle to last three days: he was making his generosity felt in a really wide sphere; in point of fact his desire to win recognition from the public brought him on that occasion as far as Thessaly with the idea of buying there the most magnificent beasts and well-known gladiators.

It was not only in colonies in the East that a taste for gladiators and wild beast shows prevailed: elsewhere (4, 13f.) Apuleius gives a vivid description of preparations made by a leading man of Plataea for the same kind of show; but as Roman entertainments they were particularly expected from priests of the imperial cult.

Straight entrance fees occur in some parts of the Roman world, notably in the African provinces.

87. *AE* 1968, 591, cf. Garnsey 1971b, 123, no. 7; from Mustis in Africa Proconsularis Zeugitana

Consecrated to the Augustan Mercury for the welfare of Imperator Caesar Marcus O[pellius] Severus [Macrinus] the Pious and Fortunate, Augustus, Father of his Country, and of Marcus [Opellius] Antoninus [Diadumenianus] Caesar Augustus by Lucius Nonius Rogatianus Honoratianus, annual priest, aedile, duovir, priest for life: although he had estimated ten thousand sesterces for the office of priest for life, besides having paid five thousand into the city Treasury, as the standard sum for the office mentioned, he increased the amount manifold and dedicated the work that he had promised for a site in public ownership with Orfia Fortunata, daughter of Marcus, his wife, and Nonius Orfianus and Nonius Fortunatus, his sons, besides providing a banquet for the city wards.

The names of the Emperors, afterwards erased, yield the date: 217-18. Future priests for life at Mustis normally (but not necessarily by law) gave five thousand sesterces for the honour. This man set the sum aside and gave it to the city Treasury (on entering office, as Garnsey suggests); he estimated the cost of the public work he also undertook to provide (a statue) at ten thousand, but in the event paid more for it. Note the formal 'estimate', 'promise' and 'standard sum' of a well-established procedure.

6

Communications, Transport
and Supplies

88. Josephus, *Jewish War* 2, 352f.; Greek

'Agreed: there is no remedying the brutality of the Roman under-
lings; still, it is not all the Romans who are ill-treating you, and not
Caesar either, and it is against them that you are starting a war. It is
not on their instructions that a man comes from them who is a criminal;
from where they are in the west they can't keep an eye on their men
in the far east; it isn't easy over there even to hear the news from here
with any speed. (353) It is preposterous to make war on vast numbers
because of a single man, and to do it for a flimsy reason when they are
so powerful, especially when they don't even know what our grievance
is!'

So (according to Josephus) spoke Agrippa II of Chalcis in 66;
distance from Rome may also have been a factor in the brutality of
officials in Britain under Claudius and Nero (**140**). It is a different story
told by Aelius Aristides a century later, in which the Emperor knows
everything almost as soon as it has happened (**113**): evidently emperors
needed reassurance. It was not so much that they feared rebellion: the
nearer armies of the Rhine were the most dangerous, but a quick
response to any initiative was much to be desired.

89. Suetonius, *Deified Augustus* 49, 3

And to make it possible to have news brought more quickly and
promptly and to know what was happening in each province, he
arranged first for able-bodied men and eventually for carriages to be
stationed at frequent intervals along military roads. The latter arrangement has been found the more convenient as it enables the men who
carry the letters from the scene of action to answer questions as well if
that is what the situation demands.

The normal speed of the couriers was about 50 Roman miles a day, as
opposed to the 20 of the army on the march.
Travel over the open seas, feasible from 11 March to 10 November
(Vegetius, 4, 39, cited by Rickman 1980, 15) was at a rate of 4-6 knots,

2-2½ against the wind (3.7-11 km an hour). Several prefects of Egypt made very good time on their 1,600 km voyage to the province.

90. Pliny, *Natural History* 19, 2-4

Flax is a plant we cultivate from seed . . : what part of our life is there in which it is not to be encountered? And what would constitute a greater marvel than the existence of a plant that brings Egypt within reach of Italy? They are so close that Galerius arrived at Alexandria from the straits of Sicily after six days and Balbillus after five. (They were both prefects of Egypt, but in the summer fifteen years later Valerius Marianus, a senator of praetorian rank, arrived there from Puteoli after eight days, carried by an extremely smooth breeze.) What could be a greater marvel than the existence of a plant that puts Gades at the Pillars of Hercules within seven days' sail of Ostia, Tarraconensis within four, the province of Narbonensian Gaul within three, Africa within two (which was the case with Gaius Flavius, legate of the proconsul Vibius Crispus, even with a very gentle breeze behind him)?

The voyages (under sails made of flax) belong to the reigns of Tiberius, Nero and Vespasian. Pliny does not mention the contrary winds that loaded grain vessels had to meet on their way from Alexandria to Rome, which made them take anything from three weeks to two months (Rickman 1980, 15). As an instance of a hurried journey by sea and land, made in winter and spring, one might cite that of the messengers who carried the news of Gaius Caesar's death at Myra in Lycia on 21 February, 4, to reach Pisa, presumably after being announced at Rome, on 2 April: nearly six weeks for about the same distance as the direct Alexandria run (EJ 69).

The burdens imposed on Rome's subjects by the imperial post and its abuse are amply documented by Mitchell (and see **54**). The document he published was the product of one of the earliest attempts to remedy them; it also offers much information on the way the service was meant to operate.

91. S. Mitchell, *JRS* 66 (1976), 106ff.; *ZPE* 45 (1982), 99f.; marble stele found at Burdur in Pisidia and now in the museum there; bilingual with variations

Edict of Sextus Sotidius Strabo Libuscidianus, praetorian legate of Tiberius Caesar Augustus: It is in the highest degree unjustifiable for me in my edict to tighten up regulations drawn up with the utmost care by the Augusti, one of them supreme among divinities, the other among Emperors, to prevent the use of transport facilities without payment. But since there are persons whose lack of discipline calls for punishment here and now, I have put up in individual cities and villages a list of the services that I judge ought to be provided, with the object of seeing it observed, or, if it is disregarded, of backing it up not only with my own power but with the majesty of the best of Emperors from whom I received instructions on this very point.

The people of Sagalassus must provide a service of ten carts and the same number of mules for the legitimate purposes of persons passing through, and receive from the users ten *asses* per *schoenus* for each cart and four *asses* per *schoenus* for each mule: if they prefer to provide donkeys they are to give two in place of each mule at the same rate. Alternatively, if they prefer to give for each mule and each cart what they were going to receive if they were providing them themselves, they are to pay it to members of another town or village who will actually perform the service, so that they may take it on. They shall be obliged to provide transport as far as Cormasa and Conana.

However, the right to use these facilities shall not belong to everybody, but to the procurator of the best of Emperors and ?to his son, a right to use them which extends to ten carts, or three mules in place of each cart or two donkeys in place of each mule, used on the same occasion, for which they are to pay the fee established by me. Besides them, it shall belong to men on military service, and those who have a warrant, and those who travel from other provinces on military service, on the following terms: to a senator of the Roman people are to be supplied not more than one cart, or three mules in place of the cart or two donkeys in place of each mule, for which they are to pay what I have laid down; to a Roman knight in the service of the best of Emperors must be given three carts or three mules in place of each or in place of each mule two donkeys, on the same terms; if he requires more he shall hire them at the rate decided by the person who is hiring them out; to a centurion a cart or three mules or six donkeys on the same terms. To those who are carrying grain or anything else of the kind for their own profit or use I wish nothing to be supplied, nor anything for a man's baggage animals or those of his freedmen or slaves. Board and lodging ought to be provided without charge to all who are members of my own staff and to persons on military service from all provinces and to freedmen and slaves of the best of Emperors and their baggage animals, on condition that they do not demand other services free from those unwilling to provide them.

Mitchell dates Strabo's governorship of Galatia to the period covering the death of Augustus and the accession or Tiberius, the 'best of Emperors' being Augustus who appointed him; and he emends the puzzling 'to his (the procurator's) son' to 'of his (i.e. Augustus') son', that is, of Tiberius. Conceivably it could be a little later, but still in the first half of Tiberius' reign, when there is room for Strabo on the list. For the boundaries of Sagalassus, see **50**. Other cities in the area were subordinated to it for the purpose of requisitioning transport and it commanded an immense area in mountainous Pisidia (Mitchell, *JRS 66* (1976), 119), Cormasa being 55 km (34 miles) south-west, Conana 34 km (21½ miles) north of it. The mountainous nature of the terrain makes the use of the Persian *schoenus* or parasang natural: it is the distance that might be covered in an hour.

Not messages but the conveyance of officials and their supplies are the burden of this document. The importance of the service to the procurator is evident: he was responsible for supplying and paying the troops and for maintaining the entourage of the Emperor when he was on his travels (see **7**).

Cities and villages situated where routes crossed or converged were particularly hard pressed by the demands of officials: for Byzantium, see Tacitus, *Annals* 12, 62, under 53, for Juliopolis on the border of Bithynia and Galatia, Pliny, *Letters* 10, 77. Italy, whose burdens were noted in an edict of Claudius (Smallwood, *Gaius-Nero* 375), was relieved of them by Nerva.

92. Smallwood, *Nerva-Hadrian* 30; sestertius

Obverse: Head of Nerva, wearing laurel wreath; legend: Imperator Nerva Caesar Augustus, Supreme Pontiff, holder of tribunician power, three times consul, Father of his Country.

Reverse: Two mules grazing in front of a tipped up cart; legend: Italy exempted from transport service. By decree of the senate.

The coin was struck at Rome in 97. Other parts of the Empire continued to bear the burden. There were good reasons for exempting Italy, but this was not the only way in which the privileged position of the imperial people was recognised well into the Principate (**64, 109**), when the process of levelling out had long been begun.

The warrants mentioned in **91** consisted of a pair of folded waxed tablets (*diplomata*) issued by the governor; by the reign of Domitian it was the Emperor's prerogative (MW 466: 'my diploma') to pass on a batch every year to governors: that way he could keep a closer check on their issue.

93. Pliny, *Letters* 10, 45f.

Gaius Pliny to the Emperor Trajan. With regard to time-expired travel warrants, my Lord, whether you would like them to be valid at all and for how long, I beg you to write and banish my uncertainty. I am afraid of making a slip in one direction or the other, either by passing invalid warrants or by putting obstacles in the way of essential missions.

(46) Trajan to Pliny. Time-expired warrants ought not to be in use. That is why I give priority among the duties I have to perform to that of distributing fresh warrants to all the provinces before they can possibly be required.

Pliny's last surviving letter (120) likewise shows how sensitive Emperors were known to be on the subject of warrants and their use (cf. **132**): he had, he confesses (and confession proved to be the right policy, for Trajan condoned what he had done), issued one to his wife after the death of her grandfather (**12**), so that she could reach her aunt in Italy more quickly.

When the industrial revolution began in eighteenth-century Britain, the best roads were the remains of those made by the Romans. Their fame as road builders is justified, and the number of milestones and other monuments that commemorate road works, bridges, and so on is enormous. The sample offered here illustrates their military purpose and construction: in recent parlance they are 'walls in the ground'.

94. EJ 294; milestone from Comama in Pisidia

Imperator Caesar Augustus, son of the deified Caesar, Supreme Pontiff, eleven times consul, designated for his twelfth consulship, hailed Imperator fifteen times, in his eighteenth year of tribunician power, built the Augustan Road, his praetorian legate Cornutus Aquila taking charge of the work.

Several milestones from this road, which was given a hybrid Latin and Greek name, Via Sebaste, have been found; this comes from the first stretch, constructed in 6-5 BC to curve round the mountains of Pisidia and link the colonies that Augustus planted there to control the as yet unconquered mountain people. It is possible that the inhabitants of Sagalassus were liable for travel facilities on part of this road (see Mitchell, *JRS* 66 (1976), 122).

95. EJ 290; milestone from between Tacape and Capsa in Africa

Imperator Caesar Augustus (i.e., Tiberius), son of Augustus, in his sixteenth year of tribunician power: Asprenas, consul, proconsul, member of the board of seven in charge of sacred banquets, saw to the construction of the road from the winter camp at Tacape. The Third Legion, Augustan. 10[- - -]

Early in the autumn of 14: the proconsul of Africa did not know that Augustus had been deified. This is milestone 101-104 or 109 on a road that was part of the gradual penetration south and west into the interior of north Africa (see also **3, 12, 153**). It would be used to speed the arrival of supplies and troops coming to the camp at Ammaedara from the port of Tacape, and to regulate the seasonal movement of tribes.

96. *CIL* 3, 3198a = 10156 + 3200 (= EJ 266); one of three plaques from Salona in Dalmatia

[He constructed the road] from the colony of Salona to the boundary of the province of Illyricum [- - -], a road which was 167 miles in length, using detachments of the Seventh and Eleventh Legions. [- - -] Likewise he engineered and constructed the Gabinian road from Salona to Andetrium, using the Seventh Legion.

Other inscriptions of the period 16-20 (EJ 292f.) attest the activity of the governor Cornelius Dolabella, which has been elucidated by J. Wilkes, *Dalmatia* (London, 1969), 452ff. Dolabella's soldiers did not have to do all the work themselves: there were prisoners from the rebellion of 6-9. The present inscription records the longest known stretch of road for which Dolabella was responsible, but it is not certain whether it ran to Siscia or the Italian frontier or whether it was the military road to the south. The second stretch, named after Caesar's proconsul Gabinius, was only 24 km (15 miles) long. But the main purpose of the whole programme was to open up the interior of the province, bring the Save valley closer to the coast, and make future rebels accessible to counter-measures.

Under Tiberius two legions spent part of the year 33-4 improving the towpath that ran along the Danube at the Iron Gate in Upper Moesia (EJ 267). The path was used for dragging vessels upstream against the rapids (for a sketch of the installation, see A. Mócsy, *Pannonia and Upper Moesia* (London, 1974), 46); the Romans had maintained a fleet on the Danube since the beginning of the reign. In Trajan's time the installation had to be modernised (Smallwood, *Nerva-Hadrian* 413) and further measures taken: the cutting of a canal to bypass the rapids.

97. J. Šašel, *JRS* 63 (1973), 80ff.; marble slab from Karataš at the Iron Gate

Imperator Caesar Nerva Trajan Augustus Germanicus, son of the deified Nerva, Supreme Pontiff, in his fifth year of tribunician power, Father of his Country, four times consul, diverted the river on account of the danger caused by the cataracts, and made the Danube safe for navigation.

Šašel provides maps of the Iron Gate and its neighbourhood. He links the works with Trajan's imminent war with the Dacians. Nor is there any doubt of the original military purpose of the route over the Alps that Claudius' father drove under Augustus.

98. Smallwood, *Gaius-Nero* 328; milestone from near Merano

Tiberius Claudius Caesar Augustus Germanicus, Supreme Pontiff, in the sixth year of his tribunician power, designated consul for the fourth time, hailed Imperator for the eleventh, Father of his Country, constructed the road which his father Drusus had laid out after his wars had opened up the Alps, from the River Po to the River Danube over a distance of 350 miles.

AD 46. The road wound through the Alpine valleys, including that of the Adige, in a north-westerly direction until it reached the valley of the Inn and other easy routes to the upper Danube. The inscription is one of two known from this road: *ILS* 208 from Feltria mentions Altinum near Venice as the starting point.

99. Smallwood, *Gaius-Nero* 351; 36 km from Philippopolis in Thrace

Nero Claudius Caesar Augustus Germanicus, son of the deified Claudius, grandson of Germanicus Caesar, great-grandson of Tiberius Caesar Augustus, great-great grandson of the deified Augustus, Supreme Pontiff, in his seventh year of tribunician power, hailed Imperator eight times, four times consul, Father of his Country, ordered that rest houses and official quarters should be constructed along the military roads by Tiberius Julius Justus, procurator of the province of Thrace.

Nero's name was posthumously struck from the inscription, which was cut in the year 61-2. Thrace had become a province governed by a procurator (see **4f.** and **10n.**) fifteen years previously. Besides presenting difficulties of its own (it had to be given a senatorial governor in 106: see **15**), it lay on routes leading from Germany and the Adriatic to the east. The main such route was to become increasingly significant: it ran from Aquileia down the Save to the Danube at Singidunum, then south to Naissus and Philippopolis and so to the Bosporus, affording a vital link between the two halves of the Empire. For the size and nature of the rest houses see S. Mitchell, *Anatolian Studies* 28 (1978), 95, where one with a colonnade is reported. For the comfort of high officials travelling to the eastern provinces, the provisions made by Nero, which are mentioned in another copy of the text set up near Serdica (*AE* 1912, 193), were important.

Only incidentally — but unmistakably — did these works promote civilian communications, commerce and the spread of Romanisation, especially through the development of towns along the routes; but so did they help to unify the Empire: consider the journeys made only by persons mentioned in this volume!

It was excellent communications that gave Gaul much of the impetus for its economic and cultural advance. The rivers were vital to it (Strabo, *Geography* 4, 1, 14, p. 188f.), but very early in that advance Strabo was aware of the importance of the roads.

100. Strabo, *Geography* 4, 6, 11, p. 208; Greek

Lugdunum is in the middle of the country, like the citadel of a Greek city, both because of the rivers that meet there and also because it is close to all parts. That was why Agrippa, when he engineered his roads, made it the starting point. One of them went through the Cemmeni mountains as far as the Santoni and Aquitania, one to the Rhine, and a third to the Ocean, to the Bellovaci and Ambiani. A fourth leads to Narbonensis and the coast round Massilia.

The date of Agrippa's roads is uncertain (M. Reinhold, *Marcus Agrippa* (Geneva and New York, 1933; repr. Rome, 1965), 90 n.76); and the fourth road is probably not his, to judge by Strabo's language.

Interested parties might attempt to influence the course of an official road.

101. Smallwood, *Gaius-Nero* 332; from Materia, about 19 km south-east of Tergeste

This road, laid out by the centurion Atius in accordance with the decision given by Aulus Plautius, legate of Tiberius Claudius Caesar Augustus Germanicus, and rerouted thereafter from the Rundictes towards the property of Gaius Laecanius Bassus, was restored on the orders of Tiberius Claudius Caesar Augustus Germanicus Imperator by Lucius Rufellius Severus, leading centurion.

The original route across the Pola peninsula was laid down by the distinguished general who invaded Britain in 43; it is not clear what functions he was performing as Claudius' legate at the time he gave his judgement: perhaps governor of Pannonia (39-42). Later the route was changed at the instance of another senator, Laecanius Bassus, suffect (substitute) consul in 40, presumably to facilitate transport of wares to and from his property in the district, where he had an important tilery and brickworks (M.H. Callender, *Roman Amphorae with Stamps* (London, etc., 1965), 104f., no. 365); the Pola peninsula was covered with estates producing olive oil (Rostovtzeff 1957 (1), 235 and 611 n.26). The change was disallowed by Claudius, no doubt on appeal from the tribe. Both times the work of planning the road was carried out by centurions, naturally with the help of small detachments of soldiers.

As time went on, local communities found themselves paying for the repair even of military trunk roads as well as the local networks for which they had always been responsible.

102. *ILS* 5864; rock-cut inscription on the Wadi Barada, near Abila on the road from Berytus to Damascus

Imperator Caesar Marcus Aurelius Antoninus Augustus Armeniacus and Imperator Caesar Lucius Aurelius Verus Augustus Armeniacus cut through the mountain and restored the road, which had been broken away by the violence of the river. The work was carried out by Julius Verus, praetorian legate of the province of Syria and friend of the Emperors, at the expense of the people of Abila.

The inscription belongs to 164-5.

In the third century milestones were commonly set up by cities and dedicated to emperors. The following example explicitly states that the road was built by the city.

103. *IGR* 4, 1206; from Thyatira in Lydia; the dedication in Latin, the rest in Greek

(Latin) Good Fortune! To Imperator Caesar Marcus Aurelius Antoninus, Pious and Fortunate, Augustus, three times consul, Father of his Country. The most distinguished city of the Thyatirans constructed the road in the proconsulship of Aufidius Marcellus. 1 mile.

Elagabalus, whose name has suffered partial erasure, was consul for the third time in 220, and the milestone, which comes from the Thyatira-Sardis road, belongs to this or the following year. The city may have done its work at the suggestion of the Roman authorities: repairs were being carried out in other parts of Asia Minor at the same time (Magie 1950 (1), 1558, n.4); but the demarcation of distances close to cities was often of importance to them as showing the extent of their obligations to the imperial post.

For all these efforts, the cost of transport by land in the ancient world remained high enough to make it surprising that any but luxury goods travelled that way: Rickman 1980, 14, gives comparative figures for transport by land and sea, based on information in Diocletian's edict on maximum prices (LR 129): a waggon-load of wheat would double its price on a journey of 480-640 km (300-400 miles), while the freightage of wheat to Rome by sea from Alexandria, even following a circuitous route (see **90**), increased it only by about 16 per cent.

From the government's point of view, what mattered was the transport of army supplies of all kinds, of state-owned bullion (of which little is known) and grain. It was a primary aim to secure this to the people of Rome (cf. **167**), and Emperors took various measures to ensure the supply.

104. Suetonius, *Claudius* 18, 2; 19; 20, 3

But once during a grain shortage due to a series of droughts he was trapped by a crowd in the middle of the Forum and subjected to such a shower of abuse mingled with bits of bread that he hardly managed to get away into the Palace — through a back gate, too. After that he devised every means he could to bring in supplies even during the winter season. For one thing, he offered businessmen guaranteed profits, personally insuring them against any loss caused to any of them by storm damage; for another he established substantial privileges appropriate to their rank for all who built merchant ships: (19) a citizen was to receive exemption from the Papian-Poppaean law; a Latin full citizen rights; women the privileges due to those with four children. The privileges he established are still maintained today . . .

(20, 3) He constructed a harbour at Ostia, bringing jetties round both right and left hand sides and throwing a mole in front of the entrance where the water became deep; to give the mole greater stability he began by sinking the ship in which the great obelisk had been transported from Egypt and drove serried ranks of piles in round it; he crowned the structure with an extremely high tower like the Pharos at Alexandria, so that ships could steer a course towards its beacon-fires at night.

The Papian-Poppaean law of 9 restricted the right of the unmarried and childless to inherit and make bequests; women who had three (or if freedwomen, four) children were permitted to manage their affairs without a guardian (Gaius, *Institutes* I, 194).

The date of Claudius' measures is not known: there was a grain shortage at the time of his accession (Seneca, *Shortness of Life* 18, 5), but the incident in the Forum belongs to 51 (Tacitus, *Annals* 12, 43, 2). Rickman 1980, 76, is probably right to see the insurance as a temporary emergency measure; the privileges for those who provided ships (of a capacity of at least 10,000 *modii* for at least six years) survived in the jurists (Gaius, *Institutes* 1, 32^c).

The harbour was only a partial success (Tacitus, *Annals* 15, 18, 3, mentions the loss of nearly 200 ships in it in 62); it was improved by Trajan: see R. Meiggs, *Roman Ostia* (2nd edn, Oxford, 1973), 54ff.

105. Callistratus, Judicial Enquiries, Book 1, in *Digest* 50, 6, 6(5), 3

Businessmen who facilitate the supply of grain to the city, and likewise shippers who are engaged in its service, obtain exemption from state burdens as long as they continue their activities. For the view has properly been taken that the dangers encountered by those persons ought to be compensated for, indeed that they should be encouraged to undergo them, by the offer of rewards, so that those who perform functions abroad that are, after all, public, and which involve them in hard work and danger, should be freed from difficulties and expenses in the management of their own affairs; it would not be out of place to claim that while they are in the service of the grain supply they are abroad on public service.

This last formula had long secured immunity against prosecution for soldiers and generals. The exemption confirmed here shows, as Rickman points out, 1980, 90, that the activities of shippers had come to be regarded as a public duty.

106. *ILS* 6987; fragment of a bronze tablet re-used as a bowl which came to light near Berytus

[- - -J]ulianus sends greetings to the marine shippers of Arelate, members of the five associations. What I have written, after having read your resolution, to [- - -] the excellent procurator of the Emperors, I have ordered to be appended. I hope that you enjoy good health and the highest success.

Copy of letter. I have appended a copy of the resolution passed by the marine shippers of Arelate, members of the five associations, and likewise of the transactions that have taken place before me. And since their complaint is becoming widespread and others besides these men are begging for the help that fair treatment would secure them, adding something of a threat that they will instantly abandon their duty if the wrong done them is not righted, I am asking that attention should be paid to preserving the accounts from financial loss and also to the peace of mind of men pledged to the service of the grain supply. You are to order the marking out of iron measuring rods and the assignment of escorts from your office who are to deliver in the city of Rome the weight that they have collected.

The writer is probably the prefect of the grain supply (*PIR*^{2}C 899, *c.* 201), who was in overall charge of securing grain for Rome, and the addressee of his reproof the official earlier attested in Arelate, the procurator of the grain supply of the province of Narbonensis (*ILS* 1432); his name has been erased from the bronze. The shippers by now, as Rickman points out, 1980, 91, were probably concerned only with transporting the grain, not with procuring it; most of it was coming from state-owned sources. They were threatening to strike evidently because some of the cargo was disappearing before it was measured in the granary at Rome and they were being held responsible. Rickman is rightly cautious (226ff.) about the development of such corporations as the shippers of Arelate had organised as evidence for their subjection to state control: they simply needed to be organised in their own interests.

The state had an indirect concern with the grain supplies of local communities. Throughout the Mediterranean region the supply was patchy and uncertain (Rostovtzeff 1957 (1), 599f.). Local shortages could not easily be remedied because of transport costs. Such shortages led to hoarding and profiteering by the rich — and rioting on the part of the suffering poor.

107. Dio of Prusa, *Discourses* 46 (Delivered in his native city, before his career as a Philosopher), 8; 11-13; 14

Further: as far as the present shortage goes, nobody is less to blame than I am. Have I harvested more grain than anyone else and shut it up, increasing the price? No. You know yourselves what my estates are capable of producing; that I have sold grain hardly ever, if at all, even when there is a bumper harvest. In all these years I have not even had enough; all my earnings come from wine and cattle-grazing. As to the objection that I lend money but won't provide any for the purchase of grain, I don't have to say anything about that either; you know both types in the city, the men who lend money, and those who borrow . . .

(11) . . . I am saying this for your own good. If you think otherwise you are very much mistaken. (12) If you are going to be like this and if, every time you are in a rage with someone — in a city you can expect a lot of things to happen, right and wrong —, you are going to see fit to avenge yourselves by actually cremating him on the spot, along with his children, and force some of his women, persons of free status, to let you see them with their clothing all torn and going on their knees to you as they would in war; is there any man alive who is such a fool, so misguided, as to choose to live in a city like that for a single day? It is much better to be an exile, to live as an alien in a foreign country than to put up with behaviour like that. Look, as it is there is the 'reason' that people say you had for turning back from my house — that the depth of the narrow lane made you uneasy — consider what a flimsy thing it is! (13) If it was that that saved me it is already high time to treat the city we are living in as if it were a camp and take over the inaccessible parts of it for future occupation, and the high points or cliff tops . . .

(14) And nobody is to think that my motive for saying this has been indignation on my own account, not fear on yours, in case you find yourselves some time accused of being violent and lawless. Nothing in the cities goes unnoticed by the authorities, and by 'authorities' I mean more important ones than those we have here. No. Children who are too unruly at home are reported by their relations to their teachers. It is the same with the populace of the cities when they go wrong; it is reported to those authorities of whom I speak.

This speech, probably delivered in the city theatre before the assembly, belongs to the seventies (see Jones 1978 (9), 19ff.). Probably some of Dio's wine was being shipped to troops stationed in the Danubian provinces or to private buyers there; commercial, political, strategic and diplomatic links between the Balkans and Asia Minor were strong and becoming more so (Levick 1979 (10), and Mitchell 1983 (6)).

Dio's threat to leave was a serious one: he was one of the men whose private funds helped finance civic services and amenities (**67ff.**), and he had influence with the Flavian Emperors. These rather than the proconsuls are the 'authorities' to whom Dio refers, and with them we return to the theme of imperial intelligence: it is natural to ask who on this occasion was going to deliver the information.

Hostility between rich and poor and the dangers it presented were one reason for imperial concern over grain supplies to the cities (**110**); they are the main theme of chapter 11.

A well-known monument of the early nineties shows one of the lesser 'authorities' in action during a grain shortage.

108. MW 464; from Pisidian Antioch

(Col. 1) To Lucius Antistius Rusticus, son of [Lucius], of the Galerian Tribe; consul; praetorian legate to Imperator Caesar [Domitian] Augustus [Germanicus] of the provinces of Cappadocia, Galatia, Pontus, Pisidia, Paphlagonia, Armenia Minor and Lycaonia; prefect of the state Treasury of Saturn; proconsul of the province of Further Spain (Baetica); legate of the deified Vespasian and of the deified Titus and of Imperator Caesar [Domitian] Augustus [Germanicus] of the Eighth, Augustan, Legion; curator of the Aurelian and Cornelian roads, co-opted among the senators of praetorian rank by the deified Vespasian and the deified Titus; awarded military decorations by them, the Mural Crown, the Fortification Crown, the Golden Crown, three Banners and three Untipped Lances; military tribune of the Second, Augustan, Legion; member of the judicial board of 15; patron of the colony: for his diligence in providing for the grain supply.

(Col. 2) Edict of Lucius Antistius Rusticus, praetorian legate of Imperator Caesar Domitian Augustus Germanicus: Since the duovirs and members of the council of the most splendid colony of Antioch have written to me saying that the harshness of the winter has caused the price of grain to rocket, and have requested that the mass of ordinary people should have some means of buying it (in margin: ? Good Luck!), all persons who are either citizens or resident aliens of the colony of Antioch are to declare before the duovirs of the colony of Antioch within thirty days of the posting of my edict how much grain each has, and where it is, and how much he is drawing for seed or for the annual supply of his household; and he is to make all the rest of the grain available to the buyers of the colony of Antioch. I appoint a period for selling to end on 1 August next. If anyone fails to act accordingly, let him know that for whatever is kept contrary to my edict I shall impose penalties for the offence, establishing an eighth share as the amount to be allocated as the reward for informers. Further, since it is declared to me that before this persistently cold winter weather the price of grain in the colony was eight or nine *asses* per *modius* and since it would be the height of iniquity that anyone should make a profit out of the hunger of his fellow-citizens, I forbid the sale price of grain to rise above one *denarius* per *modius*.

(Col. 3) [- - -] Rufus, imperial procurator.
. . .

For the date of the famine, see R. Syme, *Historia* 32 (1983), 369. The colony had a fairly extensive and fertile territory (Levick 1967 (3), 42ff.), and its difficulties are the more striking. The normal price of grain in the colony is not far from that prevailing in the Empire (Rickman 1980, 145ff.: 2-3 sesterces; 5-6 at Rome), and the limit set by the governor was not stringent, as it allows a rise of 100 per cent. Column 3 reveals that the monument was erected in one of the main public centres of the city.

It has often been thought that Rusticus was acting on the direct orders of Domitian, but there was hardly time for that (Levick 1982, 57ff.). What an Emperor could and could not do may be seen from Domitian's edict on viticulture.

109. Suetonius, *Domitian* 7, 2

On one occasion, when there was a bumper vintage combined with a shortage of grain, he came to the conclusion that excessive enthusiasm for viticulture was causing arable farming to be neglected, and issued an edict to the effect that nobody should plant new vines in Italy, and that in the provinces vines should be cut down, leaving only half at most. He did not persist in carrying out the plan.

This sweeping measure, which also belongs to the early nineties, could not have been carried out because Domitian did not have the staff to oversee it. The object of the edict seems to have been to increase grain production throughout the Empire and perhaps to lessen the pressure of competition on Italian farmers producing wine.

110. Philostratus, *Lives of the Sophists* 1, 21 (520); Greek

The embassies to the Emperor of which he was a member were numerous; a degree of good fortune used to accompany him on his embassies, but the most successful was on behalf of the vines, when he was sent, not only on behalf of the people of Smyrna, as on most of his embassies, but on that of the whole of Asia at once. I shall reveal the purpose of the embassy: the Emperor's view was that Asia ought not to have any vines, because he thought that men become seditious under the influence of drink; the existing vines were to be uprooted and others were not to be planted any more. What was needed was a joint embassy and a man who was going to use his charm on their behalf like another Orpheus or Thamyris. Accordingly they all chose Scopelian, and he was more than successful on the mission, so much so that he came back in possession not only of permission to plant, but with actual penalties to be imposed on those who were failing to do so.

Scopelian's achievement had evidently become a legend, but the motive that Philostratus ascribes to Domitian may represent a popular interpretation of the Emperor's notorious concern for public order. Thamyris was a charmer less well known than Orpheus: a Thracian musician, he was blinded for his boast that he could win a contest even against the Muses.

Philostratus' mistake about the penalties is also interesting: he seems to be running together concern for grain supplies with another imperial preoccupation: that the land should be cultivated, since it was this that afforded tax revenue (**68f.**). The two documents that follow illustrate the details of plans to bring land into production.

111. *FIRA* 1² 101; from Ain-el-Djemala in the Bagradas valley, Numidia

(Side 1) [- - - they - - -], we ask you, procurators, by the forethought which you exercise in Caesar's name, that you may be willing to show consideration towards us and for his advantage and give us those lands which are situated in marshes and woods, to plant with olives and vines under the Mancian Law on the same terms as the Neronian estate that borders on us. As we were preparing our petition here it was already clear that the aforementioned Neronian estate was undergoing an increase in population [- - -].

(Side 2) [- - -] you order. Statement of the procurators of Imperator

Caesar Hadrian Augustus: Because our Caesar, with the untiring devotion with which he constantly watches over the welfare of mankind, orders that all parts of lands which are suitable, whether for olives, vines, or grain, should be brought under cultivation, for that reason permission is given to all, with the blessing of his foresight, also to take over parts that are included in the allotments of the Blandian and Udensian estate that have been leased out, and are in those parts formerly of the Lamian and Domitian estate [which have been detached and joined to the Tuzritanan (*sic*, for Thusdritanan) and which are not worked by the lessees. And to those have taken them over the same right of possession, exploitation and inheritance is given which is provided for in the Hadrianic law on virgin lands and those which have been left uncultivated for ten years in succession].

(Side 3) [Nor shall anyone be liable to hand over to the lessees a higher proportion of crops obtained from the Blandian and Udensian estate than is provided for in the Mancian Law; but he who] takes over those areas neglected by the lessees shall pay the usual dues, one third the produce. On those areas also, formerly of the Lamian and Domitian estate, which have been detached and joined to the Tuzritanan, he shall pay the same portion. From olive trees which an individual plants [in trenches or grafts on wild olives no part of the produce obtained shall be taken for the first ten years; but neither shall they from fruit trees for the first seven years; nor shall any other fruit become subject to the division except those offered for sale by the occupiers. The proportion of dried produce that each individual shall be liable to provide he shall give for the first five-year period to the person during whose lease he has taken over the land, after that to the administration of the imperial ?Treasury].

(Side 4) Earinus and Doryphorus send greetings to their friend Primigenius. Copy of the letter written to us by the distinguished personage Tutilius Pudens, for you to know the contents; and you are to post up what is appended in the most frequented places.

Verridius Bassus and Januarius send greetings to their friend Martialis. If any lands are lying fallow and are uncultivated or if there are any wooded or marshy lands on that estate, you are not to forbid those who wish from cultivating those lands on lines laid down in the Mancian law.

The inscription is one of a celebrated quartet from the imperial estates in the area, ranging in time from the end of Trajan's reign to that of Septimius Severus; they have been elucidated by Flach, 1978. The first, from Henchir Mettich (*FIRA* 1^2, 100), calls itself a law 'based on the Mancian Law' and determines the obligations of farmers on the imperial estate of Villa Magna to its lessees and their managers. The second, translated above, is Hadrianic, a request from farmers for permission to take over land left uncultivated. The third, from Ain

Wassel (*FIRA* 102), reiterates the 'Hadrianic Law' in 198-212 (and serves to fill gaps in the text translated above). The fourth, from Souk el-Khmis (*FIRA* 103), is a petition from farmers of the Burunitan estate to Commodus against the excessive demands for service and the brutality of lessees, one Allius Maximus in particular, together with Commodus' reply of 180-3 assuring them that his procurators would keep demands to the stipulated level.

The 'Mancian Law' of these documents was hardly a true law but a formula, devised perhaps by Curtilius Mancia, consul in 55, as governor of Africa or practised on an estate named after him; (see J. Percival in *The Ancient Historian and his Materials*, ed. B. Levick (Farnborough, 1975), 213ff.). It was 'a form of tenure arising from the clearing and cultivation of waste land, available primarily (if not exclusively) to *coloni* on estates already existing'. It was followed up by a measure of Hadrian (above, side 2), also designed to promote cultivation not only of land left unallocated but of neglected allocated land and conferring rights of inheritance, whether the object was to increase production for its own sake or to increase imperial revenue from the estates or both.

The farmers at Ain el-Djemala sought to take advantage of these terms and wrote to the procurators for permission (side 1), pointing out the gains to the imperial administration that were already to be observed in a neighbouring estate where permission had been given. In Flach's view of the documents that follow their petition was addressed to Verridius Bassus, procurator of the imperial estates in the Carthaginian region, and his favourable answer is contained in his letter (side 4) to Martialis, procurator of several or a single estate in that region; his letter actually repeats phrases from the petition. In Flach's view the intervening documents are evidence relating to the neighbouring estate, appended by the petitioners to their request. The main document (sides 2-3) is a formal statement by Tutilius Pudens, a predecessor of Verridius Bassus, giving permission for the Neronian estate farmers to take over wasteland; it is sandwiched between (a) an introductory letter of Tutilius Pudens to Earinus and Doryphorus, his subordinates, handing on his statement, and (b) the letter of Earinus and Doryphorus handing on Tutilius Pudens' statement to Primigenius, who held a position similar to that of Martialis.

On side 4 Tutilius Pudens' statement is to be posted up; just as the current petition, the evidence submitted by the villagers, and Verridius Bassus' decisions were all recorded; cf. **119**.

The last clause of side 3 is just defensible as a reference to 'dried produce' of the land taken over by the occupiers; but Dr Mackie is probably right to suggest that the lapicide has erred.

7

Loyalty: The Role of the Emperor

Up to a point Rome herself engaged the loyalty of her subjects.

112. Rutilius Claudius Namatianus, *Poem on his Homecoming*, 1, 47-58; 63-6

O hear us, fairest queen of all your world,
    Whose home is now in starry heaven, our Rome,
O hear us, mother of mankind and gods;
    Not far from heaven when we are in your shrines,
'Tis you we hymn, and shall while fate allows;
    No man can live and thrive, forgetting you.
The Sun may sooner plunge in cruel neglect
    Than worship due to you fade from our hearts:
The gifts you offer equal radiant Sun's,
    Whatever land the waves of Ocean lap.
The Sun is master of the world and yet
    From where he rises to his horses' stable
Is all yours: the course is run for you.
   . . .
One nation you have made from tribes unlike;
    Men alien to law have made their way
As captives in your power to partnership
    In rights: a city what was once a world.

Namatianus' panegyric is the work of a native of Gaul, perhaps Tolosa, although he held high office at Rome. Composed probably in 417 (A. Cameron, *JRS* 57 (1967), 31ff.), it echoes phrases of the second-century panegyric of Aelius Aristides (sections 4 and 10) but carries more conviction for not being a display piece.

113. Aelius Aristides, *Oration* 26, Panegyric on Rome, 30-3; Greek

No distinction is drawn any more between continent and island; like one continuous stretch of country, one race, everything is quietly obedient, (31) . . . The governors who are sent to the cities and provinces are each and all rulers of them in their own right, but in regard to themselves and in their relation to each other they are likewise all subjects, and indeed it is in this respect that one would distinguish them from their subjects, that they offer the leading example of how a subject should behave. Such is the awe universally instilled of the mighty ruler who presides over the whole. (32) So they consider that he knows better what they are doing than they do themselves, and they feel more fear and respect than a man would for the master who was present and standing over him telling him what to do. None is so self-confident that he can so much as hear the name without being affected. No, he rises, sings his praise, offers homage and joins in a twofold prayer, one on the Emperor's behalf to the gods, one to the Emperor himself concerning his own affairs. And if they have even the slightest doubt as to the merits of the claimants in lawsuits and petitions, whether public or private, brought by their subjects, they send to him at once with an enquiry about the best course of action and wait until he gives them an indication, for all the world like a chorus awaiting the sign from their coach. (33) So there is no need for him to wear himself out touring the entire Empire, nor for him to visit one people after another to settle each individual question for them when he sets foot in their country. No, it is perfectly easy for him to sit down and govern the world by correspondence. It is as if the letters were carried on wings, so brief is the lapse of time between writing and arrival.

Aristides, who may be sniping at the peripatetic Emperor Hadrian (see below) or justifying his successor's failure to visit the provinces, shifts attention to the most important factor in securing the loyalty of the Empire: the Emperor. Not only was his power legally and in fact superior to that of governors (**2ff.**), who were known at close quarters and not always loved (see **59**, **88**, and chapter 11); it was in his interest that his subjects should not be fleeced by them, and to a limited extent he depended on their support as a counterweight to hostility in the senatorial order (the point is made negatively in **76**, and note Claudius' action in **101**).

Nothing brings home the way even quite humble subjects began at once to regard the Emperor as a source of help than Strabo's encounter with some fishermen on a journey in the Aegean.

114. Strabo, *Geography* **10**, 5, 3, p. 485f.; Greek

My ship anchored at one of these islands (the Cyclades), Gyarus, and I noticed a little village inhabited by fishermen. When we sailed we took one of them on board; he had been elected to go as envoy from the village to Caesar, who was at Corinth on his way home to celebrate his triumph for his victory at Actium. On our voyage he would tell enquirers that his mission was to get a reduction of tribute: (p. 486) they were assessed at 150 drachmas, when they would have been hard put to it to pay 100.

29 BC. Harbourless, rocky, desolate, destitute of water and vegetation except brushwood and oleanders, Gyarus was a place of exile and finds no mention in the *Blue Guide*: it is not surprising that the fisherman sought tax relief. That they might expect to be heard is suggested by an anecdote about Hadrian, tellingly cited by Millar, 1967 (2), 9. A woman who put a request to him as he went past on a journey got the answer 'I've no time'; but when she shouted after him that in that case he had better stop being Emperor she was given the chance to put her case (Cassius Dio, *Roman History* 69, 6, 3).

Recently discussion has centred on the conception of the Emperor that the forms of cult or homage offered him and his family imply (see Hopkins 1978 and Price 1980). The very power of the Emperor made it appropriate to see him as more than human, akin to the gods, capable even of miracles (see Suetonius, *Deified Vespasian* 7, 2f.). But the second part of the 'twofold prayer' of **113** shows that the cult had a practical purpose, which explains its strength, however different the forms it took in different parts of the Empire (another reason for its strength). The Emperor could give practical help; as Aristides put it in another work (*Oration* 19, 5), 'we pray to the gods for the same things we ask from you most divine rulers' (he was requesting help for Smyrna after the earthquake of 178). This practical aspect of the cult, in which homage was offered in return for protection and favours, is well illustrated in an inscription that is not directly concerned with cult at all.

115. EJ 319; Greek, from Aezani in Phrygia

[Letter of Tiberius Caesar] conveyed [from] Bononia in Gaul. Tiberius Caesar [sends greetings to the council] and people of Aezani. [Having known] long since of your [devotion and] affection for me it was also with the greatest pleasure that on the present occasion I received [from] your envoys [the decree which] demonstrates the good will of the city towards me. I shall [accordingly] endeavour [to the best of] my ability to play my part in promoting [your interests on all] occasions on which you request [my help].

This letter was written soon after Tiberius became known as the future Emperor in 4. The people of a secondary town in central Asia Minor went to the trouble and expense of sending envoys all the way to the Channel coast to offer him their good wishes. Tiberius knew what was expected in return. His reply, inscribed on stone, was set up in the city where it could be read and pondered by any (governor, procurator, military man, visiting Roman, member of another city) who thought of treating the people of Aezani with less than strict justice and courtesy.

There was nothing to prevent cities and individuals from establishing cults at will, but the wish to be sure that they were acceptable. The following document from the west shows what form city ceremonies might take.

116. EJ 100; altar from Narbo

(a) In the consulships of Titus Statilius Taurus and Lucius Cassius Longinus, 22 September: vow taken to the guiding spirit of Augustus by the mass of the ordinary people of Narbo, in perpetuity:

May it be good, well-omened and fortunate to Imperator Caesar Augustus, son of the deified Caesar, Father of his Country, Supreme Pontiff, in the thirty-fourth year of his tribunician power; to his wife, offspring and family; to the senate and people of Rome and to the colonists and resident aliens of the colony of Julia Paterna Narbo Martius, who have bound themselves to do homage to his spirit for ever. The mass of the ordinary people of Narbo have placed an altar in the market place of the city, at which annually on 23 September, the day on which the good fortune of our epoch brought him forth to the world as its ruler, three Roman knights, members of the people, and three persons of freedman status are to offer up an animal sacrifice each and are to provide the colonists and resident aliens with incense and wine at their own expense on that day so that they may offer supplication to his guiding spirit. And likewise on the 24th, and likewise on 1 January, they are to provide them, and also on the 7th, the day on which his future rule over the world was first inaugurated by him with signs from heaven, they are to offer supplication with incense and wine and to sacrifice an animal each and to provide the colonists and resident aliens with incense and wine on that day; and on 31 May, because on that day in the consulships of Titus Statilius Taurus and Manius Aemilius Lepidus he put the decisions of the mass of the ordinary people on an equal footing with those of the city council, they are to sacrifice an animal each and provide the colonists and resident aliens with incense and wine so that they may offer supplication to his guiding spirit. And from the said three Roman knights and the said [three] persons of freedman status, one [- - -].

(b) The people of Narbo dedicated an altar of the guiding spirit of Augustus [2 lines erased] under the regulations which are inscribed below.

Guiding spirit of Caesar Augustus, Father of his Country, when I make over and dedicate this altar to you today I shall do so under the regulations and in the quarters which I shall proclaim here today, as the lowest depths of the soil belong to this altar and inscriptions: if anyone wishes to clean, adorn, or repair it, let what may be of service to it be allowed by laws human and divine; or if anyone performs a sacrifice of an animal victim, even if he does not proffer additional entrails, none the less let it be proper in that respect for it to be done.

If anyone wishes to make a gift to this altar and to magnify it, he is to be permitted and the same regulation is to be extended to that gift as governs the altar. The remaining regulations for this altar and its inscriptions are to be the same as those that govern the altar of Diana on the Aventine Hill. Under these regulations and in these quarters, just as I have said, I make over and dedicate to you this altar on behalf of Imperator Caesar Augustus, Father of his Country, Supreme Pontiff, in the thirty-fifth year of his tribunician power; on behalf of his wife, offspring and family; of the senate and Roman people; of the colonists and resident aliens of the colony of Julia Paterna Narbo Martius, who have bound themselves to offer homage to his guiding spirit for ever, so that you may be graciously pleased to be favourable.

This inscription, though dated to 11, with 12-13 for the final dedication, was re-engraved in the second century, confirming the earnestness of the original dedicator(s). As elsewhere in the west, cult is offered, not to Augustus directly, but on his behalf to his guiding spirit (*numen*); the *genius* is akin.

The Roman knights are wealthy persons who happened not to be members of the council and the participation of freedmen shows how a numerous and in some cases well-off class of the population, but one debarred from membership of the council, was brought into the celebrations — and made to pay for the privilege.

The rules governing the plebeian shrine of Diana on the Aventine at Rome are invoked because it was the oldest of its kind, but the invocation strengthens the popular tone of the document, as well as emphasising the identity of the colonists as Romans (I owe this point to Mrs Shortland-Jones. For the interpretation of Augustus' action I am indebted to Dr Mackie.) Conflict of interest between classes may also be seen in **186** and **207**. In the sequel, the people had their celebrations subsidised, Augustus and his family were honoured, the knights and freedmen performed a prestigious duty in full publicity, and the colony was drawn (favourably, this time) to the attention of the Emperor.

For the language of the dedication see *ILS* 4907, a dedication to Jupiter made at Salona in 137.

The knights and freedmen constituted a group of six men, which in some communities took the form of a college open to freedmen.

117. *ILS* 6914; from Suel, near Malaca in Baetica

Sacred to the Augustan Neptune. Lucius Junius Puteolanus, member of the board of six Augustales, in the municipality of Suel,?the first to be elected by the decree of the council and for life, honoured with all the offices open to men of freedman status, provided a banquet (? and set up the monument) from his own resources, by decree of the council.

For the impressive figure that a member of a board of six Augustales could cut, see Petronius, *Satyricon* 65, where the author claims to be terrified by the arrival of one with his white robes and attendant. At Suel, if the word 'first' in the text is temporal rather than indicating primacy in the college, the priesthood was not introduced until Vespasian granted Latin rights (Mackie 1983 (2), 76, n.36).

When not individuals or cities but associations of communities, province-wide, wished to establish cult the Emperor was consulted before that public and expensive undertaking was launched.

118. Cassius Dio, Roman History 51, 20, 6f.; Greek

In the meantime Caesar, apart from the other business that he was dealing with, also gave permission for the creation of sacred precincts dedicated to Rome and to Caesar his father, under the title of the deified Julius, in both Ephesus and Nicaea. (These were the cities that had attained pre-eminence respectively in Asia and Bithynia.) (7) And he enjoined the Roman citizens resident amongst their inhabitants to do honour to those deities, but gave permission to the non-Romans ('Greeks', he called them) to consecrate certain areas to himself, the inhabitants of Asia in Pergamum, the Bithynians in Nicomedia. And this was the start of a practice that has continued under the later Emperors as well, not only among the Greek-speaking peoples but among the others besides that are subject to the Romans.

Dio dates this development to 29 BC, when the future Augustus was in the east (**114**). He makes it clear that the Emperor regulated the scheme, but the initiative came from leading figures in the provinces concerned. Early in the century 'peoples and tribes distinguished for their goodwill towards the Romans' had collaborated to establish games in honour of a proconsul (Sherk, *Docs.* 47) and the 'community of Greeks in Asia' had received a letter from Mark Antony in the triumviral period (EJ 300; cf. **162**). The organisation existed, and the occasion made a gesture imperative; the east as a whole had been behind Pompey, the Liberators and Antony. The provinces of Asia Minor needed the goodwill of the victor of 30 BC, not least because of the way their resources had been plundered by the men whose causes they had supported. As time went on the precious ties were strengthened by the construction of temples in other cities, one for each new Emperor. There was strong competition for the privilege of being awarded a temple — and for the business and prestige it brought with it (there were eleven cities in competition in 26 for the second temple in Asia: Tacitus, *Annals* 4, 55f., and see **178**), but the high priest might come from another town, and even ordinary delegates had a share of the prestige.

In accepting these honours Emperors were aware that they were accepting obligations, something made crystal clear by Tacitus' account of Tiberius' refusal of a temple in Baetica in 25 (*Annals* 4, 37f.). That was one (tacit) reason for moderating or refusing them. Some Emperors made it clearer what they were or were not willing to accept than others did.

119. EJ 102; Greek, from Gytheion in Laconia, Achaea

(a) [- - - (?the magistrate in charge of the market)] is to set on it [- - - on the first ?pedestal an image of the deified Augustus Caesar] the father, on the [second] from the right one or [Julia Augusta], on the third, one of Tiberius Caesar Augustus; [the] images are to be provided for him by the city. [And] a table is also to be set out by him in the centre of the theatre, and an incense burner placed upon it, and members of the council and all the authorities are to offer sacrifice [upon it] for the welfare of our leaders before the entry of the performers.

He is to devote the first day to the deified Augustus, son of the deified Caesar, saviour and liberator, the second to Imperator Tiberius Caesar, Augustus and Father of his Country, the third to Julia Augusta, the Good Fortune of our league and city; the fourth to the Victory of Germanicus Caesar, the fifth to the Aphrodite of Drusus Caesar, the sixth to Titus Quinctius Flamininus; and he is to be responsible for the orderly conduct of the contestants.

He is to render account to the city for the entire cost of hiring the performers and of the administration of the sacred funds at the first assembly after the games; and if he is found on inquiry to have misappropriated funds or to have falsified his accounts he is to be banned from all further office and his property is to be confiscated to the people. As to the funds of any persons whose property is ever confiscated, this money is to be sacred and additional amenities are to be provided out of it by the annual magistrates. Any native of Gytheion who wishes is to be permitted to institute proceedings concerning the sacred funds with immunity from consequent prosecution.

The magistrate in charge of the market, after completing the days of theatrical performances devoted to the gods and leaders, is to bring the performers on to the stage for two further days, one devoted to the memory of Gaius Julius Eurycles, who was an outstanding benefactor of the league and the city, and the second in honour of Gaius Julius Laco who is the present guarantor of the defence and security of our league and city.

He is to hold the performances starting on the day of the goddess on such days as he is able; and when he goes out of office he is to hand over to the magistrate in charge of the market who succeeds him a list drawn up for public use of requisites for the performances, and the city is to receive a copy from the man who takes it over.

Whenever the magistrate in charge of the market holds the theatrical performances he is to conduct a procession from the temple of Asclepius and Hygieia which is to be accompanied by the young men in training, the younger members of the citizen body, and the rest of the citizens, wearing wreaths of laurel and dressed in white. The sacred virgins and the married women are also to join in the procession, wearing sacral dress. When the procession arrives at the shrine of Caesar the overseers are to sacrifice a bull for the safety of the leaders and gods and for the continuation of their rule for ever; and when they have sacrificed they are to constrain the communal messes and their fellow-magistrates to sacrifice in the market place. If they fail to secure that the procession takes place, or do not sacrifice, or if when they have sacrificed they fail to constrain the communal messes and their fellow-magistrates to sacrifice in the market place, they are to pay the gods a sacred fine of 2,000 drachmas. Any native of Gytheion who wishes is to be permitted to prosecute.

Terentius Bias and his fellow-overseers in office with Chaeron, general and priest of the deified Augustus, are to contribute three carved representations of the deified Augustus and Julia Augusta and Tiberius Caesar Augustus and the benches in the theatre for the chorus and four doors for the stage performances and a platform for the musicians. They are also to set up a stone plinth, inscribing the sacred law on it, and are to deposit in the public archives a copy of the sacred law, so that being placed both in a public place and in the open air and where it is visible to all the law may display for all men to see how [enduring] is the thankfulness of the people of Gytheion to the rulers. But if they do not inscribe this law or set up the plinth in front of the temple or write out the copy [- - -]

(b) [- - -] but if anyone [- - -] shall be [- - -] neither decree [- - -] let him be barred from all treaty [- - - ?his property] is to be consecrated to the rulers [- - -] the honours due to the gods, if he is caught [let him perish as an object of horror], the man who kills him being [exempt from prosecution].

[Letter of Tiber]ius. [Tiberius Caesar] Augustus son of [the deified Augustus], Supreme Pontiff, [in the sixteenth year] of his tribunician power, sends greetings to the overseers of Gytheion and to the city. Decimus Turranius Nicanor, the envoy sent by you [to] me and to my mother, has delivered to me your letter, to which had been appended the legislation passed [by you] providing for homage to my father, honour to ourselves. I thank you for them; but my understanding is that what is fitting for all mankind in general and your city in this particular case is to keep in reserve choice honours suitable to the greatness of the benefits conferred by my father on the whole world; I myself am satisfied with those more modest and suitable for a mortal man. My mother, however, will send you an answer when she hears from you what your decision is concerning the honours offered to her.

The 'sacred law' belongs to the early months of Tiberius' reign, March-June 15, and in their enthusiasm the drafters credited him with titles he was never officially to accept, notably that of Father of his Country. The Gytheates had two special reasons for zeal: the Claudian family to which both Tiberius and his mother belonged were hereditary patrons of nearby Sparta, of which Gytheion was the port, and the League of Free Lacedaemonians to which it belonged and of which the 'overseers' (ephors) were magistrates had been freed from direct Spartan control by Augustus (Pausanias, *Guide to Greece* 3, 21, 6,), or had had their freedom confirmed by him (in the Greek he and Julius Caesar are 'gods'). The Empress Livia, called Julia now by the name conferred on her in Augustus' will, is identified with the Fortune that had long guided the destinies of cities and Hellenistic monarchs. Flamininus, who had originally liberated the Greeks from the control of such monarchs in 196 BC, was long revered and had a festival of his own at Gytheion (Plutarch, *Flamininus* 16, 5; *ILS* 8766); for the family of Eurycles and Laco, which enjoyed a dynastic position in the area and in the reign of Trajan reached membership of the Roman senate, see G. Bowersock, *JRS* 51 (1961), 112ff.

The sacred law, though mutilated, clearly ends with dire threats against violators, and with a self-referential instruction to inscribe it (cf. **111**).

Tiberius' reply has attracted most attention. Unlike the surviving part of the law, it distinguishes what is to be offered Augustus and what himself. It is unlikely that honours more extravagant than those offered Tiberius had been proposed for Augustus at the beginning of the inscription, or the Emperor would not have had to make the point he did. Probably the authorities inscribed his letter out of respect, ignoring his imprecisely formulated request. The vagueness is due to the new Emperor's need to steer between courtesy to extravagantly expressed goodwill (with implied willingness to confirm favours in return) on the one hand and attested personal dislike of adulation on the other.

Tiberius' imprecision has been contrasted unfavourably with the crisp selection made by Claudius in a letter sent in 41, soon after his own accession, to the people of Alexandria; equally crisp is his selection of Alexandrian requests.

120. Smallwood, Gaius-Nero 370; Greek papyrus

Edict of Aemilius Rectus: since the entire city was unable on account of its size to be present at the reading of the letter, most sacred and beneficial to the city as it was, I have considered it necessary to post up the letter so that you may read it individually and admire the greatness of our god Caesar and feel gratitude for his goodwill towards the city.

In the second year of Tiberius Claudius Caesar Augustus Germanicus, Imperator, on the fourteenth of the month of the New Augustus.

(Col. 2) Tiberius Claudius Caesar Augustus Germanicus, Imperator, Supreme Pontiff, holder of tribunician power, designated to the consulship, sends greetings to the city of Alexandria.

Tiberius Claudius Barbillus, Apollonius son of Artemidorus, Chaeremon son of Leonidas, Marcus Julius Asclepiades, Gaius Julius Dionysius, Tiberius Claudius Phanias, Pasion son of Potamon, Dionysius son of Sabbion, Tiberius Claudius Archibius, Apollonius son of Ariston, Gaius Julius Apollonius, Hermaiscus son of Apollonius, your envoys, have handed me your decree and given me a long account of the city, evidently drawing my attention to the goodwill towards us, which, you may be sure, you have stored up with me for many years; you are naturally disposed to be devoted to the Emperors, as has been known to me for a long period of time, but you have given particular attentions to my own house, attentions which have been returned. To mention only the consummate instance and pass over the others, my brother is the prime witness to it in the speech he addressed to you in his own very genuinely felt words.

That was why I was glad to receive the honours conferred on me by you, although I am not given to such things. And first I grant you leave to celebrate my birthday as Augustus-Day in the way you have chosen, and I acquiesce in your setting up statues of me and my family everywhere throughout the city for I see your keenness to establish monuments everywhere of your devotion to my house.

But as to the two gold statues, the one of the Claudian Augustan Peace shall be set up at Rome, as my most honoured friend Barbillus proposed, winning his point by perseverance, although I was inclined to refuse as I was likely to appear to be acting in rather bad taste, (col. 3) while as to the other, it shall take part in processions held in your city in the way you think best on the days named after me, and the chair (? or chariot), decorated in the way you wish, may accompany it in the procession.

And it would be silly, perhaps, when I have agreed to honours of this magnitude, to decline to introduce a Claudian Tribe and to diverge from the customary practice in Egypt of dedicating sacred groves; for which reason I grant you these things also. And set up the equestrian statues of

Vitrasius Pollio my prefect, too, if you wish.

The erection of four-horse chariots which you wish to set up for me at the entries to the country I acquiesce in, one to be set up near the place in Libya called Taposiris, the other near the lighthouse at Alexandria, the third near Pelusium in Egypt.

But I beg to be excused a high priest of my own and the establishment of temples, as I wish not to show bad taste in the eyes of my contemporaries, and judge religious cult and things of that kind to have been rendered by every age solely and exclusively to the gods.

Concerning the requests which you have been anxious to obtain from me, my decisions are as follows. For all persons who have passed through their training period up to the time of my accession I preserve intact their Alexandrian citizenship, on the basis of all the rights and privileges at the disposal of the city, with the exception of any persons who have insinuated themselves among you and completed their training in spite of having been born from slave women; and it is equally my wish that all the favours granted you by Emperors before me and by kings and governors should be confirmed, as the deified Augustus also confirmed them.

(Col. 4) As to the temple wardens of the shrine that belongs to the deified Augustus in Alexandria, I wish them to be selected by lot in the same way as those of the deified Augustus are selected in Canopus. With regard to the proposal that civic offices should be of a three year duration, this seems to me to be a really good plan: we shall find that the officials will conduct themselves in a restrained fashion for their term of office for fear of being held responsible for failings in their administration.

Concerning the city council, what was your custom once upon a time under the old kings is something I cannot comment on, but you know perfectly well that you have not had one under any of the Emperors before me. This is certainly a plan mooted for the first time, and it is unclear whether it will be advantageous to the city and from my point of view; I have written to Aemilius Rectus to look into it and inform me whether the institution should be established, and, if it were to prove advisable to summon one, in what way it shall be put into effect.

As to the disturbances and rioting against the Jews — rather, the war against them, if I am to use the accurate term — and the question which side was originally responsible, although your envoys, especially Dionysius son of Theon, have zealously maintained their case at length in the confrontation, I have none the less been unwilling to examine the matter in detail, reserving implacable wrath for those who started it up again. I tell you plainly, that if you do not put an end to this disastrous, ?outrageous frenzy against one another, I shall be forced to show you what a well-disposed Emperor is like when he becomes justifiably angry.

Accordingly even at this late stage I conjure the Alexandrians to show humanity and good will towards Jews who have been living in the same city with them for many generations, (col. 5) and not to do anything to desecrate the practices connected with the cult of their god, but to allow them to keep to the same customs as they followed under the deified Augustus, which I too have confirmed after having heard both sides. And as to the Jews, I tell them straight out not to waste time working for any more privileges than they had before, nor in future to send two separate delegations as if they were living in two separate cities, which is something that has never happened before; nor are they to force their way into games arranged by gymnasiarchs or *cosmetici*, since as it is they enjoy their own privileges as well as benefiting from an abundance of unstinted advantages when they are living in a city that does not belong to them. And they are not to bring in or admit Jews sailing from Syria or Egypt, which will inevitably increase our suspicions. Otherwise I shall proceed against them in every way as spreading what amounts to a world-wide epidemic.

If your two parties renounce those courses and are willing to live together in a civilised way, treating each other like human beings, I too shall give careful attention to the city which comes into our hands like a house inherited from our ancestors.

I testify that my friend Barbillus is unremitting in the care he gives to your affairs in my presence; even now he has been showing the greatest zeal in the struggle on your behalf. The same goes for my friend Claudius Archibius. My good wishes for your welfare.

The date of the document is 10 November, 41, the second year of Claudius' reign on Egyptian reckoning because the Egyptian new year had fallen on 29 August.

For Claudius' brother Germanicus' actual words to the Alexandrians, see EJ 320 and 379; they evidently did receive him with great enthusiasm (see Tacitus, *Annals* 2, 59).

For a new and inexperienced Emperor, Claudius showed himself firm. The Alexandrians failed in their main request for a city council, for all the honours they had offered (it was granted only by Severus: *The Augustan History, Septimius Severus*, 17, 2), and they made no headway in their feud with the Jews.

For the prized citizenship of Alexandria, see **135**. There had been Jews in Alexandria since its foundation, occupying first the Ghetto to which they had been assigned, then another of the five divisions of the city. They had no rights as citizens but an organisation of their own, an ethnarch and council of elders, and their numbers, cohesion and wealth made them much better off than the non-citizen peasantry of Egypt (**202**); for graded rights in Cyrenaica see **46**. After Alexandria's humiliation at the hands of Rome in 30 BC (the parallel of Germany after her defeat in 1918 suggests itself irresistibly), resentment was vented on the Jews who, having supported Julius Caesar in Egypt in 48 BC were favoured by the Romans (for community strife elsewhere, see **39**). It was aggravated by pressure exerted by some members of the Jewish community for admission to the citizenship proper, or to rights that went with it. The present document and its context have been elucidated by V.A. Tcherikover and A. Fuks, *Corpus Papyrorum Judaicarum* (Cambridge, Mass., 1957), 1, 67ff. and 2 no. 153. A prefect in bad odour with the Emperor Gaius Caligula connived at Greek attacks on synagogues, including the setting up of the Emperor's statues in them; the Jews were forced back into the original Ghetto and their homes looted. The prefect's successor Vitrasius Pollio referred the question of Jewish rights to Gaius (Philo, *Embassy to Gaius*), who was shortly assassinated. Now Jews brought in co-religionists from outside (Josephus, *Antiquities* 19, 278) and began a counter-pogrom. Disturbances at Rome (Cassius Dio, *Roman History* 60, 6, 6) may also have added to Claudius' irritation, and if the reference to two delegations is to two Jewish delegations (conciliatory official and radical separatist?), by that too; he may be objecting only to the Jews sending one separate embassy of their own, Philo's, but if so he should not have said that it had never happened before.

The institution of cult was not always the work of provincials acting on their own initiative with the idea of putting moral pressure on the Emperor. In the west the council of Gauls and the altar of Rome and Augustus that the tribes supported was a Roman creation.

121. Livy, *History of Rome, Epitome of Book* 139

The German tribes situated on both sides of the Rhine were reduced by Drusus and the disturbance that had broken out in Gaul because of the census was brought to an end. An altar to the divine Caesar was dedicated at the confluence of the Saône and the Rhône, and Gaius Julius Vercondaridubnus, an Aeduan, was elected priest.

13-12 BC. This illuminating passage reveals the occasion for the Roman action: incursions of the Germans and discontent at the prospect of taxation (cf. **196**). Now the leading members of all the sixty or so tribes were induced to contribute to construction and maintenance of the altar and join an annual assembly at which men of good will (the wealthy, whom the Romans supported in power) could confer and take part in ceremonies that would enhance their own dignity (and commit them to Rome). The festival, for which see **148** and **173**, was timed for 1 August, coinciding with the eisteddfod simultaneously held at Autricum (Chartres), which like Lugdunum could claim to be the centre of Gaul (Caesar, *Gallic War* 6, 13, 10), in celebration of the Celtic harvest festival of Lammas ('loaf mass') Day, as Dr Nash has kindly pointed out to me. The site of the new altar, at the confluence of two rivers, was acceptable to Gallic paganism (see A. Ross, *Pagan and Celtic Britain* (London, 1967), 46ff.), but immediately outside the gates of a Roman colony and at the mercy of the garrison.

The first holder of the priesthood had received the Roman citizenship and was a member of the tribe of the Aedui who, having enjoyed treaty relations with Rome since the twenties of the second century, were always thought to deserve the highest privileges (Tacitus, *Annals* 11, 25, 1f.).

It was not long before an altar of similar type and purpose was erected amongst the loyal tribe of the Ubii near Cologne on the Rhine (Tacitus, *Annals* 1, 57, 2); in AD 9 a supposedly loyal member of the German Cheruscan nobility was high priest. Even the Elbe saw the erection of an altar to Augustus, prematurely as it turned out (Cassius Dio, *Roman History* 55, 10a, 2).

In the succeeding reigns, areas securely within the western Empire, such as Baetica, petitioned to be allowed to erect temples (**118n.**): as time goes on, evidence for cult accumulates.

122. MW 128; bronze tablet found at Narbo

[Honours due to the high priest - - - at Na]rbo [- - - when the high priest performs the rites] and [sacrifices], the lictors [who attend on magistrates are to attend on him. - - - According to the] law and right of that province [- - -] he [is to have the right of giving his opinion and voting] among the members of the council or senate; likewise [- - - he is to have] the right of viewing [public games of that province] from the front seats [among members of the council or senators [- - -. The wife] of the high priest, clad in white or purple garments [on festal days - - -] nor is she to take oath against her will or [is she to touch] the body of a dead person [nor - - - unless] it is of a person [related to her. And [it is to be permitted] for her [to be present - - -] at public shows in that [province].

Honours due to one who [has been] high priest. If a [man who has been] high priest has done nothing in breach of this law, then the incumbent high priest [is to ensure - - - that - - - by ballot] and under oath they decree and make it their pleasure that a man who has vacated the high priesthood should be permitted [to set] up a statue [of himself]. The man to whom they have so decreed that he has the right of setting up a statue] and [of inscribing] his own name and that of his father, his place of origin and the year of his high priesthood is to have the right of setting up the statue [at Narbo] within the confines of that temple, unless Imperator [Caesar ?Vespasian Augustus has accorded] someone [the right. And he] is to have the right in his local council and in the provincial council of Narbonensis of giving his opinion and voting among (men) of his rank according to the law [- - -]; likewise, when a public show [is given] in the province, of [attending among members of the council] in a magistrate's toga, and of those days on which he made sacrifices when he was high priest [or wearing in public] the dress [which he wore in making them].

Possible lack of high priest in the community. If there ceases to be a high priest in the community and no substitute has been elected for him then as each [high priest - - - is at Narbo] within three days of his being informed and being able he is to perform the rites at Narbo and is to conduct [all those rites throughout the rest] of the year [according to this law] in the order in which [the rites] of the annual high priests [are conducted, and if he conducts them for not less than] thirty days the same law, right and claims are to apply [to him] as apply to one [who has been elected] high priest of Augustus [according to the prescription of this law].

Place in which the [provincial] council is to be held. Those who assemble for the provincial council in Narbo are to hold it there. If any business is transacted at a council held outside Narbo or the boundaries of the territory of the people of Narbo it [is not to be held] lawful and valid.

Money [earmarked for rites]. A man who has vacated the high priesthood is to use [the surplus] of the money [which has been earmarked for the rites, to dedicate] statues and images of Imperator Caesar [? Vespasian Augustus] within the said temple [at the discretion of the incumbent] governor of the province. [- - - And he is to prove] before the official who [computes the finances of the province that he has] in that respect done [everything as provided in this law - - -] temple [- - -].

Vespasian is now agreed to be the object of the cult (cf. Mackie 1983 (2), 148 n.17). A motive for offering it to him is not hard to find: Narbonensis had supported Vitellius in the civil wars of 69-70, though only out of fear (Tacitus, *Histories* 1, 76); compare the motivation of Asia and Bithynia in 29 BC (**118**).

The regulations, as Dr Mackie points out, drawing attention to the phrase 'within the confines of that temple', seem to be based on a general law (cf. M.W. Frederiksen, *JRS* 55 (1965), 191). Hence the non-committal word 'community' in the following paragraph where one might have expected 'province' or 'colony'. The view that the paragraph refers to the loss of Roman citizenship by the high priest is implausible: why should that be envisaged — or so expressed?

The attraction of all the outward and visible honour that the high priests and their wives enjoyed (especially the purple-bordered toga worn by magistrates at Rome) once again shows the imperial cult as a means of acquiring dignity and recognition; in Narbonensis, which was very Romanised, the high priests were normally members of the equestrian order and their honours correspondingly striking.

123. ILS 6930; seen at Tarraco in the sixteenth century

To Gnaeus Numisius Modestus, son of Gnaeus, of the Sergian Tribe, native of New Carthage, who has held every office in his city and was elected by the provincial council to tend (? or to gild) the statues of the deified Hadrian, and who was high priest. At public expense, in his honour. At public expense, in his honour (*sic*).

The date of this inscription cannot be much after the death of Hadrian in 138. The priesthoods passed among the wealthy of the cities and tribes of western provinces like Tarraconensis as they did in the east (cf. **122**).

124. EJ 120, cf. AE 1955, 212; from near Divona Caducorum

To Marcus Lucterius Leo, son of Lucterius Senecianus, who held every office in his native land, priest of the altar of Augustus between the confluence of the Saône and the Rhône: the community of the Cadurci set up the monument at public expense for his services.

A remarkable testimony to the success of Roman rule in Gaul: Lucterius' ancestor had been an energetic and determined opponent of Caesar's in the revolt of Vercingetorix, 52 BC (see *Gallic War* 7, 5ff.; 8, 30ff., 39 and 44, where he is handed over to the Romans, presumably to be executed with Vercingetorix in 46).

Another means exploited by provincials of drawing attention to their loyalty and by Roman authorities of assuring themselves of it was by the taking of an oath. A handful of specimens remain, all belonging to the first century of the Principate, but the practice of taking or exacting them continued on the accession of a new Emperor.

125. EJ 315; Greek, from Phazimon-Neapolis in Paphlagonia

In the third year from Imperator Caesar Augustus, son of the deified Caesar, holding the consulship for the twelfth time, on 6 March in Gangra in [the market place], oath sworn by the inhabitants of Paphlagonia [and] by the Romans residing among them for business purposes.

I swear by Zeus, Earth, Sun, all the gods [and] goddesses, and by Augustus himself that I will be loyal to Caesar Augustus and his children and descendants for all the time of my [life], in word, deed and thought, considering as friends whomsoever they consider so, and reckoning as enemies whomsoever they themselves judge to be so; and that in their interests I shall spare neither body nor soul nor life nor children, but in every way for those things that pertain to them I shall endure every danger; and that if I see or hear anything hostile to them being either

said or planned or carried out, this I will reveal and shall be the enemy
of [the man] who is saying or planning or doing any of these things. And
whomsoever they themselves may judge to be their enemies, these I will
pursue and defend them against, by land and sea, by sword and steel.

But if I do anything contrary to this [oath] or do not conform to the
letter with the oath I swore, I myself bring down on myself and my body,
soul and life, and on my children and all my family and all that belongs
to me utter and total destruction down to my every last connection [and]
all my descendants, and let neither land [nor] sea receive [the bodies] of
either me or mine, nor let them produce fruit [for them].

All the inhabitants of [the countryside] also took the oath in the same
terms in the shrines of Augustus in the districts at the altars [of
Augustus].

Likewise the people of Phazimon who inhabit the town [now] known
as Neapolis one and all [took the oath] at the [altar] of Augustus.

Gangra was the capital of Paphlagonia, annexed as part of Galatia in
6 BC, Phazimon one of the lesser city centres in which the oath was taken
three years later. In this backward, mountainous, wooded, and newly
annexed part of the Empire the savage terms of the oath are not
surprising: there may have been real danger of unrest. In 29 BC (**118**)
Augustus had renounced cult from Roman citizens; here they too take
the oath, and by gods that include the Emperor himself. The distinction
was hard to maintain in a society in which provincials were being
admitted to Roman citizenship in increasing numbers. Besides, public
pronouncements made in Asia were a different matter from the
enforcement of oaths in Paphlagonia.

Next in time comes an oath taken on the accession of Augustus' heir.

126. EJ 105*; Greek, from near Palaepaphos, Cyprus

[By] our goddess Artemis Acraea and our goddess Core and our god
Apollo Hylates and our god Apollo Cerynetes and our saviours the
Twins and the goddess who belongs to the entire island, Hestia who presides over the council, and the gods and goddesses who are the ancestral deities common to the entire island and the descendant of Aphrodite,
the god Augustus Caesar, and by Rome who lives for ever and all the
other gods and goddesses, we ourselves and our descendants swear to
hearken and be obedient by land and sea, to show good will, to
reverence (space for 12 letters) Tiberius Caesar Augustus, son of
Augustus, with all his house, and to have the same man as friend and
enemy that they have, and along with the other gods to introduce and
vote for [?religious rites] only for Rome and Tiberius Caesar Augustus,
son of Augustus (space for 12 letters) and for the sons of his blood and
for nobody else whatsoever [- - -].

This oath was taken spontaneously: the participants would be able to show what they had done. In offering cult to Tiberius and the sons 'of his own blood' they have happened on an unfortunate phrase, but it is unlikely that they meant to rate Tiberius' adopted son Germanicus lower than Drusus Caesar. It is other claimants to the throne that they mean to exclude, such as the disgraced rival Agrippa Postumus.

Uncertain about the titles that the new Emperor meant to take, they twice left a space to be filled in later, when they were known; the people of Gytheion were less cautious (**119**).

127. Smallwood, *Gaius-Nero* 32; bronze tablet found at Aritium, Lusitania

Under Gaius Ummidius Durmius Quadratus, praetorian legate of Gaius Caesar Germanicus Imperator.

Oath of the people of Aritium.

It is my heartfelt intention to be a personal enemy to those whom I discover to be enemies of Gaius Caesar Germanicus, and if anyone causes or shall cause any danger to him or his security, I shall not cease to pursue him with the sword and relentless war by land and sea until he has paid the penalty to Caesar; nor shall I hold myself or my children dearer than his safety, and those who are of hostile mind to him I shall consider to be enemies to me.

If I knowingly forswear myself or break my oath in future, then may Jupiter Best and Greatest and the deified Augustus and all the rest of the immortal gods make me forfeit my native land, my personal safety, and all my property.

11 May in the township of old Aritium in the consulships of Gnaeus Acerronius Proculus and Gaius Petronius Pontinus Nigrinus, the officers in charge being Vegethus son of Tallicus and [- - -]ibius son of [- - -]arionus.

Here again an oath is taken to a new Emperor (Tiberius had died on 16 March, 37). The governor is named, which suggests that in remoter or less reliable provinces he was responsible for administering the oath of loyalty (see Tacitus, *Annals* 1, 34, 1, for its administration in Belgica in AD 14).

A different tradition has been detected behind eastern and western oaths (see Herrmann 1969; Gray 1970). In the east they have been derived from oaths belonging to the city's internal political life which in the Hellenistic age were adapted to relations of alliance with kings, in the west from the oath taken to Caesar at the end of the civil war, when he dismissed his bodyguard, and from those sworn to Octavian before the Actian campaign in Italy and by the provinces of Gaul and Spain, Africa, Sicily and Sardinia (*Achievements of Augustus* 25, 2, where the editors (Brunt and Moore) attribute the inappropriately warlike terms of the Aritium and Gangra oaths to the circumstances in which the model was drawn up in 32 BC).

Alike in eastern and western parts of the Empire, the loyalty of the troops, whether legionaries or auxiliaries, was a prime consideration. It was secured by the attention paid to their material welfare and to their self-regard, but also by a traditional set of military festivals observed throughout the year.

128. Fink *et al.*, 1940; papyrus found in the temple of Artemis Azzanathkona, Dura on the Euphrates

(Co. 1) [1 January - - -;

5 January, because vows are made and fulfilled], and for the welfare of our Lord Marcus Aurelius Severus Alexander Augustus and for the Eternity of the Empire of the [Roman] people, [an ox to Jupiter Best and Greatest, a cow to Juno, a cow to Minerva], an ox to [Jupiter Victor];

[6-8 January, - - -], a bull to Father Mars, a bull to Mars Victor, a cow to Victory [- - -];

9 January, [because honourable discharge with access to full] privileges [is granted to those who have served their time, or stipends] are paid [to the troops, an ox for Jupiter Best and Greatest, a cow to Juno], a cow [to Minerva], a cow to Welfare, a bull to Father Mars [- - -];

10 January, for the birthday of the deified [female member of the imperial family], supplication to the deified [- - -];

[11-14] January, for the birthday [of Lucius Seius Caesar, father-in-law of Augustus, an ox to the Genius] of Lucius, father-in-law of Augustus, Seius Caesar (*sic*);

24 January, for the birthday of the [deified Hadrian, an ox to the deified Hadrian];

28 January, for the victories in Arabia, Adiabene, and the greatest Parthian Victory of the deified Severus, and for [the imperial power of the deified Trajan, a cow to the] Parthian [Victory], an ox to the deified Trajan;

4 February, for the imperial power of the deified Antoninus the Great [- - -], an ox to the deified Antoninus the Great [- - -];

1 March, for the birthday celebrations of Father Mars the Victor, a bull to Father Mars the Victor;

6 March, for the imperial power of the [deified Marcus Antoninus and the deified Lucius Verus], an ox to the deified Marcus, an ox to the deified Lucius [- - -];

13 March, because Imperator Marcus [Caesar Marcus Aurelius Severus Alexander was hailed] Imperator, an ox to Jupiter, [a cow to Juno], a cow to Minerva [- - -], an ox to Mars; and because Imperator

[Caesar Marcus Aurelius Severus Alexander Augustus] was first hailed as Imperator by the soldiers, [a supplication - - -;

14 March, because Alexander our Augustus was named Augustus and Father of his Country and Supreme Pontiff], supplication; [a bull to the Genius of our Lord Alexander Augustus];

(col. 2) 19 March, for the day of the Quinquatria, supplication; [?continued supplication until 23rd];

4 April, for the birthday of the deified Antoninus the Great, an ox to the deified Antoninus;

9 April, for the imperial power of the deified Pius Severus, an ox to the deified Pius Severus;

11 April, for the birthday of the deified Pius Severus, an ox to the deified Pius Severus;

21 April, for the birthday of the Eternal City of Rome, a cow to the Eternal City of Rome;

26 April, for the birthday of the [deified] Marcus Antoninus, [an ox] to the deified Marcus Antoninus;

7 May, for the birthday of the deified Julia Maesa, [supplication] to the deified Maesa;

10 May, for the Rose Festival, supplication to the military standards;

12 May, for the Circus games in honour of Mars, a bull to Father Mars the Avenger;

21 May, because the deified Severus Imperator was hailed [- - -], to the deified Pius Severus;

24 May, for the birthday of Germanicus Caesar, supplication to the memory of Germanicus Caesar;

31 May, for the Rose Festival, supplication to the military standards;

[9] June, for the Festival of Vesta, supplication to Mother Vesta;

[26] June, because our lord Marcus Aurelius Severus Alexander was hailed as Caesar and was clad in the toga of manhood, a bull to the Genius of Alexander Augustus;

[1] July, because Alexander our Augustus was designated consul for the first time, supplication;

[4] July, for the birthday of the deified Matidia, supplication to the deified Matidia;

[10] July, for the imperial power of the deified Antoninus Pius, an ox to the deified Antoninus;

[12] July, for the birthday of the deified Julius, an ox to the deified Julius;

[23] July, for the day of the Festival of Neptune, supplication and sacrifice;

[1 August], for the birthday of the deified Claudius and the deified Pertinax, an ox to the deified Claudius, an ox [to the deified Pertinax];

[7 August], for the Circus Games of Welfare, a cow to Welfare;

[16-31 August], for the birthday of Mamaea [Augusta], mother of our

Augustus [- - -] to the guiding Juno of Mamaea Augusta;
[17-31 August, - - -];
18-31 August], for the birthday of the deified Marciana, [supplication to the deified Marciana]; (col. 3)
[31 August, for] the birthday of the [deified Commodus, an ox for the deified] Commodus;
[7] September [- - -;
?8-17 September - - -;
18 September, for the birthday of the deified Trajan and for the imperial power of the deified Nerva, an ox to the deified Trajan, an ox to the deified Nerva;
19 September, for the birthday of the deified Antoninus Pius, an ox to the deified Antoninus Pius;
[20-22 September], for the birthday of the deified Faustina, supplication to the deified Faustina;
[23] September, for the birthday of the deified Augustus, [an ox] to the deified Augustus;
[about 9 entries]; (col. 4)
17 December [- - -] continued supplication until 23rd;
[- - -].

The pantheon honoured in this calendar, which belonged to the Twentieth Cohort of Palmyrenes, presents figures from the beginning of the Principate as well as those to be expected in the reign of Alexander Severus, members of the Severan dynasty such as Julia Maesa and the Emperor's mother Mamaea, and of the dynasty of Trajan, Hadrian and the Antonines from whom the Severans claimed descent in an appeal for legitimacy (Marciana was Trajan's sister, Matidia her daughter; whether Faustina is the elder, wife of Antoninus Pius, or the younger, wife of Marcus Aurelius, is uncertain).

The calendar has more to do with tradition, *esprit de corps* and Romanisation than with the purposeful arrangements considered earlier in this chapter. But the figures of Augustus and Trajan, and especially that of Germanicus, who was never deified, may have been genuinely important to the military: so too the contemporary female members of the imperial family: Julia Domna, wife of Septimius Severus, had been exploited as 'Mother of the Camps', like the younger Faustina before her; Mamaea was virtually commander in chief.

The animals offered are always appropriate to the person concerned: the living Emperor gets a bull, deceased male members of the imperial family an ox, and females of any standing a cow. The 'supplication', originally an act of propitiation offered to the regular gods after a military victory such as Caesar's in Gaul, had changed its character.

8

Patronage

In a sharply stratified society, each level defined by birth and wealth, jealous of status and privileges and inclined, if only in self-defence or in reaction from oppression from above, to oppress social inferiors, patronage was vital. It alleviated (a Marxist would say masked) conflicts of interest between classes, securing loyalties in a series of vertical ties not only between but within them — as between Roman senators governing provinces and their fellow landowners in the cities and tribes.

The operations of patronage were not merely negative (protection) they were a recognised means by which a man could advance in official posts to a higher social position. The Emperor, who had taken over so many functions of his peers, usurped the powers that patronage affords. His superior military command put army commissions in his hand, for example. He became the fount of patronage; often using his influence to unite communities and individuals (**154**).

129. Dio of Prusa, *Discourse on Kingship*, 3, 129-32; Greek

Most dynasts see only the men who have got close to them, no matter how, and those that are willing to toady to them; the rest they drive away, the best of them even more than the others. (130) But the true king makes his choice from all . . . For he has at his disposal every means of making friends: praise wins over to loyalty those who wish to be well thought of, a share of power those who have a talent for leadership, while some form of military activity wins over the fighting men, and managing affairs those who like responsibility; certainly keeping warm-hearted people at one's side wins them over. (132) Who then is better placed to appoint governors? Who needs more men to take on responsibilities? Who can give men a share in enterprises that are more important? Who is in a better position to entrust military matters to a deputy? Who can confer honours of greater distinction? Who has a table in better repute? But if friendship is up for sale, who is better provided with funds to eliminate any potential rival?

How far Dio's speeches on kingship of 100 or later were intended to influence Trajan, and how far they were intended to reveal him as the ideal ruler, is a matter for discussion (see Jones 1978 (9), 115ff.); the two are not incompatible, given the obligations imposed by homage. Here he defends himself from any accusation of flattery.

The document that follows provides an actual example of an imperial letter of appointment, showing the qualities that were supposed to win and keep the Emperor's favour.

130. *AE* 1962, 183; Bulla Regia, Africa Proconsularis

To Quintus Domitius Marsianus, son of Lucius, of the Quirina Tribe; imperial procurator in charge of the Emperor's inherited property in the province of Narbonensis, imperial procurator in charge of the iron mines, imperial procurator in charge of taking the Gallic census of the provinces of Belgica, in the territories of the Tungrians and Frisavones, and lower Germany, (? in the territories of the Canninefates) and Batavians; prefect of soldiers; co-opted on to the jury panels by the Emperors Marcus Aurelius Antoninus and Lucius Aurelius Verus Caesar. When the city council had voted that an equestrian (statue) should be erected to him at public expense, his brother Lucius Domitius spared the cost to the public and erected it at his own expense.

Copy of commission:

Caesar Antoninus Augustus sends greetings to his friend Domitius Marsianus. I have long been eager to advance you to the distinction of a procuratorship of two hundred thousand sesterces and take advantage of the opportunity which has now presented itself. Succeed then to the post of Marius Pudens, with a hope of enjoying my uninterrupted favour proportionate to the scrupulous regard that you will pay to the need for integrity, application and acquired expertise. Farewell, Marsianus, my dearest friend.

This native of Bulla Regia had been enrolled as a member of the Roman jury panels in 161-9 and as prefect had commanded a troop of irregulars raised after plague had decimated the army (see H.-G. Pflaum, *La Gaule et l'Empire romain: Scripta Varia* 2 (Paris, n.d.), 14). As a census official his work straddled provincial boundaries, as did that of the imperial procurator of Belgica and the *two* Germanies (Pflaum, *ibid.*, 15f.). But the Emperor's properties in Narbonensis were so important that, according to Pflaum (*ibid.*, 23) Marcus Aurelius waited until he had the chance of promoting Marsianus to precisely this post in Gaul where he already had had so much experience; that view puts much stress, perhaps too much, on the polite language of the letter of appointment (for these see Millar 1977 (1), 288ff.).

Even the fount of patronage could be influenced by suggestions from men and women close at hand, who were the dispensers of secondary patronage suggestively called 'brokers' by Saller 1982. Under the

Republic some of the favours concerned might have been directly in their gift, and lesser favours still remained within the power of private individuals: a long-established relationship would involve dispensing both kinds of favour, direct and indirect.

131. Plutarch, Precepts for Politicians, 13, 18-20 (Moralia 808B-C); Greek

For the rationale of politics does not force us to come down heavily, at least on the less serious offences of our friends; rather it permits us, once we have put the most important public affairs on a secure basis, to use spare resources to help our friends, to stand by them, and to work all out with them in their interest. (19) There are favours that involve causing no offence, such as giving a friend preferential help in obtaining a post, putting some prestigious administrative function into his hands, or a friendly embassy, such as one involving honours to a governor or one to a city aimed at securing friendship and co-operation. (20) But if there is some laborious but distinguished and important activity, to this a man should appoint himself first, and then his friend to help.

Plutarch is addressing himself to men involved in the politics of the Greek cities; the same opportunities of dispensing patronage are available as in Roman politics.

132. *The Augustan History*, Pertinax 1, 4-2, 1

As a boy he was taught basic literature and arithmetic, and was also entrusted to a Greek teacher of grammar and then to Sulpicius Apollinaris; on leaving Apollinaris Pertinax himself set up as a teacher of grammar. (5) But when the income he made out of that proved inadequate he applied, with the assistance of Lollianus Avitus, a man of consular rank who was his father's patron, for a commission as a centurion. His next move was to set out for Syria in the reign of Titus Aurelius (Antoninus Pius) as prefect of a cohort, where he was compelled by the governor of Syria to travel on foot from Antioch to his post because he had used the official transport system without having warrants.

(2,1) Winning promotion by his efforts in the Parthian war, he was transferred to Britain and retained there; (2) after that he commanded a cavalry squadron in Moesia. His next post was the charge of distributing provisions on the Aemilian road; (3) that led to command of the German fleet . . . (4) Then he was transferred to Dacia and a post that brought in 200,000 sesterces, but the machinations of certain persons brought him under Marcus (Aurelius') suspicions and he was removed from it; afterwards he was given employment as commander of legionary

detachments through the influence of Claudius Pompeianus, Marcus'
son-in-law, whose aide he was thus to become. (5) In this office he won
approval and was enrolled in the senate. (6) Eventually, after further
successful service, the plot that had been orchestrated against him was
exposed, and the Emperor Marcus, in order to make up to him for the
wrong done him, raised him to the rank of an ex-praetor and gave him
command of the First Legion; his immediate action was to free Raetia
and Noricum from enemy occupation. (7) The notable purposefulness he
showed brought him appointment from this post to the consulship, with
the Emperor Marcus' support. (8) His speech praising Pertinax survives
in Marius Maximus' work; it includes everything he did — and
everything that happened to him. (9) And apart from that speech, which
would take too long to append, Pertinax was very frequently praised by
Marcus, in addresses to the soldiers and in the senate; Marcus made no
secret of his regret that Pertinax was a senator and was not available to
him for appointment as prefect of the Guard. (10) After Cassius' revolt
had been put down Pertinax set out from Syria to protect the Danube,
and then undertook the governorship of Upper and Lower Moesia (11)
and eventually that of Dacia. Success in those provinces earned him the
governorship of Syria.

The patronage of the eminent was not always effective. In spite of the
support of Avitus (his own as well as his father's patron in the strict
sense of the word, if his father had been freed by Avitus), Pertinax does
not seem to have been successful in his application for a centurionate.

His achievements in the Parthian War belong to the years 161/2-165,
and the service in Britain immediately afterwards took the form of two
separate posts (*PIR*^{2} H 73, with details). What happened in Dacia is
unclear; perhaps he fell foul of the governor: disagreements between
senatorial and equestrian officials were not uncommon, and they are well
illustrated by an episode in Britain under Nero (Tacitus, *Annals* 14,
38f.). Claudius Pompeianus, a fellow-student of literature who put
Pertinax's career back on course and who may have helped him before
that (cf. Cassius Dio 74, 3, 1), became Marcus' son-in-law in 165. Once
in the senate, Pertinax enjoyed a steady rise through Marcus' favour: his
suffect consulship was held in 175.

In the patronage system merit often took second place to influence
(see Tacitus, *Annals* 11, 49, 1); but Pertinax clearly was more than
adequate to the posts he held and much of his advancement was due to
successful military service.

The following letter shows a 'broker' in action, and what counted as
merit in a man seeking admission to the senate.

133. Pliny, *Letters* 10, 4

Gaius Pliny to the Emperor Trajan. Your generosity, most excellent Emperor, from which I am benefiting in its fullest form, encourages me to venture to put myself under an obligation to you on my friends' behalf as well. Of them the one who claims a quite special position is Voconius Romanus, with whom I have been intimate since our student days together in early youth. (2) For these reasons I had also requested your deified father to advance him to a place in the supreme council of state. But this prayer of mine has been left for your own goodness to fulfil, because Romanus' mother had not yet fully complied with the legal requirements in transferring the gift of four million sesterces which she had undertaken in a memorandum to your father to bestow on her son; this she afterwards did on being reminded of it by us: (3) she has alienated the estates and completed the remaining transactions which are normally required in bringing this kind of conveyance to completion.

(4) The factor that was delaying the fulfilment of our hopes has thus been eliminated. That being so, it is not without considerable confidence that I offer you my guarantee of the character of my friend Romanus. A broad-based education has given it grace and so has his remarkable devotion to his family, which has won him the generous act on the part of his mother which I have just mentioned, and in close sequence an inheritance from his father and adoption by his step-father. (5) These claims are enhanced by the distinction of his birth and his father's wealth; each I am sure will gain a good deal of additional favour in your generous eyes from my pleas.

(6) I ask you, then, my Lord, to grant me a reason for rejoicing over something that is very near to my heart, and afford my affections, which are, I hope, worthy ones, an opportunity to take pride in your favourable judgement, not only of me, but of my friend.

The year is 98 and the Spaniard (from Saguntum in Tarraconensis) for whom Pliny is writing was probably hoping for admission at the rank of ex-praetor, as Sherwin-White suggests in his commentary, rather than mere permission to stand for senatorial office; he had already held the high priesthood of the imperial cult in his province. The qualifications are wealth and good family (as in **159**); the candidate's education was also in his favour, as it stood Pertinax in good stead. Specialised qualifications are not required.

Whether Pliny was successful in his request we have no firm evidence. But it is worth looking at the letter of commendation that Pliny had written on Romanus' behalf to a consular governor (2, 13); more informal in style, it expatiates on Romanus' literary ability (not of much interest to the uncultured Trajan, suggests Sherwin-White) and on Pliny's affection.

In another recommendation, made on behalf of a knight to a senatorial governor, Pliny is brisk.

134. Pliny *Letters* 7, 22

Gaius Pliny greets his friend Falco. You will be less surprised at the pressing nature of my request that you confer a military tribunate on a friend of mine, when you know who he is and what he is like. Your promise makes it possible for me now to give you his name and a description of the man.

(2) He is Cornelius Minicianus, whose rank and character alike add lustre to my native district. His birth is distinguished and he is well off, but his devotion to literature is that of a man who has to earn his living. Added to that, his integrity as a judge, courage as counsel and loyalty as a friend are unsurpassed. (3) You will believe that it is you who are being done the favour when you get to know the man at closer quarters: he is equal to any office and any distinction (he is very unpretentious and I don't want to say anything too extravagant about him). All good wishes.

This letter belongs to *c*. 106-7, when Pompeius Falco was praetorian governor of Judaea. Again we have birth, wealth, and culture, this time with the addition of legal experience. Pliny (who had indeed written Minicianus, a native of Bergamum, two letters concerned with criminal trials, 3, 9, and 4, 11), is referring here, as Sherwin-White points out, to his qualities as a civil judge, which are surprisingly appropriate for a military tribune, who acted as advocate and social worker for the men under his charge (Isidore of Seville 9, 3, 29). In spite of these qualifications, Pliny's request for a tribunate was unsuccessful; instead the inscription *ILS* 2722 shows Minicianus as prefect of the First Cohort of Damascenes in Palestine, a typical first post in equestrian military service; his tribunate was to be held in Africa.

Grants of citizenship to deserving subjects were also made on the intervention of patrons.

135. Pliny, *Letters* 10, 6f.

Gaius Pliny to the Emperor Trajan. I offer you thanks, my Lord, for having granted without delay the full right of citizenship to the freedwomen of a lady closely connected to me and Roman citizenship to my masseur Arpocras.

However, when I was producing his age and property qualification, as you enjoined me, I was advised by persons of more experience than myself that I ought first to have obtained him the citizenship of Alexandria, then that of Rome, as he is an Egyptian. (2) But as I understood there to be no difference between Egyptians and other non-citizens I had confined myself to writing to inform you only that he had been freed from slavery by a woman who was not a citizen and that his patroness was long since deceased. I do not deplore my own ignorance when the result of it was that I had the opportunity of putting myself under a second obligation to you on behalf of the same person.

My request then is that you bestow on him the Alexandrian citizenship as well, so that I may lawfully benefit from your favour. His age and property rating I have sent to your freedmen, as you ordered, to remove any further delay to the exercise of your generosity.

(7, 1) Trajan to Pliny. It has been a principle of mine to follow the practice of my predecessors in not granting the citizenship of Alexandria without good reason. But, since you have already secured Roman citizenship for your masseur Arpocras, I do not see my way to refusing this supplementary request of yours. You will have to let me know from what district he is so that I can send you a letter for my friend Pompeius Planta, the Prefect of Egypt.

Pliny's original letter asking for citizenship for Arpocras (10, 5) is separated from his final letter of thanks (10, 10) by a few months, 98-9. For Alexandria and its privileges, see **120, 167**: it was their depressed and unurbanised condition that made real Egyptians unlikely candidates for Roman citizenship; a professional man recommended by Pliny was unexceptionable. For the districts (nomes) into which Egypt was divided, see **167**.

Another aspect of the working of patronage is to be observed in Trajan's reference to the Prefect of Egypt: he is a 'friend', holding office as such.

The two freedwomen who had also benefited from Pliny's earlier request had been of an inferior 'Latin' status because they had been freed by a woman who was not independent (*Monograph on Rules attributed to Ulpian* 1, 17).

Pliny was sure of his protégés' merits. At the other extreme we have cold-blooded financial transactions, which may be denied the dignified title of patronage because no permanent bond is set up: the value of the transaction is known and the debt is extinguished. But there is no hard and fast distinction, and the part that money played pervaded the system. Claudius Lysias, the military tribune who had paid 'a great sum' for his citizenship (*Acts of the Apostles* 22, 28) is well known, and it is in his time, the reigns of Claudius and Nero, that the sale of citizenship became a matter of scandal, involving imperial freedmen and even the Emperor's wife.

136. Cassius Dio, *Roman History* 60, 17, 5f.

For since Romans enjoyed a higher status than non-citizens in practically every respect, many people were applying for citizenship from Claudius himself and were buying it from Messalina and the imperial freedmen. (6) And for that reason although it was sold at first for large sums, as time went on the price was so lowered because it was easy to get that a saying was coined that a man could become a citizen even by giving someone glassware all in fragments.

Dio puts this state of affairs in the period 43-8, but sales of citizenship, office and privilege did not end with the death of Messalina.

137. Suetonius, *Deified Vespasian* 23, 2

One of his favoured servants was asking for a cashier's post for someone, pretending he was his brother. Vespasian put him off and summoned the candidate to him in person. Having levied the sum that the man had agreed upon with his promoter, Vespasian appointed him without more ado. When his servant asked about it afterwards he said, 'You find yourself another brother; this one, who you thought belonged to you, is mine'.

Vespasian, who had started at the bottom of the ladder, as Pertinax was to do, could work the system. He owed his appointment to a legionary command in Germany to the favour of Narcissus, Claudius' influential freedman (Suetonius, *Deified Vespasian* 4, 1).

An Emperor, his courtiers and officials, were well placed not only to make gifts of places but more dubiously, as Saller remarks, 1982, 56, to intervene in the judicial process. He cites the intervention of Antoninus Pius' heir Marcus Aurelius in the interest of the Athenian millionaire Herodes Atticus.

138. Marcus Cornelius Fronto, *Correspondence with Marcus Caesar* 3, 2

Aurelius Caesar sends greetings to his friend Fronto. I know that you have often said to me that your object was to find whatever gave me greatest pleasure. Now is the time; now you can increase my affection for you, if it is capable of increase.

A trial is coming on, in which men are evidently not only going to give a favourable hearing to your oratory; they will look askance at the sight of your righteous anger. And I see no-one who would venture to advise you in this matter: those who are less friendly to you prefer to watch you acting rather inconsistently, while those who are better friends are afraid of seeming too friendly to your adversary if they induce you to give up attacking him in a way that is entirely natural to you. Then again, they cannot bring themselves to silence you and so to deprive you of the utterance of some particularly elegantly turned phrase that you have thought out for that occasion. For that reason, whether you rate me an ill-advised counsellor, an adolescent too bold for his years, or too much of a friend to your adversary, I shall not be unduly backward in offering you my advice, because I judge it to be better. But why did I say 'advice'? It is a request I am making of you, an earnest request, and if I am successful I give you my word that I shall be under an obligation to you in return for it. But you will say, 'What! If I am attacked, am I not to pay him back with the same language?' Actually, you will get more credit out of it yourself if you say nothing in reply even if you are attacked. However, if he attacks first you may be excused for replying as best you can; but I have asked him not to be the first, and I believe I have gained the point. I am attached to both of you each for his own merits, and I am aware of the fact that while he was brought up in the house of my maternal grandfather Publius Calvisius, I was your pupil. That is why I am extremely anxious that this most distasteful business should be brought to a conclusion in the most reputable way possible. I hope that you approve my advice; my intentions you certainly will. My own preference at any rate is to fail in good sense by writing rather than to fail in friendship by remaining silent.

Good wishes to you, my dearest and most affectionate Fronto.

Some time late in the reign of Pius the controversial Athenian magnate and sophist (see **163**) Herodes Atticus was prosecuting one of his compatriots; Cornelius Fronto, the young Marcus' tutor in oratory, was appearing for the defence, and Marcus intervened to prevent any allusion to the brutality and dishonesty that Herodes' political opponents laid at his door (see Bowersock 1969 (9), 99f.).

The letter that follows shows even the Emperor's designated successor as a 'broker'. This request seems improper to modern eyes.

139. Marcus Cornelius Fronto, *Correspondence with Marcus Caesar* 5, 34f.

My Lord: Saenius Pompeianus has had me defending him in a very large number of cases; since he undertook the contract for the African tax he has been assisting me in my private affairs in an equally large number. I commend him to you so that, when his accounts are examined by our Lord your father, you may be induced both by my recommendation and by your own habit to grant him the benefit of that kindness which is your nature and which you extend to all as a matter of course. My good wishes, sweetest Lord.

Reply: Pompeianus has won my favour too by the same good offices that have made you his friend. For that reason I want everything, in conformity with the Lord my father's forbearance, to go his way. For whatever turns out for you as you wish is a cause of rejoicing to me. My good wishes, most agreeable of masters. Faustina and our little girls send you greetings.

The exchange belongs to the decade 149-59.

Pompeianus' tax farming (see *ILS* 1463 and **65**) gave him the opportunity to look after the interests of the absentee African landowner Fronto.

Governors at least of senatorial provinces still regarded themselves at the beginning of the Principate as wielding power that was virtually monarchical: witness the story of the proconsul of Asia who stalked amongst the corpses of the three hundred persons he had executed on one day congratulating himself on a royal deed (Seneca, *On Anger* 2, 5, 5; Tacitus, *Annals* 3, 68, 1; the man was exiled). Their favour was worth having after as well as during their term of office. In particular, as Saller 1982, 151f., observes, their judicial functions made them very desirable patrons for advocates; he cites the example that follows.

140. *CIL* 8, 2734; from Lambaesis

To Marcus Aurelius Cassianus, praetorian legate of the Augusti, a man of the highest distinction, their patron: Titus Flavius Silvanus, Roman knight and advocate, Quintus Pinarius Urbanus, duovir, and Lucius Gargilius Felix, high priest of the provinces, who have so often [admired] the judgments delivered in his court, [and his sense of justice].

This badly damaged monument was erected to a governor of Numidia *c*. 244-9. Saller suggests that dedications of this kind advertised a connection with the governor that made the advocate likely to win his cases.

Partiality is seen from a different point of view in another passage cited by Saller, 153f. The author Lucian is put ashore by a ship's captain who had been paid to murder him at sea.

141. Lucian, *Alexander, or, the False Prophet,* 57; Greek

There I encountered some envoys from the Bosporan kingdom who were coasting past. They were going from King Eupator to Bithynia to deliver the annual tribute. I explained to them the danger in which we had been involved, obtained a pledge of help from them, was taken up into their boat, and arrived safely at Amastris, after coming within a hair's breadth of dying.

From that point it was my turn to arm myself, against him, and I began to crowd on sail in my eagerness to retaliate against him. I detested him even before the plot against me; his filthy character made me find him utterly hateful. I addressed myself to the prosecution with a number of supporters, the most prominent among them being the philosophers descended from Timocrates of Heraclea. But the then governor of Bithynia and Pontus himself held me back, all but going on his knees and entreating me to give up. The reason was that his loyalty to Rutilianus made it impossible for him to punish Alexander even if he caught him red-handed. So my efforts were frustrated, and I did give up; I didn't have the requisite nerve with a judge who took an attitude like that.

The governor so embarrassed by the prosecution was Lucius Lollianus Avitus, 165-6; his friend Mummius Sisenna Rutilianus, whom Lucian presents as the besotted patron of the charlatan Alexander, was the consul of 146, whose daughter Alexander had married (section 35).

The word *patronus* was used in a technical sense, in the legal context in which we continue to use the word client. The barrister was supposed to act as a friend, putting his clients under a debt of gratitude, and Republican restrictions on fees were reiterated under the Principate. In political cases and when communities were involved, as Cirta was in the following document, this was an important manifestation of patronage.

142. Marcus Cornelius Fronto, *Correspondence with his Friends* 2, 11

To the triumvirs and members of the city council. ?How much care I have [- - -]; and I should much prefer the protection of my native city to be enhanced, rather than my own influence. That is why I advise you to select the following, who currently hold leading places at the bar, to be your patrons, and to send them decrees on the subject. Aufidius Victorinus you will have on your roll of citizens, if heaven favours my plans: I have betrothed my daughter to him and I could not have formed a better plan, whether I was thinking about posterity for myself or about my daughter's whole future life, than by choosing a son-in-law with a character like his and with his great talent for public speaking. You will also be able to claim Servilius Silanus, an excellent man and a highly gifted speaker, as a patron and member of the city, since he comes from the neighbouring and friendly community of Hippo Regius. Postumius Festus you will find you have done right to make your patron on the basis of his character and oratorical talent; he, too, belongs to our province and comes from no distant city. Of these no ordinary patrons [- - -] as long as my youth and strength were undiminished, our business [- - -] that our ?city has been founded on the support of men who are leaders of the bar and still relatively young [- - -] that we have a man who is well known to the people and who is man of consular rank entitled to interpret the law of the state to enquirers. I too, I hope, took no inconspicuous part in civil functions while I was young and strong. There is a very large number of men from Cirta in the senate, men of the highest distinction. The last honour is the greatest, in that three of your citizens [- - -] but it is also agreeable [- - -] but it is better that you should now sometimes [- - -].

Cirta had been a colony since the beginning of the Principate and was the dominant member of four communities in its district, Rusicade, Chullu and Milev being the others which from Trajan onwards also enjoyed colonial status and joined Cirta in the unique group known as 'the four Cirtan colonies': E. Champlin, *Fronto and Antonine Rome* (Cambridge, Mass., etc., 1980), 6f. Presumably as a survival from its pre-colonial constitution, Cirta was governed by a board of three.

Fronto has been asked to represent Cirta in court but pleads age and ill-health. His substitutes, who will become citizens of Cirta on being appointed patron, are not only well-qualified to plead the city's case (and interested in it), but men of influence at Rome: they all reached the consulship, respectively in 115, 152 and 160; for the oratory of Victorinus, see Cassius Dio, *Roman History* 73, 11, 2, of Festus *ILS* 2929.

From suggesting patrons Fronto passes to a rehearsal of successes in public life achieved by citizens of Cirta; the jurisconsult who possessed the right of giving officially recognised interpretations of the law is identified by Champlin, *Fronto and Antonine Rome* 11, with Pactumeius Clemens, consul 138.

For an individual to describe a man as 'patron', except in the technical sense of 'advocate', made him likely to be taken for a freedman, and he would probably avoid it (cf. **140**: perhaps there was a particularly open attitude to the relationship in north Africa — as in Gaul: **173**). Municipalities need feel no such inhibitions, and more than a thousand such patrons of municipalities are known (Harmand, 1957). They may be imperial officials or local notables; they are chosen by local councils (**26** section 61) and the formal act commemorated by the cutting of bronze tablets, one kept by the city, the other given to the patron. Tablets are common in Tarraconensis and Africa Proconsularis, but occur also in Baetica, Mauretania, Sardinia, Thrace and Italy (Nicols 1980b, 538).

143. *ILS* 6109; bronze tablet found on the Aventine Hill, Rome

In the consulship of Imperator Caesar Marcus Aurelius Severus Alexander, 13 April: the council of the community of the people of Clunia co-opted Gaius Marius Pudens Cornelianus, legionary legate, a man of the highest distinction, as its patron for itself, its offspring and posterity, because of his many outstanding services to them as individuals and collectively; the envoy used was Valerius Marcellus of Clunia.

The year is 222. The senatorial patron, who had presumably been serving in Spain with the Seventh Legion, must have received his commemorative tablet at Rome.

In the East, where the name and formal institution of patronage were alien, a different vocabulary was in use.

144. Smallwood, *Gaius-Nero* 265; Greek, from Iconium on the border of Phrygia and Lycaonia

The People of Claud[iconium] honoured Lucius Pupius Praesens, son of Lucius, of the Sabatina Tribe, military tribune, prefect of the Picentine Cavalry Squadron, Procurator of Caesar of the Tiber Banks, Procurator of Tiberiius Claudius Caesar Augustus Germanicus and Nero Claudius Caesar Augustus Germanicus of the province of Galatia, their benefactor and founder.

Praesens may be seen on his duties in (51). The benefactions he conferred on Iconium were not mere administrative favours: the word 'founder', which is not uncommon in inscriptions from the Greek-speaking part of the Empire, precisely implies substantial building or rebuilding in the city concerned.

It was not only imperial officials who were thought worth electing as patrons: a favourite son of the city who had done well might also be co-opted, even if he had not risen as high as the men listed by Fronto in **142**.

145. Smallwood, *Nerva-Hadrian* 300; from Matilica in Umbria

To Gaius Arrius Clemens: private soldier in the Ninth Cohort of the Praetorian Guard; mounted trooper in the same Cohort; decorated by the Emperor Trajan with the Twisted Necklets, Armbands and Chestpieces for service in the Dacian War; aide to the prefects of the Praetorian Guard; detailed to charge of the watchword; candidate for the centurionate; officer in charge of the pay chest; clerk to the military tribune; recalled for service as a veteran; centurion of the First Cohort of Watchmen; of the Imperial Messengers; of the Fourteenth Urban Cohort; of the Seventh Cohort of the Praetorian Guard; officer on special duties; decorated by the Emperor Hadrian with the Untipped Spear and the Golden Crown; centurion of the Third, Augustan, Legion; leading centurion; quinquennial duovir; patron of the municipality; curator of the community: the members of the city council, the Augustales members of the board of six, and the citizens of the municipality of Matilica.

Clemens' rise from private soldier to leading centurion made him one of the most prominent men in his town, second only to any men of equestrian rank that it may have possessed; and his service in the Urban and Praetorian Cohorts at Rome gave him contacts that might be valuable to Matilica. It is not surprising that he not only held the chief magistracy there but also was appointed curator by the Emperor (**190ff.**) and elected patron by the city council.

The institution of patronage gave wide scope for abuse, functioning as it did as a partial substitute for a fully developed system of law and a fully developed bureaucracy in which promotion was based entirely on merit and seniority. Justice could suffer (**140f.**) and money do for merit (**136f.**). It was unsatisfactory for another reason: lip service and some genuine attention were paid to merit even when patronage was in operation (**133f.**); a fictional letter ascribed to Marcus Aurelius makes it clear that there were posts (an equestrian military command is the subject) which Trajan and Hadrian 'would grant only to the most tested officers' (*Augustan History, Pescennius Niger* 4, 1). An unsuccessful applicant would never know whether he had failed for lack of merit, of influence, or of money.

146. Arrian, *Discourses of Epictetus*, 4, 1, 91-8; Greek

This is what travellers do, too, those who are not inclined to take chances. A man has heard that there are robbers on his route. He does not venture on his way by himself, but waits about for a group belonging to an envoy, pro-quaestor or proconsul; he attaches himself to it and goes on his way safely. (92) This is what the sensible man does in the world at large. 'Robbery is widespread; so are dictators, storms, problems, the loss of all that means most to one. (93) Where is one to find refuge? How is one to continue on one's way without falling a victim to robbers? What group is one to wait for so as to go on one's way in safety? To whom should one attach oneself? (94) To so-and-so the rich man, the ex-consul? And what good does that do me? He too is stripped, groans, grieves. What if my travelling companion himself turns on me and behaves to me like a robber? What shall I do? (95) I shall become a friend of Caesar's; nobody will do me any harm when I am of his company. First of all, to become his friend the number of things I have to do and to put up with! The number of times I have to be robbed, and by how many people! And then if I do become his friend, even he is mortal. (96) And suppose for some reason he becomes my enemy, wherever had I better retire? To a desert? (97) Why, doesn't fever come there? What is to become of me, then? Isn't it possible to find a reliable fellow-traveller, one that one can trust, strong, incapable of treachery?' (98) He puts his mind to this and comes to the conclusion that if he attaches himself to God, he will get through safely.

Epictetus, the freedman of an imperial freedman who was killed for his part in the murder of Domitian, was well placed to assess the value of patronage, but many others must have shared his view. The passage provokes reflections on the swift progress of monotheism in the society of the Empire. Christianity gave access, on a basis of merit and effort and through an incorruptible intermediary, to a reliable authority.

9

Assimilation

Resources from outside Italy maintained the Empire (Chapters 5 and 6). It needed not only the money but the manpower of the provinces. Their contribution had to be recognised, and it led to the transformation of an Empire under the Italian people to a class structure extending over both Italy and the provinces. In the west, Roman success gave the process additional impetus: the subjects were eager to emulate the ruling people and to become real Romans.

Romanisation cannot adequately be illustrated in this book. For one thing it would have meant very different things to an Italian of the second century BC, a Gaul of the first century AD and a Greek of the same period. For another, the changes it implies were often non-verbal, in dress, food and housing. None the less a high proportion of the documentary evidence already cited here could be enlisted to illustrate it (for example, **20**, **27**, **55**, **81f.**, **86**, **108**, **112**, **123**, **142**), and it must be asked if the Romans ever or anywhere sought to promote such changes. The answer must be a qualified 'yes': for certain purposes (not for its own sake), at certain times, and in certain areas: above all, it was a means of dispensing with force.

147. Tacitus, *Life of Agricola* 21

The winter that followed was spent on some very constructive schemes. To let people who were scattered, backward, and therefore given to fighting have a taste of the pleasures of a peaceful and untroubled existence, and so to accustom them to it, Agricola gave encouragement to individuals and assistance to communities in the construction of temples, markets and private houses. If they showed willing he had praise for them, if they hung back, a rebuke. In that way, instead of being put under duress they were spurred on by rivalry for marks of his esteem. (2) Not only that: he was having the sons of the chieftains educated in the liberal arts, and Agricola preferred the keen-witted Britons to the Gauls, cultured though these were; so that the very people who a short time before would have nothing to do with Latin were eager for the training of an orator. (3) Then our way of dressing came to be held in regard, and the toga was often to be seen. Little by little they went astray, taking to the colonnades, bath-houses and elaborate banquets that make moral failings attractive. They were naive: they called it 'civilisation' when it helped to ensure the loss of their freedom.

Tacitus, as Ogilvie and Richmond point out, ignores the conglomerations that existed before the Roman invasion. The Britons had not only hill-forts such as Maiden Castle in Dorset but settlements which the Romans merely developed as tribal capitals (Calleva Atrebatium, for example). Where they did not exist towns were created from scratch: Isca Dumnoniorum began as a Claudian fort. Camulodunum, Lindum, Eboracum and Glevum became colonies (**40**) and Verulamium a municipality, but even the unprivileged towns became a focus of tribal activity.

As to the buildings mentioned by Tacitus, Ogilvie and Richmond draw attention to the market-place at Verulamium, with an inscription over its entrance mentioning Agricola (*AE* 1957, 169) and a Flavian temple in the same city, constructed like other specimens of the period as a square shrine surrounded by a portico; they also show plans of late first-century town houses there.

As Tacitus points out, the Romans had already found the Gauls amenable to literary education.

148. Suetonius, *Caligula* 20

He also gave shows in the provinces: at Syracuse in Sicily he gave city games, and at Lugdunum in Gaul a mixed programme, where he also held a contest in Greek and Latin oratory, and they say that in that contest the vanquished provided the prizes for the victors, and were also obliged to write eulogies on them; but the competitors who had been particularly unsuccessful were ordered to erase their composition with a rubber, or with their tongue — unless they preferred to be caned or plunged into the nearby river.

The Romanised eisteddfod at Lugdunum — Lugos was an intellectual deity sometimes identified with Mercury (see A. Ross, *Pagan Celtic Britain* (London, 1967, repr. 1974), 320f.) — ended with what looks like a bowdlerised sacrifice to the river. But schoolboys were already at work on their Latin and Greek in the new tribal capital of Augustodunum, which replaced Bibracte. The very name of the new city was a hybrid of Roman and Celtic forms (**196**).

For some duties a Roman citizen required a knowledge of Latin: Suetonius, *Claudius* 16, 2, reports that Emperor as striking a leading Greek not only off the roll of jurors but off the list of citizens altogether because of his ignorance of Latin. On what was presumably a separate occasion he was equally severe.

149. Cassius Dio, *Roman History* 60, 17, 3f.; Greek

The Lycians had rebelled and had gone so far as to kill some Roman citizens. He deprived them of their freedom and assigned them to the province of Pamphylia. (4) In the course of this enquiry (he was holding it in the senate) he asked a question in Latin of one of the Lycian envoys, a man who was originally a Lycian but had become a Roman. When the man failed to understand what Claudius said he took away his citizenship with the remark that a man who didn't understand the language of the Romans had no right to be one.

This took place in or soon after 43. We have to remember that the circumstances were unfavourable to the envoys, and that Claudius, who may have conferred the citizenship on the man in the first place, may also have been aware of charges that he was over-generous with it (**150**). This, or plain peevishness, could account for the sharp reaction; but the criterion was available for use as a barrier.

In quite another sphere there was a definite attempt in some eastern provinces to modify city councils so that their members, like those of the Roman senate, sat for life; the roll was supervised by officials analogous to the Roman censors. This was done not for cultural reasons but to promote stable government by the wealthy upper class.

150. Pliny, *Letters* 10, 79

Gaius Pliny to the Emperor Trajan. There is a provision, my Lord, in the Pompeian law which was issued to the people of Bithynia, against anyone holding a magistracy or being a member of a local council at the age of less than thirty. The same law provides that those who have held a magistracy are to be members of the senate. (2) Then followed an edict of the deified Augustus, in which he gave permission for men to hold the lower magistracies from the age of twenty-two.

(3) The question is, then, whether those who have held a magistracy at less than thirty years of age may be enrolled in the council by the censor and, if they may, whether on the same understanding men who have not held a magistracy may be enrolled as councillors from the same age as that from which it has been permitted that they may hold a magistracy. This has frequently been done before now in any case, and is said to be essential, on the grounds that it is a good deal better that the sons of men of standing should be admitted to the council than men from the mass of the people.

(4) My view, when the censors-elect asked me what I thought, was that at any rate those who had held a magistracy at less than thirty years of age could be enrolled in the council under the provisions both of the edict of Augustus and of the Pompeian law: Augustus had given

permission for those less than thirty years of age to hold magistracies and the intention of the law was that the man who had held a magistracy should be a senator. (5) However, concerning those who had not held a magistracy, although they were of the same age as those who had been permitted to hold one, I was undecided. That was what made me consult you, my Lord, as to what rule you would like followed. I append to the letter the sections of the law and the edict of Augustus.

Trajan's reply showed him in agreement with Pliny: men of less than thirty who had held a magistracy might be enrolled; the others he excluded. The 'Pompeian law' was drawn up by Pompey in the late sixties BC for the former kingdoms of Bithynia and Pontus. Like other such provisions it laid down guidelines for the administration of the province, defining the rights of the local communities in relation to the governor, and established the tax system for the area. As Sherwin-White points out in his commentary, it made more detailed provision than would have been necessary in areas that had developed further under a Hellenistic bureaucracy.

In Germany the general Gnaeus Domitius Corbulo inflicted drastic changes on the recalcitrant Frisians.

151. Tacitus, *Annals* 11, 19, 1-3

That policy of intimidation, however, affected troops and enemy in different ways; we found greater courage, while the savage spirit of the barbarians was shattered. (2) After the rebellion that opened with the disaster to Lucius Apronius, the tribe of the Frisians had been untrustworthy when it had not been openly hostile. Now it handed over hostages and settled on lands marked out for it by Corbulo; and he likewise imposed a council, magistrates and a binding constitution on them. (3) And to prevent them neglecting his orders he set up a garrison on the spot.

In 47 it was nearly twenty years since the poverty-stricken tribe, provoked by exorbitant demands for tribute, had revolted and crushed Roman units with the destruction of 1,300 men; the governor Lucius Apronius had left the reverse unavenged (4, 72ff.). Corbulo was more enterprising: having swept one north German tribe from his province and imposed the severest discipline there (Tacitus' 'intimidation'), he intended to make further inroads into Germany, against the Chauci, but was stopped by Claudius.

What Corbulo was doing to the Frisians is explained by E.A. Thompson, *The Early Germans* (Oxford, 1965), 104ff.: he was destroying the old assembly, council and war-chieftainship, and consolidating the position of the nobility, freeing them from the control of the warrior tribesmen. Corbulo's success was only temporary; by 58 the Frisians were again under two 'kings' (a common feature of tribal structure in free Germany) and squatting on land outside their reservation (Tacitus, *Annals* 13, 54, 2). Tacitus goes on to tell how, while the kings Verritus and Malorix were at Rome negotiating for squatters' rights, which the Romans would not grant, Nero offered them a bribe, the Roman citizenship. In accepting the honour, however, they would be committing themselves to loyal service to Rome: the citizenship implied a succession of duties, military and political (see above on **149**). Some of those obligations had often been discharged before the gift was conferred, especially in the form of military service to Rome; the principle is clearly stated in Cicero's speech delivered on behalf of Cornelius Balbus, the enfranchised citizen of Gades, in 56 BC (section 51). In its developed form this principle meant the enfranchise-ment of the auxiliary troops that made up more than half the total strength of the army. After twenty-five years' service, often away from their homes (the removal of able-bodied men from recently pacified districts diminished the danger of rebellion there too) and with honourable discharge, they were qualified for Roman citizenship, and their sons as Roman citizens for service in the legions. From the time of Claudius onwards there survive as evidence of honourable discharge and the grant of citizenship the hinged pairs of small bronze plaques known as military *diplomata*, which give details of service, name of the beneficiary, position of the original authorising document in the archives at Rome and the names of witnesses (*diplomata* seem to have been issued to enfranchised civilians also: Suetonius, *Nero* 12, 1).

The number of Roman citizens created by this method would be considerable, but it depends on length of service (25 years is the minimum), on the mortality rate amongst the troops and on their own and their wife's fertility; the figure of ten thousand new citizens a year (Webster 1974, (3), 279) seems high.

In the early forties of the second century it was found necessary to restrict the privileges of discharged auxiliary soldiers, as later diplomas show.

152. *ILS* 2006; bronze diploma found near Maros-Keresztúr in Transylvania, not far from Apulum in Dacia

Imperator Caesar Titus Aelius Hadrian Antoninus Augustus Pius, son of the deified Hadrian, grandson of the deified Trajan Parthicus, great-grandson of the deified Nerva, Supreme Pontiff, in his twenty-first year of tribunician power, hailed Imperator for the second time, four times consul, Father of his Country, granted to the mounted troops and infantry who have served in the three squadrons called First Batavian of a thousand men, First Spanish of the Campagones, and First Gallic and

Bosporan, and in the First Cohort of Thracian Archers, the Fourth Spanish, and the First Augustan Ituraean, and to the detachments from Africa and Mauretania Caesariensus who are serving with the Moorish Irregulars in Upper Dacia and are under the command of the legate Statius Priscus, to those who have served twenty-five campaigning seasons and have been granted honourable discharge, whose names have been inscribed below, Roman citizenship to those who did not possess it and legitimate marriage with the spouses they had at the time when citizenship was granted to them or with those they married thereafter, to the limit of one spouse to each man.

On 8 July in the consulships of Marcus Servilius Fabianus and Quintus Allius Bassus.

Of the First Gallic and Bosporan Squadron, under the command of Licinius Nigrinus, to the common soldier Heptaporis, son of Isus, a Bessian.

Copied and authenticated from the bronze tablet which has been fixed up at Rome behind the temple of the deified Augustus near the shrine of Minerva. Seals of Marcus Sentilius Iasus, Tiberius Julius Felix, Gaius Bellius Urbanus, Gaius Pomponius Statianus, Publius Ocilius Priscus.

The diploma belongs to 158. All the units mentioned were stationed in Dacia, that of the discharged Thracian Heptaporis apparently at Apulum itself; his commanding officer achieved the consulship the following year.

What has now been lost to the discharged auxiliaries is the citizenship for their children and descendants. Some of the men themselves already possessed the citizenship, as the language of the diploma shows, and enfranchised sons were probably becoming unwilling to join up, or, if M.-P. Arnaud-Lindet, *Revue des Études Latines* 55 (1977), 282ff., is right, the authorities shrank from awarding non-citizen veterans privileges greater than those that could be given to citizens who were forbidden to marry during their term of service.

Special rewards for services rendered might be made to communities.

153. Smallwood, *Gaius-Nero* 407b; from Volubilis in Mauretania

To Marcus Valerius Severus, son of Bostar, of the Galerian Tribe, aedile, sufet, duovir, first high priest in his municipality; prefect of auxiliary troops against Aedemon in the military operations that crushed him: in honour of this man the council of the municipality of Volubilis (set up a statue) for his services to the community and for his successful conduct of the mission on which he obtained for his fellow-citizens from the deified Claudius Roman citizenship and the right of contracting legitimate marriages with non-citizen wives; exemption from taxes for ten years; settlers; the property of citizens killed in the war who had no surviving heirs. Fabia Bira, daughter of Izelta, his wife, in honour of a most considerate husband, accepting the distinction declined to accept the cost of erecting the monument and dedicated it as a gift from her own money.

The inscription belongs some time after 54. Early in his principate Augustus had made Mauretania into a client kingdom, but Gaius had summoned the ruler Ptolemy to Rome in 39 and had him executed. Ptolemy's freedman Aedemon led a revolt against Roman rule which was put down in 40-1 (Pliny, *Natural History* 5, 11). A second rebellion, this time apparently amongst native Moorish tribesmen, was repressed in 41-2 (Cassius Dio *Roman History* 60, 9). Volubilis, just north of the Atlas Mountains that sheltered the nomad rebels, played a loyal part, rewarded in 44 at latest, as Smallwood, *Gaius-Nero* 307a, shows. It was not only troops raised by Valerius that had taken part: Volubilis itself seems to have been attacked and in part burnt and it is clear from the inscription that whole families had been wiped out; the remission of imperial taxes was probably a necessary boon.

The inscription does not show whether Valerius, whose father's name, like that of his wife and father-in-law, makes his native origin evident, was himself a citizen before the grant to Volubilis, nor whether his Punic post of sufet was held before or after the grant of municipal status. If after, the people of Volubilis kept on the old title in combination with the new office of duovir. The city was surrounded by unenfranchised tribesmen, so the right of making legitimate marriages with non-citizen women was a valuable one for its inhabitants. As to settlers, they would be, in Dr Mackie's view, fresh inhabitants brought in to replace those lost during the war or, as Sherwin-White 1973, 243, holds, resident aliens from whose taxes the town was to benefit.

The victory did not bring permanent peace to Mauretania Tingitana. Its equestrian governor was an acting legate commanding legionary troops (Smallwood, *Gaius-Nero* 307a) and the Moors were threatening incursions into Spain in the reign of Marcus Aurelius. Volubilis could still play an important part in maintaining order in the province.

An equally famous grant of citizenship, not for services against nomad rebels but at sea in the civil wars against the Republicans, was made by Octavian.

154. EJ 301; Greek, from Rhosus in Syria

1. In the year [- - -], the month Apellaeus [- - -]. Imperator Caesar, son of the deified Julius, hailed Imperator for the fourth time, twice consul, designated consul for the third time, sends greetings to the magistrates, council and people of the city of Rhosus, sacred, possessor of the right of

asylum, and [free]. (If you are flourishing, well and good); I too and the army [are in good health].

What is written below has been excerpted from a pillar on the Capitol at Rome, and [I think that it should] be filed in your public records. Send a copy [of it] also [to] the council and people of Tarsus, of Antioch, and of [?Seleuceia], so that they may file it. Good wishes.

2. [Caesar], Imperator, Triumvir for the establishment of the constitution have (*sic*) granted citizenship and tax exemption on all existing property in accordance with the Munatian Aemilian law, as follows: since Seleu[cus] son of Theodotus, citizen of Rhosus, has fought alongside us in the [?East (or Sicily)] at the time when we were in supreme command, and has borne many grave hardships and run many great risks on our behalf without flinching from anything in his resistance to the dangers that threatened, [and] has displayed complete steadiness and loyalty in the cause of the [Republic], and has united [his own fortunes] with our welfare, and has endured every form of loss for the [Republic] of the Roman People, and has been of service [to us] whether we were present or absent:

(1) [To him and] his parents, his children and descendants, and the wife whom he shall have [- - -], we grant citizenship and exemption from tax on his property on the same terms as those who are citizens in possession of the fullest legal rights and privileges [are exempt; and he is to have] freedom [from military service] and all forms of public financial obligation.

(2) The man whose name is inscribed above, [himself and his parents, his children] and descendants are to be members of the Cornelian Tribe, [and their vote ? is to be cast] in that tribe and they are to be permitted to [cast their vote and be enrolled in it]. And if they wish to be enrolled in absence [or if] they wish to be [enrolled in one of the towns] of Italy [- - -].

(3) [Insofar as] the aforementioned [(and his wife and parents], children [and descendants) ?was exempt from tax] before he became a tax-exempt [Roman] citizen [? and possessed certain privileges], now too that he has become an exempt Roman citizen, if [he wishes, ? as is his] right, ?to make use of them, [he may possess and enjoy the] priesthoods, [- - -], honours, privileges, [- - -] and [?properties just as a citizen of the fullest] legal rights and privileges possesses [and enjoys them].

((4)-(7) are mutilated; they contain references (4) to exemption from the duty of undertaking 'the least tax-farming contract' (cf. **167**(1)), or providing 'hospitality or winter quarters' for officials; (6) to the 'right of contracting legitimate marriage' (for Seleucus' descendants) and to the 'Atilian and Julian laws on the appointment of guardians' (the first provided for the appointment by Roman magistrates of a guardian for a minor if none had been appointed by will, and the Julian(-Titian) law for the same to be done by governors in provinces (Gaius, *Institutes* 1,

185)); and (7) to the import and export by Seleucus of goods to and from any 'city or territory of the provinces of Asia and Europe for his own use' on which 'neither local community nor Roman customs official might levy duty'.)

(8) If anyone wishes to accuse them, bring a charge against them, establish a court against them or grant jurisdiction [- - -], in respect of all these matters, [?it is my pleasure, whether] they wish to go to court in their own city under their own [?legal system or in the] free cities or before our magistrates or pro-[magistrates - - -], that the choice should rest with them, and that no-one should [?take any action] otherwise [than is prescribed] in these clauses, or give judgement concerning them when referring their case, or deliver a sentence on them; [and if any legal process concerning them is instituted] contrary to these terms, it is [not to be] valid.

(9) [If anyone consents] to entertain an accusation against the aforementioned person, their (*sic*) parents, wife, children and descendants, and make a preliminary decision concerning their status [- - -], it is our pleasure that the aforementioned persons have the right to send representatives to appear before our senate and our magistrates and pro-magistrates, and to send representatives concerning their own affairs. Any community or any magistrate [who does not act as required by these terms and acts contrary] to them or takes a ?partisan judicial decision (or, one that nullifies them), [or - - -], or exacts pledges and by wilful malice [prevents] these persons aforementioned from being able to make use of the privileges formally granted them, is to stand liable to pay the Roman People the sum of one hundred thousand sesterces, and the suit for and exaction of this sum is to be open to anyone [who wishes] to undertake it, [whether] he wishes to sue for it and exact it in the province before our magistrates and promagistrates or at Rome; but it is our pleasure that he provides adequate security for these [matters] when he [brings proceedings]. Our magistrates and pro-magistrates who are charged with the administration of justice there are to deliver judgement and ensure [that] the aforementioned provisions are carried out as prescribed above.

3. [In the year - - -], Dystrus 15th. Imperator Caesar, son of the deified Caesar, hailed Imperator for the sixth time, three times consul, designated consul for the fourth time, sends greetings to the [magistrates], council, and people of the city of Rhosus, the sacred, possessor of the right of asylum, and free. If you are flourishing, well and good; I too and the army are in good health. The envoys sent by you, Seleucus my admiral, Heras son of Calli [- - -], Symmachus, worthy men from a worthy people, our friend and ally, have arrived in Ephesus and have discussed their mission with me. I have, then, received the men, finding them patriotic and worthy, and have accepted the honours and the crown, and I shall endeavour when I come to your area to be the cause

of some advantage to you and to be vigilant for the privileges of the city; and I shall do so more gladly because of Seleucus my admiral who has fought at my side for the duration of the war and has shown the highest valour throughout and given a perfect demonstration of loyalty [and] fidelity. He has let slip no opportunity of petitioning on your behalf and of applying zeal and enthusiasm in furthering your interests. Good wishes.

4. [In the year - - -], Apellaeus 9th. Imperator Caesar, son of the deified Caesar, hailed Imperator for the sixth time, four times consul, sends greetings to the magistrates, council and people of the city of Rhosus, the sacred, possessor of the right of asylum, and free. If you are flourishing, [well and good]; I [too] and the army are in good health. Seleucus who is both your fellow-citizen [and] my admiral, who has fought at my side in all the wars and has given many proofs of his loyalty, fidelity and courage, has been distinguished, as was fitting when men fought alongside us and showed valour in war, with privileges, grants of immunity and citizenship. I therefore commend him to you: men of his character add a particular warmth to good will felt towards their [native cities]. Accordingly, as I am going to do all in my power for you the more gladly [for] Seleucus' [sake], send your requests to me, whatever they are, with confidence. Good wishes.

Rhosus' position on the Gulf of Alexandretta made it a natural place to produce a naval man. The date of 1 is uncertain, probably 36-4 BC, if the consular dating is correctly interpreted. The document on the Capitol, 2, must have been a comprehensive grant containing other names than that of Seleucus, as the slips in the text show; as Sherk suggests, it may be an ancestor of the military diploma (**152**). The legal basis for the grant is a law of 42 BC conferring power to create citizens on the Triumvirs — the last known enactment specifically conferring such a power.

In the list of privileges given Seleucus the first two sections deal with his rights as a Roman citizen, the rest with his relations with Rhosus (Sherwin-White *JRS* 63 (1973), 92, n.33). At Rhosus Seleucus may keep his rights but is freed from burdens: contrast both Cicero's doctrine of the incompatibility of citizenships and the attitude taken by Augustus in 47-6 BC (**84**).

In (8) the translation follows Sherwin-White in dividing the four actions indicated between those of would-be prosecutors and magistrates, rather than Riccobono (*FIRA* I² 55) in distinguishing between criminal and civil suits: Sherwin-White sees Seleucus and his kin as vulnerable to political attack in their native city (cf. **149**).

Damage to the central part of the clause makes it unclear exactly what the choice reserved for Seleucus was: between types of court or systems of law. The clause raises the larger question of how far Roman law ran in the provinces and how far it was affected by them (see Sherk's discussion, *Docs.* p. 305ff., and below on **157**).

The stiff penalty for infringing privileges granted with regard to capital cases (9) shows how determined the Triumvirs were to defend the interests of their protégés.

3. belongs to the months after Actium (2 September) and it was probably received in the Macedonian month that spanned February and March, 30. For the mechanism at work here, see **115**.

4. belongs to 30 BC when Octavian passed through Syria (Cassius Dio, *Roman History* 51, 18, 1; cf. **114**).

Not all grants of citizenship were linked with military service: political and cultural distinction also qualified individuals. But one concession going back to the latter part of the second century BC allowed the magistrates of cities with the 'Latin right' to become Roman citizens, helping to ensure the loyalty of all but one of the Italian towns that possessed it when the Social War broke out in 91 BC. This concession led to the enfranchisement of a substantial segment of the upper class in the cities favoured although the numbers who benefited from it in each would decline rapidly after the dominant oligarchy had been served.

The right was exported to the provinces and Vespasian granted it to Spain (**26**).

155. MW 480; from Iluro, Baetica

To Imperator Domitian Caesar Augustus Germanicus: Lucius Munius Novatus of the Quirina Tribe and Lucius Munius Aurelianus, son of Lucius, of the Quirina Tribe, having obtained Roman citizenship by holding the office of duovir, (set up the monument) from their own funds by decree of the council (or, presenting it as a gift).

Under Hadrian a more generous form of Latin right emerged: the entire council attained citizenship (Gaius, *Institutes* 1, 96).

156. *ILS* 6780; from Gigthis on the Lesser Syrtis

To Marcus Servilius Draco Albucianus, son of Publius, of the Quirina Tribe, duovir, priest for life: in recognition of the fact that, over and above his many services to the community and his most open-handed eagerness to confer benefactions, he has twice undertaken an embassy to the city of Rome at no cost to the community for the purpose of petitioning for the greater Latin right, and has eventually brought news of success, the council decreed the erection of the monument, and although he was satisfied with the honour alone and reimbursed the community for the cost, the people set it up from its own funds.

From the less urbanised area of Mauretania Tingitana comes a tablet recording another successful request, made on behalf of leading tribesmen in the reigns of Marcus Aurelius, Verus and Commodus.

157. Sherwin-White *JRS* 63 (1973), 86ff.; bronze tablet from Banasa, Mauretania Tingitana

(1) Copy of the letter of our Emperors Antoninus and Verus Augustus to Coiiedius (*sic*) Maximus. We have had the memorandum of Julian, the Zegrensian, attached to your letter, and although the Roman citizenship has not normally been granted to members of those tribes unless the imperial generosity has been elicited by merits of the highest order, none the less, since you assert both that he is one of the leading members of the tribes to which he belongs and that he shows ready obedience and extreme loyalty in our affairs, and since we did (*sic*) not consider that many clans among the Zegrensians could make comparable claims on the basis of their services ?although we might wish very many of them (or, and since we wish as many of them as possible) to be roused by the honour conferred by us on that house to emulation of Julian, we do not hesitate to grant Roman citizenship, without prejudice to the rights of the tribe, also on Ziddina his wife herself, likewise on their children Julian, Maximus, Maximinus, and Diogenianus.

(2) Copy of the letter of the Emperors Antoninus and Commodus Augustus to Vallius Maximianus. We have read the memorandum of the chieftain of the Zegrensian tribes, and we have noted the favour shown in advancing it by your predecessor Epidius Quadratus; wherefore, profoundly moved both by his written support and by the merits of the man himself and by the evidence that he adduces, we have granted Roman citizenship, without prejudice to the rights of the tribe, to his wife and sons; ?in order that the fact may be recorded in our files, ascertain the age of each, and write to us.

(3) Copied and authenticated from the file of persons granted Roman citizenship kept by the deified Augustus, Tiberius Caesar Augustus, Gaius Caesar, the deified Claudius, Nero, Galba, the deified Augusti Vespasian and Titus, Caesar Domitian, the deified Augusti Nerva and Trajan Parthicus, Trajan Hadrian, Hadrian Antoninus Pius, Verus Germanicus Medicus Parthicus Maximus, Imperator Caesar Marcus Aurelius Antoninus Augustus Germanicus Sarmaticus, and Imperator Caesar Lucius Aurelius Commodus Augustus Germanicus Sarmaticus; the freedman Asclepiodotus produced the file: statement below.

In the consulships of Imperator Caesar Lucius Aurelius Commodus Augustus and Marcus Plautius Quintilius, 6 July, at Rome.

Faggura, wife of Julian, chieftain of the Zegrensian tribe, aged 22; Juliana, aged 8; Maxima, aged 4, Julian, aged 3; Diogenianus, aged 2, children of the afore-mentioned Julian.

At the request of Aurelius Julian, chieftain of the Zegrensians, made by memorandum, with the support of Vallius Maximianus, by letter, we have granted Roman citizenship, without prejudice to the rights of the tribe, to these persons, with no diminution of tribute and taxes due to the people and to the imperial Treasury.

Transacted on the same day, same place, under the same consuls. Checked by the freedman Asclepiodotus.

Sealed by (twelve names follow).

Coiedius Maximus was equestrian governor of Tingitana *c*. 168; the second and third documents belong to 177. The two petitions probably came from father and son, the latter being the Julian mentioned with his three brothers at the end of (1).

The grants were unlike that made to Seleucus (**154**) in that no immunity from tax is conferred; but they raise the same question of how the grant affected the beneficiaries' relations with their native community (see on **84** and **154**). Their public rights and duties were maintained as before; the grant of citizenship to the wives and children, guaranteeing succession like the less comprehensive grant of legitimate marriage made at Volubilis (**153**), shows the irrelevance of local private rights in a context of Roman law.

The file of individual grants of citizenship (grants to discharged veterans were recorded elsewhere, see **152**), is referred to by Trajan in Pliny's *Letters* 10, 105.

The men who affixed their seals, twelve members of Marcus' advisory board, half ex-consuls, half knights, including the prefect of the Guard Bassaeus and the jurisconsult and prefect of the Watch Scaevola, played a part in the decision to award the grant; compare the role of the governor's advisory board in **50**.

If services rendered to Rome earned citizenship, grants of citizenship provided Rome with men to serve her: three attested Roman citizens are among the native dignitaries enlisted in the early Principate to do Rome's work for her (**17-19**). But her prime need was of legionary troops (**28**) and, as the Emperor Tiberius also complained, she was in need of able senatorial administrators (Tacitus, *Annals* 6, 27, 3). The equestrian order formed the pool from which new senators, not of senatorial family, were drawn; it is not long after the foundation of the Principate that equestrian officials of provincial origin as well as a sprinkling of provincial senators begin to be found. Nero's adviser and prefect of the Guard is perhaps the most famous of the substantial number of equestrian officials from southern Gaul.

158. Smallwood, *Gaius-Nero* 259; from Vasio, Narbonensis

The people of Vasio of the Vocontians, to Sextus Afranius Burrus, son of Sextus, of the Voltinian Tribe; military tribune; procurator of Augusta; of Tiberius Caesar; of the deified Claudius: prefect of the Praetorian Guard; awarded the insignia of a consul.

Burrus' origin is confirmed by his tribal voting unit, Roman citizens from Narbonensian Gaul were frequently in Voltinia. The way the people of his city refer to themselves, as Vocontii, members of a Gaulish tribe, shows how strong the old social structure was, even in Romanised Narbonensis (**24**).

After one season of military service Burrus became manager of imperial estates belonging successively to Livia (titled Augusta since 14), Tiberius, presumably Gaius, who is passed over in silence, and Claudius. In 51 he became prefect as the Empress Agrippina's nominee (Tacitus, *Annals* 12, 42, 1f.). Tacitus refers to his reputation as a soldier, but nothing in the record above would justify it; it may have been enhanced by a conspicuously mutilated arm (*Annals* 13, 14, 5). The high political importance of the post is measured by the honorary senatorial insignia awarded Burrus: he was allowed to wear the insignia of a consul, the highest magistrate.

Provincials who actually entered the senate also did so through imperial patronage: Burrus' associate Seneca, for example. Several score had already entered when Claudius made his speech of 48 advocating the grant of permission to stand for senatorial office to leaders of the communities of Gallia Comata, more precisely perhaps the members of the council of the Gauls (**121**, **123**), given the place where the document was found.

159. Smallwood, *Gaius-Nero* 369; bronze tablet found at Lugdunum

(Col. 1) [- - -] is of our affairs [- - -] I for my part pray to avert above all the attitude which I foresee as likely to prove quite the main obstacle in my path, your shuddering at the introduction of that proposal as a novelty. No, you are rather to reflect on this: how many innovations there have been in this state, indeed, how many different forms and conditions our constitution has assumed, right from the foundation of our city.

Once upon a time kings occupied this city; all the same it was not their destiny to hand it on to heirs from their own household. Men who had nothing to do with them took their place — foreigners, in fact: Numa succeeded to Romulus, and he came from the Sabine country, not far away, of course, but it made him a foreigner in those days; and Tarquinius Priscus succeeded Ancus Martius. He had mixed blood, being the son of Demaratus of Corinth and a mother from Tarquinii who was well born but not well off, as one would expect with a woman who had to lower herself to such a husband, and that was why he was kept from holding office at home; after he migrated to Rome he obtained the kingdom. He too and his son or grandson — there is also disagreement on this point amongst the authorities — had Servius Tullius interpolated in their succession. If we follow our Roman sources Servius was born in captivity to Ocresia, but if we follow the Etruscans he was once the most faithful comrade of Caelius Vivenna and his companion in all his adventures, and, after he was driven out through the fickleness of Fortune and was exiled from Etruria with all the surviving troops of Caelius, took over the Caelian Hill and gave it that name after his commander, changed his own name — in Etruscan his own name was Mastarna —, took the name I have mentioned, and claimed the kingdom with the greatest benefit to the state. Then, after the ways of Tarquinius Superbus came to be loathed in our community — and that goes for himself as much as for his sons —, well, we were thoroughly tired of monarchy and the running of the state was transferred to annual magistrates, the consuls.

Why should I now recall the power of the dictatorship, a power stronger than that of this very consulship itself, and devised by our ancestors for use in particularly hard-fought wars or intractable civil disturbances, or the plebeian tribunes elected to bring aid to the ordinary people? Or the power transferred from the consuls to the Board of Ten and returned once more to the consuls when the monarchical power of that board had been brought to an end? Or how the power of the consulship was split among a number of men, and the military tribunes with consular power (as they were called) elected six and often eight at a time? Or how posts were eventually shared with the people, not just magistracies carrying official power, but priesthoods as well? If I were now to tell the story of the wars which were the starting point for our ancestors, and how far we have progressed, I am afraid that you might think me unduly arrogant, and that my object has been to find an opportunity of boasting about the glory I have acquired by extending our power beyond the Ocean. No, I shall return to the point instead. The citizenship (or, our community) [- - -].

(Col. 2) [- - -] can. It was a novel policy to be sure when both my great-uncle the deified Augustus and my uncle Tiberius Caesar wished to have in this Senate House the entire flower of the colonies and municipalities no matter where it was to be found, provided of course that it consisted of men of sound character and substance. But where does one go from there? Is an Italian senator not preferable to one from the provinces? I shall show you in due course, by my actions, what my opinion is on that subject, when I come to claim your approval for that part of my censorship. But I do not think that provincials are to be turned away either, provided that they can bring honour on the House.

Here you have the most honourable and powerful colony of the people of Vienna; for how long a time has it been contributing senators to this House? That is the colony from which comes Lucius Vestinus, who does honour to the ranks of the knights as few others do; for him I feel the affection of the closest of friends, and have him engaged in my service today; his offspring I hope may eventually enjoy priesthoods of the highest standing as in the course of years they secure advancement in rank. Not to mention the repulsive name of a thug — and I detest that prodigy of the wrestling ring who conferred a consulship on his house before his colony had acquired the privilege of Roman citizenship *en bloc* — I am in a position to say the same of his brother; it is indeed a pitiful and completely undeserved stroke of bad luck that he cannot be useful to you in the capacity of a senator.

It is time now, Tiberius Caesar Germanicus, for you to reveal to the members of the senate the direction of your speech; for you have already reached the outer limits of Narbonensian Gaul. Here, under my eye, are all these distinguished men in the prime of life. It would not be a cause of regret if they were senators any more than it is to Persicus, a man of the highest consular lineage and a friend of mine, to read the name of 'Allobrogicus' when he looks at the busts of his ancestors. Now if you agree that this is the case, what more do you need than for me to use my finger to point out to you that actually the soil outside the boundaries of the province of Narbonensis already sends you senators, since it is not a cause of regret that we have members of our order from Lugdunum? Diffidently indeed, members of the senate, have I passed outside the provincial boundaries that are known and familiar to you; but the case for Gallia Comata has now to be fought with no holds barred. In the course of it, if anyone has an eye to the fact that they kept the deified Julius busy fighting for ten years, let him also consider the other side: one hundred years of unshakable loyalty and a readiness to obey that has been more than tried during a number of crises in our affairs. While my father Drusus Germanicus was conquering Germany they remained quiet and so afforded him secure and untroubled peace behind him, and that when he had been called away to the war from the work of carrying out the census, a novel and unfamiliar operation to the Gauls at that time. (How arduous that operation is for us we are only now discovering by having more than enough experience of it, although the only object of the enquiry is to make known to the public the extent of our resources.)

Claudius' speech, taken down *verbatim* and immortalised in bronze, lacks the elegance of Tacitus' version (*Annals* 11, 24) and, it has been argued, its 'advanced cosmopolitanism' (Griffin 1982, 418: Claudius meant only to do *protégés* a favour). The initiative came from the Gauls and their council and not surprisingly was resisted by senators: the numbers who might receive permission to stand for office were large (Tacitus, *Annals* 23, 6) with sixty or more tribes represented on the council, some with several representatives (**173**). Their wealth was another source of fear and envy (24, 10). In the event only the favoured Aedui (**126**) were given the privilege as a first step (25, 1f.). Perhaps the Gauls wanted the honour of wearing the broad stripe on their tunics without bearing the burdens of office — or they failed to secure election. Senators from Comata are rare in the second half of the first century.

For Claudius' account of early Roman constitutional history, see A. Momigliano, *Claudius* (2nd edn, Cambridge, 1961), 11ff.

His claim in col. 2 that Augustus and Tiberius sought recruits all over Italy, which he refers to in the standard phrase as 'the colonies and municipalities', is fair enough (see EJ 193, 197, 205); Tiberius was bolder in admitting provincials than Augustus had been (T.P. Wiseman, *New Men in the Roman Senate 139 BC-AD* 14 (Oxford, 1971), 190; B. Levick, *Tiberius the Politician* (London, 1976), 98f.). When Claudius passes to Narbonensis, emotion creeps in: Vestinus became prefect of Egypt in 59 (cf. **167**) and enjoyed as much power as most senators (Tacitus, *Histories* 4, 53); the 'thug' was the senator from Vienna, Valerius Asiaticus, consul for the second time in 46, tried and forced to suicide the following year (Tacitus, *Annals* 11, 1ff.); his brother was lost to the senate for that reason (the listening Gauls may have been reconsidering their request at this point). Persicus, member of the aristocratic Fabian clan and consul 34, is brought in only as a feeble joke and as a compliment: the surname Allobrogicus had been won by an ancestor who had defeated that tribe and so established hereditary patronage over it. For the capital Vienna, see **24**; it had been made a full colony only by Gaius. As for Gallic senators from outside Narbonensis, Claudius points to himself, born at Lugdunum, the only example at the time. His enthusiastic defence of Gallic loyalty made him ignore the brief revolt of 21 (**196**) and the fact that it was unrest in Gaul that in part had decided Augustus to send Drusus on his invasion of Germany (**126**).

New men were content to take on work that senators born to the rank preferred to avoid. The same phenomenon may be seen at a lower level of society: by the end of Nero's reign nearly 40 per cent of the Rhine legionaries were being recruited from Narbonensis (Forni 1953, 157ff.) and two senators from the same province had commanded the Lower Rhine army: Pompeius Paulinus of Arelate and Lucius Duvius Avitus of Vasio (Tacitus, *Annals* 13, 53ff.; *PIR* P 479 and *PIR*[2] D 210). The influence of Nero's ministers is detectable: Paullinus was Seneca's brother-in-law and Avitus came from the same town as Burrus. Wealth and influence played an important part, but competence was a recommendation too, in the face of senatorial prejudice: the standard of provincial administration may have risen in the hands of men who depended on imperial support.

The process continued, not surprisingly at the lowest level first: there was an overall majority of provincials in the legions under Claudius and Nero, if the available evidence is adequate; under the Antonines provincials came near parity in procuratorial posts and are in the majority in the third century (Pflaum 1950, 170ff.); in the senate Italians retain a narrow majority through the Antonine age but are outnumbered after Caracalla (Hammond 1957, 77).

Prosperity, tradition, culture, opportunities for patronage and the weight of prejudice, all varied from one region to another. Upper-class easterners, lacking the military tradition so intimately connected with citizenship in Roman eyes, relied on the cultural attainments that were the prerequisite for administrative posts. Roman prejudice told against them at first, despite (or because of?) their ambition and political sophistication (see **179**, **183**).

160. Plutarch, *On Peace of Mind*, 10 (Moralia 470C); Greek

But there is a different type of person, a Chian, or a Galatian or Bithynian, who is not content if he has won the glory or power that goes with a certain position among his fellow-citizens; he is in tears because he does not wear the shoes of a patrician senator; if he does wear them, because he is not yet a Roman praetor; and if he is praetor, because he is not consul; and when he is consul, because he was not the first to be declared elected, but came in later.

The ambitions of Greek-speaking magnates were satisfied in the second century. By the reign of Marcus Aurelius more than half the provincial senators were of eastern origin and the proportion continued to rise. By contrast they provided less than half the provincial procurators, even in the third century; these quiet posts gave less scope for the display of literary and political talent than membership of the senate and the governorship of provinces.

It is worth looking more closely at the rise of one Greek-speaking family from the municipal aristocracy to the highest positions at court and in the senate — and at their fall.

161. *MAMA* 9, 26 (forthcoming); marble altar from Aezani in Phrygia; Greek

The council and people honoured Publius Aelius Zeuxidemus Cassianus: high priest of Asia, corrector, benefactor of the city.

162. *IGR* 4, 819; from Hierapolis in Phrygia; Greek

The Greeks in Asia and the council and people honoured Publius Aelius Zeuxidemus Aristus Zeno, son of Publius Aelius Zeuxidemus Cassianus, the high priest of Asia: treasury counsellor in Phrygia and in Asia.

163. Philostratus, *Lives of the Sophists* 2, 24 (606f.); Greek

The native city of the sophist Antipater was Hierapolis, a city that must be classified among the flourishing ones of Asia, while his father was Zeuxidemus, one of the most distinguished citizens it had. He went to Hadrian and Pollux for tuition (607) but was more influenced by Pollux, letting the rhythmic effects of his style dissipate the vigour of his ideas. He also went to hear the Athenian, Zeno, and learnt the finer points of the art from him. He was a natural extempore speaker who did not neglect prepared compositions either, but used to recite us set speeches for the Olympic and Panathenaic Games; and he composed an historical work on the achievements of the Emperor Severus. It was by Severus that he was put in charge of the imperial correspondence, and he achieved a brilliant reputation in the post. Let me make my own opinion clear: although there were a number of men who were better speakers and better historians than this man, there was none better at drafting a letter: he was like a brilliant tragic actor who is thoroughly conversant with stagecraft and he made his utterances consonant with the Emperor's role; what he said possessed clarity, grandeur of expression, a style adapted to the circumstances, and an agreeable use of asyndeton, which adds brilliance to a letter more than anything else.

He was enrolled among the consuls and governed the province of Bithynia, but as he was thought to be too ready to use the sword he was relieved of his command. Antipater lived to be sixty-eight years old, and he was buried in his native city. He is said to have died from self-starvation, not from disease: he was the recognised tutor of Severus' sons, and one of our ways of applauding his recitals was to call him 'teacher of the gods'; but when the younger of the two was executed on the charge of plotting against his brother, he wrote the elder a letter containing a solo funeral ode and dirge, to the effect that he had one eye left and one hand, and that he heard that the pupils he had taught to take up arms in defence of each other had taken them up against each other.

Municipal and provincial posts were all that Cassianus (**161**) achieved; he was presumably the member of the family who was given the citizenship by Hadrian. In the next generation (**162**) we find a Roman knight engaged in defending the legal claims of the imperial Treasury successively in the district of Phrygia and the Asian Province as a whole;

personal service to the Emperors rendered by the grandson (**163**) was rewarded with high senatorial office.

Antipater was too much the sophist to be a typical senator, but it is not surprising that he attained consular rank. In a world without printing, television, or telephone, in which a letter was doing well to make fifty miles a day, address and eloquence were prime assets: a man had to win over his fellow citizens to his views in assembly, council or law courts: as envoy to other cities or to the senate or emperor he needed the same talents; so did members of the provincial councils and of the senate itself; we have seen an emperor in action (**159**). There were adepts to speak for their cities (**110**), teach, offer public advice and entertain.

The 'Second Sophistic' flourished, especially in the prosperous cities of Asia Minor, in the second century. Its members were influential even when they did not hold imperial or provincial office and, as Antipater's intellectual ancestry illustrates, they contributed to the cultural unity of the Empire. His teacher, Hadrian of Tyre, became professor of rhetoric at Rome; he in turn had been a pupil of the great Herodes Atticus (**138**); Julius Pollux was himself a pupil of Hadrian, and held the chair at Athens.

Antipater may have come to know Septimius Severus when the future Emperor spent a period of retirement and study at Athens in the 180s (*Augustan History*, *Septimius Severus* 3, 7; A. Birley, *Septimius Severus*, (London, 1971), 119). Such personal connections, along with the generally high esteem enjoyed by sophists (Trajan is made by Philostratus, *Lives of the Sophists* 1, 7 (488), to put Dio in his chariot and turn to him with the words 'What you are saying I have no idea, but I love you as myself'), help to explain the special privileges granted them by the intellectual Hadrian; the number of persons eligible was restricted by Antoninus Pius.

164. Modestinus, Pleas for Exemption, Book 2, in *Digest* 27, 1, 6, 8; 2 and 7; Greek

(8) Inscribed amongst the decisions taken by the Emperor Commodus is a section from a letter of Antoninus Pius, in which it is shown that philosophers also enjoy immunity from undertaking guardianships. The wording is as follows: 'In line with all these provisions, as soon as my most divine father came to power he confirmed existing privileges and immunities by means of an edict, writing that philosophers, rhetoricians, teachers of literature and doctors were exempt from holding office as gymnasium presidents, superintendents of the market place and priests; from billeting and the duty of purchasing grain or oil; and they are not to serve on juries or embassies, nor are they to be enlisted for military service if they are unwilling to serve, nor are they to be compelled to

undertake any other duty whether provincial or other.

(2) But there is actually a fixed number of rhetoricians in each city who possess immunity, and certain conditions attached to the regulation, as is shown from a letter of Antoninus Pius which, although it is addressed to the provincial council of Asia, affects the entire world. The section subjoined here is taken from it: 'Smaller cities may have five doctors exempt from tax, three sophists, and the same number of teachers of literature; for larger cities the number of medical practitioners they may have is seven, and of teachers four in each of the two languages; the largest cities may have ten doctors, five rhetoricians, and the same number of teachers of literature. Beyond this number not even the largest city grants immunity from tax' . . . (7) Concerning philosophers the same decision of Pius has this to say: 'The number of philosophers was not prescribed, because of the paucity of practitioners. In my opinion those who are exceedingly well off will willingly provide their native cities with what is necessary out of their resources; if they quibble about their property the very fact will immediately show them up as not being philosophers.'

Eastern provinces contributed a remarkable number of men to procuratorship and senate in the second and third centuries. The African provinces matched them, as well as providing an extraordinarily high proportion of legionaries in the same period. In north Africa a vital factor must have been wealth based on expanding agriculture and nearness to Rome. The Emperor Septimius Severus came from Lepcis as a product of this success, just as Trajan and Hadrian had been natives of Spain, though ultimately of some Italian stock. The Empire had indeed been transformed from a vast area dominated by the elite of a single city or (by Augustus' time) the elite of the Italian peninsula (**159**), into a unity run by the elite of all the provinces. When Tacitus, *Annals* 11, 23, 2, makes Italians claim in 48 that Italy was still capable of producing senators for the City (*Urbs*) he exposes their narrowness of vision, which did not take in the needs and importance of the world (*orbis*: see **110**, where the words are juxtaposed).

The Danubian provinces stand apart in a significant way. They made a substantial contribution to the legions, nearly a fifth of the men of provincial origin from Hadrian onwards, but the proportion of procurators they can show is only half as high, and the number of senators negligible. Only after 235 is there a sudden leap: usurping Danubian Emperors qualify for entry in modern lists of senators! In that period the slow processes of evolution broke down under economic, social and hence political strains.

165. Eutropius, *Survey of Roman History* **9, 12-13, 1**

After him Quintillus, the brother of Claudius, was elected Emperor as the choice of the troops. A man of unmatched self-restraint and courtesy, comparable with his brother or even preferable, and given the title Augustus at the wish of the senate, he was killed on the seventeenth day of his reign. (13, 1) After him Aurelian took over the Empire; a native of Dacia Ripensis, he was a man capable in war but of an uncontrollable temper, and somewhat given to cruelty. He too gained a very hard-won victory over the Goths. In a series of wars with varying fortunes he restored Roman authority as far as the frontiers it had once reached.

For unfavourable speculation on Aurelian's parentage, see the *Epitome of Aurelius Victor*, 35, 1: he was 'the offspring of a father of middling rank, and according to some writers the tenant of an extremely distinguished senator, Aurelius'.

In Tacitus' time the Goths were east of the lower Vistula (*Germania* 43, 6), and in the mid-second century they expanded southwards to the area north of the Black Sea, from which in the mid-third century they were attacking Asia Minor and the Balkans. Quintillus' brother Claudius gained his title Gothicus from them. In spite of his victories, Aurelian had to evacuate Dacia north of the Danube in face of its occupation by the western (Visi-) Goths.

10

Failings

It may seem unnecessary to devote a chapter to the deficiencies of Roman government, when many items elsewhere came to be recorded precisely because of them. But it is worth considering which were inherent, which remediable, which chronic, and which likely to lead to breakdown.

Most in evidence are the offences typical of a conquering power against its victims. The leader of rebels in Dalmatia is represented by Cassius Dio, *Roman History* 56, 16, 3, as complaining in 6 that they had 'wolves' sent to look after them, and the same author's stories about the procurator Licinus in Gaul, who inserted two extra months into the calendar and so increased his takings by more than 16 per cent (54, 21, 2ff.), like Herodian's about Maximinus and his procurator (*Roman Histories* 7, 4, 2), show that the Emperor himself might be perceived as conniving at the fleecing of his subjects. The exploitative attitude is betrayed too by an innocent remark attributed to a high-minded Emperor (see also **209**).

166. Cassius Dio, *Roman History* 57, 10, 5; Greek

At any rate, when Aemilius Rectus once sent him from Egypt, which he was governing, an extra sum of money, beside what had been prescribed, he sent him back the message, 'I want my sheep shorn, not shaven'.

Suetonius has the sheep more drastically 'skinned' (*Tiberius* 32, 2), but Tiberius' actual purpose is the point.

Rectus was governor of the most blatantly exploited province of the Empire (correspondingly it lagged behind in privilege: **135**). Nero, especially towards the end of his reign, was less prudent than Tiberius in his calculation. At any rate it was clear that it was only at a time of crisis that the inhabitants of Egypt and Alexandria could expect even promises of relief.

167. Smallwood, *Gaius-Nero* 391 (MW 328); Greek; on the outer gateway of the Temple of Hibis, El-Khârga Oasis, Egypt

(Col. 1) Julius Demetrius, strategus of the oasis of the Thebaid: I have appended for you the copy of the edict sent to me by the Lord Governor Tiberius Julius Alexander, so that you may know and profit from his acts of beneficence. Year 2 of Lucius Livius Augustus Sulpicius Galba, Imperator, on the day Julia Sebaste, first of Phaophi.

Edict of Tiberius Julius Alexander. Since I am exercising every care that the city should remain in the condition appropriate to it and continue to profit from the acts of beneficence conferred on it by the Emperors, and that Egypt should continue in a satisfactory state and put itself with a will at the service of the corn supply and supreme happiness of the present time without being burdened by fresh and unjust exactions; and since I had hardly set foot in the city before I was mobbed by the people I encountered, both in small groups and in crowds consisting of the most respectable people here in the city and of those who farm the countryside, who were complaining of the abuses that have recently occurred, I have been unremitting in applying the authority invested in me to matters requiring urgent reform.

But in order to enhance the cheerful confidence that you feel in placing all your hopes for everything that is conducive to your security and for your material advantage on the benefactor our Emperor, whose light has shone upon us for the salvation of the entire human race, Imperator Galba, and in order that you may be aware that I have given thought to measures to relieve you in your need, I have made binding proclamations dealing with each one of the petitions that are within my authority to determine and act on; as to the more serious matters, which require the power and majesty of the Emperor, I shall explain them to him with the utmost accuracy, the gods having watched over the safety of the inhabited world up to this most sacred time of consummation.

(1) Thus I recognise above all the perfect reasonableness of your petition against the forcible coercion of unwilling persons into tax farming or other forms of lease on imperial real estate in violation of normal practice in the provinces; and that affairs have been mismanaged to no small detriment when men who are inexperienced in that kind of business have been coerced into it as a result of compulsory tax burdens being placed upon them. That is why I myself have not coerced anyone into tax farming or taking leases nor shall I do so: I know that what is to the advantage of the imperial revenues is that those who are capable of it should undertake the business voluntarily and with enthusiasm. I am assured that no-one in future will coerce tax farmers or lessees who are unwilling, but will hire out the business to those who are willing to take it on voluntarily, keeping to the time-honoured practice of former prefects rather than imitating the casual injustice of an individual.

(2) Since certain persons on the pretext of the public interest have actually taken on debts due to other creditors and have handed some persons over to the debtors' gaol and other prisons which I know to have been abolished for the very purpose of ensuring that execution of debts should be on property and not on persons, I act in accordance with the wishes of the deified Augustus and order that no one on the pretext of the public interest is to take over from other persons loans which he did not himself originally make, nor are any free persons to be imprisoned at all in any form of detention whatsoever (unless an offender is involved), nor yet in the debtors' gaol, apart from those whose debts are due to the imperial Treasury.

(3) But in order that the phrase 'the public interest' may prove no impediment to contractual agreements and that those who misuse the state's right of prior claim for improper purposes may not damage public credit, I have also published a binding enactment on this prior claim: for it has been revealed to me on a number of occasions that certain individuals have attempted in the past to invalidate contracts legally entered into and to use violence to exact debts already paid from the persons who have received them, making the purchases void and withdrawing the property from those who have bought it. The pretext is that the purchasers have contracted with persons who have obtained delays of payment from the Treasury, or with *strategi*, or with their agents, or with other persons who are indebted to the Public Revenue. I order accordingly that whoever is imperial procurator or estate manager in Alexandria and entertains suspicions of any of the persons who are engaged in public business, should take note of the man's name or publish it, so that no-one makes a contract with such, or sequester part of his property to the public Record Office as security. If on the other hand a man makes a loan to one whose name has not been noted nor his property sequestered, taking security in a legal manner, or has previously recovered his loan or actually made a purchase, when the vendor's name has not been noted nor his property sequestered, he shall have no problem.

As to dowries, which are the property of others and not that of the men who have received them, both the deified Augustus and the prefects have ordered that they should be returned from the imperial Treasury to the women involved, whose prior claim ought to be kept secure.

(4) I have also encountered requests concerning exemptions from tax and tax reductions, including cases concerned with ?tax on land formerly belonging to the state: that they should be maintained on the terms on which the deified Claudius granted them exemption in what he wrote to Postumus; and there are complaints that transactions carried out (?or properties bought) by private persons in the interval between their being subject to tax by Flaccus and being exempted by the deified Claudius have since been subjected to tax. Since both Balbillus and

Vestinus exempted these items I accordingly confirm the decrees of both governors, which themselves complied with the concession granted by the deified Claudius; this means that I remit sums not yet exacted on them, on the understanding that tax exemptions and reliefs on them are to be observed in the future.

(5) Concerning properties of the imperial Treasury sold in the intervening period, on which a tax on the produce was levied, as Vestinus ordered the established tax to be paid, I too have remitted sums not yet exacted and ordain that in the future too they are to remain at the established rate. It is an injustice when the purchasers have bought property and paid the purchase price to demand taxes from them on their own estates as if they were tenant farmers of the state.

(6) It is in conformity with the concessions granted by the Emperors that persons native to Alexandria, even when they are residing in the countryside for the purposes of their work, should not be coerced into any public service due from the country districts; (col. 2) you have often requested, and I myself confirm, that no person native to Alexandria is to be coerced into public services due from the country districts.

(7) I shall also make it my business to see that after the completion of the Audit the positions of *strategus* are put for a three year term into the hands of those who are to hold them.

(8) I issue a general order that whenever a prefect has previously taken a decision to dismiss matters brought before him, those matters shall not be brought up to the Audit again. If it is two prefects who have been of the same opinion, the official accountant is also liable to punishment for bringing the same matters up to the Audit and doing nothing short of laying up an excuse for himself and the other officials to enrich themselves. Certainly many persons have taken the decision rather to abandon their own property: they have spent more than its market value because the same matters are being brought up for judgement at each Audit.

(9) I establish the same principle for matters brought up under the special Treasury Account; so if something has been decided and dismissed or is hereafter dismissed by the official in charge of the special Treasury Account, it shall not be permissible for this (same) person again to lay information before a prosecutor or for the case to be brought to court; or the person responsible will be mercilessly punished. There will be no end to malicious prosecutions if matters that have been dismissed are brought up until someone makes an unfavourable judgement. Since the city has already become practically uninhabitable because of the horde of malicious prosecutors and every household is in turmoil, I issue a binding order that if any of the prosecutors attached to the special Treasury Account brings an indictment as counsel to another party, the accuser is to be produced by him, so that he too is not immune from risk. If he brings three indictments on his own account and fails to

prove his case, he is to be banned from bringing further prosecutions, while half his property is to be confiscated. It is the height of injustice for a man who has brought danger on a number of persons involving their property and possible penalties himself to enjoy impunity throughout. I shall also issue a general order that the code of the special Treasury Account [is to stand] now that I have corrected innovations that are in conflict with the beneficent acts of the Emperors. I shall make written proclamation [to the public of how I have] inflicted due punishment on those who have [already] been convicted of malicious prosecution.

(10) I am not unaware that you are much concerned for another thing: that Egypt should continue in good condition, and that it is a source of [? great worry to you]. As to the civic duties you perform, [then], I have made what reforms I could: those who are engaged in farming throughout the whole countryside have often sought me out and revealed that there have been a number of novel imposts. [?They have not been made out of gratuitous wickedness] but by way of exactions of grain and money, although it is not practicable for those who are so inclined to make unscrupulous innovations that will have universal application. But [I have found] these and similar imposts [extending] not only over the Thebaid nor over the distant nomes of Lower Egypt; they have already [taken over in] the suburbs of the city too and what is known as 'the territory of the Alexandrians' and the nome of Lake Mareotis. [For that reason I order] the *strategi* throughout the nomes that if any imposts have been newly imposed in the past five years on [farmers] in nomes or toparchies which were not paid before either in the whole country or over the greater part of it, they are to reduce them to the former level, abandoning demands for them, and cases that have been brought before the Audit from (?local jurisdiction I remit].

(11) I have also checked the immoderate power of the state accountants before this present occasion, when they were universally accused of drawing up very many of their estimates on the basis of [analogy]; the result of that was that they were enriching themselves, while Egypt was devastated. I now enjoin the same officials once again to make no estimate on the basis of analogy, and not to make any general estimate without a decision of the prefect. I also order the *strategi* to accept nothing from the accountants without the sanction of the prefect. And the other officials, if they are found to have drawn up any estimate that is fraudulent or contrary to what it ought to be, shall both return to private individuals the same sum that was demanded of them and shall pay the same amount into the public Treasury.

(12) Another variety of the same form of malpractice is the so-called 'demand based on estimate', which is made with reference not to the current [Nile] inundation but to an average of certain former inundations, [when all the time] it is evident that there is no juster method than that of the actual state of affairs. I want the population to take courage

and cultivate the soil with a will [in the knowledge] that the tax demand will be made with reference to the true state of the current inundation and of the [land] reached by the flood, [and] not to the chicanery of officials who draw up the assessment on the basis of an estimate. If anyone is convicted of falsifying [it], he shall pay back three times what he has obtained.

(13) Any persons who have been caused alarm by rumours about the measuring up of the old land in the [territory] of the Alexandrians and the Menelaite Nome, to which the measuring rod has never been applied, are not to entertain unfounded fears: [no-one] has [ever] ventured to [undertake] the measuring up nor shall he do so; the age-old rights to the land ought to stand.

(14) I make the same ruling also with regard to the new alluvial accretions to these districts: no changes are to be introduced as far as they are concerned.

(15) You press the matter of particularly long-standing arrears; through frequent attempts to exact or determine them certain persons have achieved nothing more than the enrichment of the officials and the oppression of the [population]. Concerning these arrears I shall write to Caesar Augustus Imperator with the other matters that I shall expound to him as the only authority able completely to do away with such problems: his unfailing beneficence and foresight are the sources of the security of us all.

In the first year of Lucius Livius Galba Caesar Augustus Imperator, Epeiphi 12th.

The edict, promulgated in Alexandria on 6 July, 68 (last section), passed on to the temple, *c.* 660 km to the south, on 28 September (*init.*).

The *strategus* was in charge of one of the nomes into which rural Egypt was divided, about 47 at the time of the edict, rising to nearly 60 by the end of the second century. They were subdivided into toparchies and these again into villages.

Alexander (*PIR*^{2} I, 139) was the nephew of the Jewish writer Philo, but had become Hellenised. He was one of the three *epistrategi* ('over-generals') of Egypt under Rectus in 42 (Smallwood, *Gaius-Nero* 156), was procurator of Judaea 46-8 (Josephus, *Jewish War* 2, 220), declared for Vespasian in July 69 and remained in office under him (Suetonius, *Deified Vespasian* 6, 3).

The prefect's picture of himself mobbed by complainants as soon as he set foot in Alexandria makes him sound a new broom, but he had been in office since 66. By securing the loyalty of his subjects he would increase Galba's security, earn his gratitude and strengthen his own hold on office. Earlier, in the Hellenistic age, periods of disturbance tended to be followed by promises on the part of the Ptolemies to end abuses and to protect rights and privileges.

In (1) the wrongdoer is Alexander's predecessor Caecina Tuscus (63-6); but complaints of enforced tax-farming and leasing of imperial estates are found previously (Smallwood, *Gaius-Nero* 383) and afterwards under Domitian (AJ 167). Equally, imprisonment for debt, repudiated in (2), went on under Augustus, if a man was indebted through his own fault and had no property he could use to pay off his debt (G. Chalon, *L'Édit de Tiberius Julius Alexander* (Olten, etc., 1964), 116f.). But it was worth invoking the charismatic name of Augustus.

In (3) officials are included among those indebted to the Revenue because they had to answer for their transactions in state money. Dowries are protected: they belong to the wife, not to the husband whose property is being confiscated as having been bought from a state debtor (or who is the original debtor: Chalon, *L'Édit* 138).

The tax-exemptions of (4) were granted in about 45-7 on transactions ('properties sold', Chalon) on which the prefect Avillius Flaccus (32-8) had levied full tax. Some transactions of the period between the two decisions had been subjected to full tax. Balbillus (55-9) and Vestinus (59-62: see **159**) had granted remission on them, and Alexander keeps to their rulings. Once again the villain of the piece is Tuscus.

From (6) may be seen the anxiety of rural officials to find men to perform the public duties for which they were held responsible. Alexander's ruling follows one of Cleopatra made in 41 BC and still in force in the mid-third century. Reluctance to serve may also be seen in (7), which concerns the actual *strategiae*: men are to take office by a certain time (thus freeing their predecessors?) and are to continue for a fixed term.

The state accountants threatened in (8) had every incentive to enrich themselves: each was responsible for the taxes of one nome, which he also assessed, and was paid *pro rata*. Their method was infallible: either the owners paid up or the legal costs eventually forced them to abandon their property.

The special Treasury Account mentioned in (9) received revenues not from taxation but (for example) from confiscation, intestacy, fines, and anything else the officials could devise: see its code (LR 99). Here was a role, an opportunity for private informers and accusers (Sherwin-White, *JRS* 56 (1966), 242). The section further gives a striking picture of these accusers sheltering behind official prosecutors. The penalties to be imposed on them may have been 'merciless', but they are not specified, unless we take it that they were liable to the same penalty as the official prosecutor who was found to be bringing malicious actions.

The prefect claims in (10) that his subjects, whom he addresses with familiar and friendly directness, can have had new burdens imposed on them only sporadically, but the districts he mentions as afflicted cover the whole country as far south as Thebes. The innovations were devised by nome officials, however, and so applicable only within individual nomes. By inventing new taxes the officials were able to produce the revenue required by their superiors.

One way the accountants had been wronging the tax payer (11) was by basing their assessment not on current income but on what had been taxable in previous years, whether the best of a run or an average over a period. This had applied in particular (12) to the Nile flood levels. The area of land inundated and so liable to tax was assessed not by inspection but by averaging out previous risings.

For the variation in the rise, see Pliny, *Natural Histories* 5, 58, and for the Nilometers that measured the floods IR 100.

Alexander devotes (13) and (14) to rebutting rumours that the territory originally assigned to the settlers at Alexandria in 321 BC was to become subject to tax, along with the land added to it by alluvial deposit.

Was Alexander dealing with a chronic state of affairs or had there been a deterioration? Nero's exactions are well known (Tacitus, *Annals* 15, 45L, 1ff.; Cassius Dio, *Roman History*, *Epitome of Book* 61, 5, 5), but Egypt had been exploited, particularly for her grain, ever since the Romans took over. Exploitation led to evasion, even to men fleeing their own estates. That in turn made it harder to find men able to carry the responsibility for extracting profit from the province in the form of tax; as the officials themselves were held responsible for the sums demanded they were naturally ruthless in exacting them. Alexander was trying to break a vicious circle with palliatives. Complaints decline in numbers after the date of the edict: that may be because conditions improved or because a settled political situation gave the victims less hope of redress. There would be no real change as long as the aim of exploiting Egypt remained dominant: and that is prominent in the edict itself.

In brief illustration two papyri will have to suffice, but see also **214** and **219**.

168. EJ 117; Greek; from Oxyrhynchus

[- - -], village secretary, son of [- - -] Eremus. [I swear by Tiberius Cae]sar the new Augustus, Imperator, son of the [deified Zeus the Liberator] Augustus, that I have [no] knowledge of anyone being shaken down in the region of the villages in question by the soldier [- - -] and his companions. [If I swear truly] may it go well with me, if I forswear myself [the reverse]. Twenty-third (year) of Tiberius Caesar Augustus, Mecheir 17th.

11 February, 37. The officials, with or without the connivance of the village secretary, had used a gang led by a soldier to enforce payment ('shake down') defaulters in a group of villages near Oxyrhynchus.

169. *P. Teb.* 2, 289; Greek

Apollonius, *strategus*, to Akous, toparch of Tebtunis, greetings. Send me immediately a supplementary classified statement of payments made up to date: then I shall know whether I am going to leave you in employment in the district or summon you and send you to the prefect for neglecting the collection. Farewell. 9th year of Tiberius Caesar Augustus, Mecheir 21st.

15 February, 23. The *strategus*, who has a Greek name, writes in peremptory style to the Egyptian village functionary (see on **167**, section (6) f.).

These documents illustrate the unenviable position of provincials and of officials constrained to 'shear' them (**166**). But it was not only in financial matters that officials could make mistakes through paying too much nervous attention to their master.

170. Philo, *Embassy to Gaius*, 299-302, Greek

Pilate was one of the officials appointed procurator of Judaea. This man, less to do honour to Tiberius than to irritate the mass of the people, set up gilded shields in the palace of Herod in the Holy City. They had no image or anything else forbidden on them, apart from the minimum of writing to indicate two things, the dedicator and the honorand. (300) But when the masses found out — and the enterprise was already notorious —, they put up as their representatives the four sons of King Herod, who enjoyed royal status and treatment, and his other descendants and their own authorities, and begged Pilate to put things right by going back on his innovation with the shields and not to infringe customs they had inherited from their ancestors which had previously been kept inviolate by kings and emperors alike from time immemorial. (301) Pilate, who was a man of unbending, arrogant and implacable character, refused point blank, and they shouted, 'Don't start a riot, don't cause a war, don't bring peace to an end! Dishonouring our ancient customs does no honour to the Emperor. Don't let Tiberius be your excuse for insulting our nation: he doesn't want any of our ways brought to an end. Or if you claim he does, you show us a decree, or a letter, or something like that, so that we can stop troubling you, choose envoys, and put our case to our master.' This last suggestion irritated Pilate most of all: he was scared that if they really did send an embassy they would impeach the rest of his governorship as well with a catalogue of his acts of bribe-taking, brutality, rapine, torture, outrage, a whole series of executions without trial, and his unremitting, utterly atrocious savagery.

Philo ends the story with an eloquent account of Tiberius' anger when he heard in a letter from the Jewish authorities what Pilate had done. But it is likely that Pilate's intention was to please the Emperor: he had also used money from the Temple Treasury to finance the building of an aqueduct to Jerusalem (Josephus, *Antiquities of the Jews* 18, 55ff.; *Jewish War* 2, 169ff.).

Exploitation for the state and for private enrichment both find a place in the story of Licinus cited at the beginning of this chapter. Domitian seems to have frightened off the merely greedy.

171. Suetonius, *Domitian* 8, 2

Further, he devoted such care to keeping domestic magistrates and governors of provinces under control that they have never shown more self-restraint or more sense of justice. Since his time we have seen men from these groups on trial for every kind of offence.

The claim that trials of former officials became more frequent after 96 is borne out by the evidence of Pliny the Younger, who was personally involved in trials arising from events in Spain, Africa and Bithynia (**59**). The prosecutions were not always straightforward: their outcome depended as much on the relations that a governor had been able to establish with a dominant group in the provincial assembly or with leading individuals in the cities as on the justice of the case.

When cliques of local magnates collaborated with a governor, ordinary provincials could only be the losers. Few were as articulate as Dio of Prusa, who compares the charges against him with those brought against Socrates — and throws light on the rearguard action taken by an offending proconsul of Bithynia with whom he is accused of being hand in glove.

172. Dio of Prusa, *Discourses* 43, 11f.; Greek

But the indictment against me was longer; dare I say grander? A covert affair, evidently: 'Dio stands guilty of failing to honour the gods either with sacrifices or with hymns, thereby abolishing our ancestral festivals; of exerting his influence on a criminal governor so as to get him to torment the people and exile as many as possible, actually to kill some of them by compelling them to commit suicide, because at their age they could not bear to go into exile or give up their native city. He stands guilty even now of collaborating to the full with the man who tyrannised over the province, ensuring (as far as it is in his power to do so) that he is successful in his struggle and will get the cities and their popular assemblies forcibly under his control; (12) and of attacking the people itself, getting up as an accuser and using his speeches and his tongue to wrong the citizens, his actual fellow-townsmen; and of doing a number of things which I am ashamed to speak of individually; and of making himself to young and old alike a model of idleness, extravagance and bad faith; and of offering bribes to the people so that nobody will confront him with what was done at that time but will let his hatred and scheming pass into oblivion.'

This speech, made by Dio not in court but to the people of Prusa, belongs to the first decade of the second century; the wicked proconsul he is accused of abetting is either Julius Bassus (**59**) or Varenus Rufus (Pliny, *Letters* 5, 20, etc.).

The workings of a provincial council, and manipulation of it by leading men of the province, may be seen from the other end of the Empire and more than a century later.

173. H.-G. Pflaum, *le Marbre de Thorigny* (Paris, 1948); marble statue base from Araegenuae of the Viducasses, Lugdunensis

(Front) To Titus Sennius Sollemnis, son of Solemninus, four times duovir without drawing lots, who held all offices and performed all public duties [- - -] in his community and at the same time as high priest of Rome [and Augustus at the altar] produced every kind of show; there were contests of gladiators totalling 32 in number, and of these over a period of four days a total of 8 were fought to the death. A bath-house, which Solemninus [- - -] had left in his will to be an amenity for his fellow-citizens in his colony [- - -], after laying the foundations he brought to completion; likewise he bequeathed [- - -] profit in perpetuity, from which it was to be equipped.

Sollemnis whom we honour was a friend of Tiberius Claudius Paulinus, praetorian legate of Augustus in the province of Lugdunensis, and his client; later he was his assessor when he was praetorian legate in Britain, with the Sixth Legion; Paulinus also sent him the stipend for his military service in gold, and other gifts much more valuable. He was the highly esteemed client of Aedinius Julianus, legate of Augustus in the province of Lugdunensis, who was afterwards prefect of the Guard, as is stated in the letter inscribed on one side of this monument. He also acted as assessor in the province of Numidia, at Lambensis (*sic*), to Marcus Valerius Florus, military tribune of the Third, Augustan, Legion.

To the magistrate with jurisdiction over the treasury of the iron mines, the three provinces of Gaul set up this monument, the first ever to a magistrate in his own community; the council of the community of the Viducasses gave the site. Set up on the 16th day of December in the consulships of Pius and Proculus.

(Right side) Copy of the letter of Aedinius Julianus, prefect of the Praetorian Guard, to Badius Comnianus, procurator and acting governor: Aedinius Julianus sends greetings to Badius Comnianus. When I was acting as praetorian governor of the province of Lugdunensis I noticed a number of worthy persons, including the man Sollemnis, a high priest native to the community of the Viducasses. I conceived a warm affection for him on account of the seriousness with which he holds to his principles and his honourable character. Furthermore, when certain persons who felt that, considering their records, they had been injured by my predecessor were attempting in the council of the Gauls to set in motion a prosecution based on the apparent agreement of the province, it was he, my friend Sollemnis, who stood out against their undertaking; that is to say he put in a plea to the effect that his native district, when it had elected him among others to be its representative, had given him no instructions about an action at law but quite the contrary had used terms of praise. By this means they were all brought finally to give up the prosecution. I have come more and more to feel affection and esteem for him.

This man, trusting himself to my high regard for him, has come to the capital to see me. On departure he requested me to give him an introduction to you: and so you will do the right thing if you acquiesce in his wishes. Etc.

(Left side) Copy of a letter from Claudius Paulinus, praetorian legate of Augustus in the province of Britain, to Sennius Sollemnis; [written] at Tampium. Although your deserts are too great for them, these things, few though they are, are offered you from me on the occasion of your appointment to office, and so I should like you to accept them with good will: a cloak made of wool from Canusium, a Dalmatian tunic from Laodiceia, a gold brooch set with jewels, two cloaks, a British tunic, a sealskin. As to the letter of appointment to a six-months' tribunate, I shall send it in the near future, as soon as there is a vacancy: the stipend for this service, namely 25,000 sesterces in gold, you are to take. With the favour of the gods and the sacred majesty of the Emperor to help you, you will directly attain rewards more worthy of the services that you have performed with such good will. In true accord.

On the front of the monument, which belongs to 238, the council of the Gauls mentions Sollemnis' relations with three high-ranking Romans; on the sides are confirmatory passages from letters written by the two who had governed Lugdunensis. Tiberius Claudius Paulinus (*PIR*[2] C 955) had been legionary legate in Britain and governor of Narbonensis before he went to Lugdunum. His escape from prosecution in 220 made it possible for him to reach the consulship and go on to govern Lower Britain, where Sollemnis joined him not as tribune but as judicial assessor at York. The knight Marcus Aedinius Julianus (*PIR*[2] A 113) was described on the front of the monument as legate but in Pflaum's view was acting-governor; he was prefect of Egypt in 222-3 and then prefect of the Praetorian Guard; it was on this appointment that Sollemnis came to congratulate him at Rome. All that was a decade and a half before the dedication of the monument; and the occasion of that in Pflaum's view was an effort by the current procurator of Lugdunensis, Furius Timastheus (*PIR*² F 581), to ingratiate himself with the two politicians and their *protégé* Sollemnis, who with the accession of Gordian III had returned to power.

Whether that is correct or not (and Timastheus must have needed other recommendations to become, as he did in 241, Gordian's father-in-law), the date of the monument is surely of political significance.

Sollemnis was currently holding a post in the gift of the council, one which showed how some of its activities were financed. But he was rich himself: Pflaum estimates the cost of the shows from which he is lauded at over 332,000 sesterces. His expenses as duovir of the Viducasses (cf. **86**) would have been little to him. Sollemnis, we are told, did not draw lots for the post. Pflaum explains this with a reference to **27** section 57; but in the third century it may mean that Sollemnis took the post on voluntarily (cf. **218**).

The tribunate promised in the letter of Paulinus but not mentioned on the front of the stone was one in command of the legionary cavalry at headquarters, and the stipend perhaps half that of a regular, annual, military tribunate (cf. Pliny, *Letters* 4, 4, with Sherwin-White 1966 (1)). Either Sollemnis never attained it and was paid the stipend in lieu, or its importance was eclipsed by his later posts as assessor.

As provincials advanced in the senatorial and equestrian orders some came to govern or collect taxes in their own or neighbouring provinces (so Tiberius Julius Alexander in Egypt, **167**). Their administration could benefit from local knowledge, but there was a dark side: they could be particularly prone to become involved in local disputes.

174. J. Reynolds, *JRS* 49 (1959), 96 no. 2; lines 8-13 Greek; marble stele in the Temple of Apollo, Cyrene

. . . (Year)142. Publius Sestius Pollio, son of Gaius Sestius Florus, descendant of Marcus Antonius Flamma; priest of Apollo, of senatorial family and quaestor at Rome, curule aedile, ex-praetor, legate of praetorian rank of Crete and Cyrene. (Year) 138 . . .

Into this running record of priests from 102 to 107, the name of the priest for 111 has been inserted (the dating is by the Actian era of 2 September, 31 BC). His ancestor Flamma is probably the man who in 70 was condemned for extortion in Cyrenaica and sent into exile (Tacitus, *Histories* 4, 45). Local feuds and their vicissitudes are seen on a wider stage, and even if Flamma was not the innocent victim of a rival faction in Cyrene, which was torn by strife (see **46**), his misdemeanours are not those of an alien imperialist but of a member of an oppressive native ruling class. Men were forbidden to govern their own provinces after the revolt of Avidius Cassius in 175 (Cassius Dio, *Roman History*, *Epitome of Book* 72, 31, 1), but the rule was made for the protection of Emperors rather than their subjects, and it was ignored when that was convenient.

The reliance placed on local communities, especially cities, in the Roman Empire was a weakness as well as a strength. If they were to provide the services demanded of them they had to enjoy an identity of their own and a measure of self-respect. Most had that; some of them, of which Athens is the most obvious example, were older and (they felt) more distinguished than Rome. While the upper crust in each society had attained Roman citizenship (if they wanted it) and felt due loyalty to Rome (see Chapter 7), the political horizon of the great mass was that of their native city.

175. Aelius Aristides, *Oration* 26, Panegyric on Rome, 97; Greek

It is as if the whole world were celebrating a festival. It has laid aside its old burden of steel, and has turned to self-adornment and all forms of merry-making; as well it may. And while all other types of rivalry have passed away from the cities, this one form of emulation preoccupies them all: how each one is going to appear as beautiful and attractive as it can. Everywhere is full of training grounds, fountains, imposing gateways, temples, workshops, schools; and one can speak with full knowledge of how the world, which has been in distress since ancient times, has been brought back to health.

Local patriotism meant local feuds. Inter-city quarrels over the land and supplies on which they depended had once issued in war. (Oliver rightly sees an allusion to Thucydides 1, 6, 1ff., who describes the Athenians as being the first to give up the habit of carrying weapons.) The old patriotism now found its outlet in investment in public buildings and amenities, salutary in itself, if not carried beyond what the city could afford (cf. **187**), but also in a preoccupation with privileges and titles, and the old feuds in verbal abuse, appeals to the Roman authorities, and occasional hooliganism.

176. Philostratus, *Lives of the Sophists*, 1, 24 (529); Greek

After that Marcus went to Megara, which had colonised Byzantium. The Megarians were giving all their attention to their feud with the Athenians, just as if the table of prohibitions against them had only recently been drawn up, and when the Athenians came to the Lesser Pythian Games they refused them admission. But Marcus spoke to them in their assembly and brought about such a conversion of the Megarians

that he persuaded them to open their houses to the Athenians and let
them mix with their wives and children.

Marcus traced his pedigree back to the original founder of
Byzantium; hence his powerful influence at Megara. The Athenians had
passed the notorious Megarian Decree at the beginning of the
Peloponnesian War, more than half a millennium previously.

Marcus was not the first well-disposed politician to try to persuade
Greek-speaking cities to give up their feuds. Dio Chrysostom had
addressed speeches on concord to the people of Tarsus (34, with several
cities of Cilicia), Nicomedia (38, with Nicaea), Prusa and Apameia
(41f.).

177. Dio of Prusa, Discourses 34, 14; Greek

At any rate the loathing and unrest of the people of Mallus ought to
make you less uneasy than it does. But these people of Soli and Adana
and others too perhaps are in the same state of mind, and are no more
inclined to restrain themselves; they feel oppressed, talk you down, and
would prefer to be subject to others. This fact gives rise to the suspicion
that perhaps the people of Aegeae and Mallus are not altogether wrong
to be angry either; that they are not alienated from you out of envy in
the one case and a greedy desire for material gain in the other, but that
perhaps there is something approaching the truth in the story about your
city somehow ill-treating people less powerful than it is and making
trouble for them.

This speech was delivered in about 100 (see Jones 1978 (9), 71ff.).
The dispute with Mallus was over territory that Dio calls worthless
(sandy coastland near the lagoon); like the dispute with Adana it was of
long standing. Another issue was whether Tarsus should remain the
centre of the assize district and seat of the provincial council, of which
the main attraction was the dignity it brought, with the business that
came too surely being an additional point.

178. The same, 47f.

So with the other cities too. I think that you should treat them with
kindness and care, with the idea of winning their respect, not as if you
hated them. If you do, everyone will be your willing follower and will
offer you admiration and affection; and that means more than that
Mallus should offer sacrifice and conduct its law-suits in your city. There
is no advantage to you whatsoever in the people of Adana or Aegeae
coming here to offer sacrifice; just vanity, self-deception, and silly,
useless ambition. (48) But good will and being seen to be exceptionally

worthy and generous, those are the things that are really good, those are worth competing for and taking seriously. And you had better pay attention to them: your present concerns are a laughing stock. And whether it is the people of Aegeae feuding against you or the Apameians with the people of Antioch or further afield the Smyrniotes against the Ephesians, the quarrel is 'over a donkey's shadow'; primacy and power are in other hands.

Fighting over a donkey's shadow seems already to have been proverbial in fifth-century Athens.

Plutarch offers an historical perspective that helps to explain the survival of inter-city rivalries.

179. Plutarch, *Precepts for Politicians* 17, 7f., 10 (Moralia 814 A-C); Greek

When we see small children trying to tie on their fathers' boots and playing at putting on garlands we laugh. But city magistrates foolishly tell the people to imitate the deeds of their forefathers, their ambitious schemes and courses of action that are out of keeping with things as they are at the present time, and put ideas into the heads of the masses. What they do may be laughable, but what happens to them is no laughing matter any more, unless they are treated as negligible. (8) It is not as if there weren't a number of other stories about the Greeks in earlier times for people nowadays to recount and so to help form character and teach sense: at Athens a man might refer not to anything to do with war, but for example to the amnesty decree passed after the fall of the Thirty. (9) . . . (10) These are things that men can emulate even now and become like their forefathers; but the battles of Marathon, the Eurymedon, and Plataea, and all the models that give the masses inflated ideas and fill them with unrealisable ambitions they should leave to the schools of the sophists.

Note the comparison between Greek politicians of Plutarch's day (he wrote the *Precepts* between 96 and 114: see Jones, *JRS* 56 (1966), 72) and children, as in **183**; we have seen the Romans comparing their subjects with sheep (**166**).

Plutarch approves an historical example that shows the mildness of the restored Athenian democracy (403 BC) rather than the victories over the Persians of 490, 479, 478 BC, and concord rather than discord (see **175f.**). For the fate of nationalistic politicians he has just cited the execution of one Pardalas of Sardis whose enmity with Tyrrhenus had brought down Rome's anger.

Only when war broke out did pent-up hatreds find open expression.

180. Tacitus, *Histories* 4, 50

His next action was to settle the quarrel between Oea and Lepcis. It had begun in a small way, with the peasants making off with each other's crops and animals, but was now being carried on in a series of pitched battles. The people of Oea, who were less numerous, had called in the Garamantians, a tribe that had never been conquered and inexhaustibly given to plundering its neighbours. As a result the Lepcitanes grew short of supplies; their territory was devastated far and wide and they cowered behind their city walls, until the auxiliary infantry and cavalry units were brought in and the Garamantians were put to flight. All the plunder was recovered except what the Garamantians had taken with them as they made their way through remote encampments and sold to those still further off.

Valerius Festus, legate of the Third, Augustan, Legion in Africa, was mopping up in the aftermath of the civil war of 68-70; Oea and Lepcis were, with Sabratha, the three cities that gave Tripolitania its name.

181. The same, 1, 65

The recent war had inflamed a longstanding feud between Lugdunum and Vienna. A number of reverses were suffered by either side in the fighting, which was too intense and too bitter for a mere struggle over Nero and Galba. Besides, Galba had used the excuse of his displeasure to divert the revenues of Lugdunum to the imperial Treasury, by contrast conferring great distinctions on Vienna. That gave rise to rivalry, and loathing bound them to enemies who were separated from them only by a single stream. So the people of Lugdunum began to egg on individual soldiers and urge the destruction of Vienna: they reminded the men that their colony had been put under siege by the people of Vienna, that Vindex's rebellion had been abetted by them, and that legions had recently been enrolled from them to ensure Galba's safety. And when they had provided the men with a good excuse for hatred they proceeded to reveal how much booty there would be. At this point they gave up buttonholing individuals in favour of appeals from the whole community to the soldiers to go and take revenge by rasing the town that was the source of war in Gaul: everything to do with it was alien, hostile; the people of Lugdunum, a Roman colony, were an integral part of the army and shared its fortunes, good and bad; if fate were turning against them it should not leave them to enraged enemies.

The mutual hostility of Lugdunum and Vienna, 30 km lower down the Rhône, went back to the Triumviral period: Lugdunum had been founded as a colony in 43 BC, for Italian refugees from the Allobroges, whose capital Vienna was (Cassius Dio, *Roman History* 46, 50, 4). Vienna had lived down the offence and was itself a colony (**24, 159**). In 68 Lugdunum, seat of the procurator, had been loyal to Nero; Vienna had followed the rebel governor Julius Vindex and provided him and his candidate Galba with troops. Like the Rhine legions, Lugdunum had backed a losing horse in Nero. Now they were out for revenge. In the event, the prayers of Vienna's inhabitants and a tip of 300 sesterces for each soldier saved them: they were disarmed and compelled to contribute supplies to the army.

In later civil wars, and elsewhere in the Empire, there were comparable outbreaks of hostility.

182. Herodian, *Histories* 3, 2, 7-9; 3, 3; Greek

But when the story of Severus' victory spread, unrest and a spirit of contention immediately became rife among the cities in those provinces. It was not so much that they felt any hatred or enthusiasm for the warring Emperors as because of their mutual jealousy and quarrelsomeness: they resented men of the same race as themselves and wanted to destroy them. (8) This is a long-standing misfortune of the Greeks . . . (9) and so in Bithynia, immediately after the events at Cyzicus, the people of Nicomedia attached themselves to Severus; they sent envoys welcoming his army and promising to put everything at his disposal. Conversely, the people of Nicaea, out of hatred for the Nicomedians, favoured the opposite course and received the army of Niger, whether they were fugitives who had taken refuge with them or men sent by Niger to garrison Bithynia . . . (3, 3) . . . The same rivalry and hatred broke out in mutual struggles in Syria and Phoenicia, where respectively Laodiceia hated Antioch and Tyre loathed Berytus.

These events of the civil war between Septimius Severus and Pescennius Niger (193-4), which followed Niger's defeat at Cyzicus, turned out badly for Laodiceia and Tyre in the short run: Niger let his Moorish spearmen loose on them. But after his final victory, Severus rewarded both of them (see G. Downey, *A History of Antioch in Syria* (Princeton, 1961), 241). Material benefits for Laodiceia included new buildings, the Italian right (**64**), becoming capital of the new province of Coele Syria and, most satisfactorily, receiving the supervision of the new 'village' of Antioch; its mint also became the chief eastern mint. These privileges conferred prestige; so too did the title metropolis, which Antioch lost. Similarly we find Nicomedia bearing the title 'Severianic' in the third century. But feud with Nicaea, like that between Tyre and Berytus, did not end in the third century: they were still at loggerheads at the Council of Chalcedon in 451, when the issue was the rights over bishoprics conferred by the status of Metropolis (see L. Robert, *Harvard*

Stud. Class. Phil. 81 (1977), 1ff.).

Inter-city quarrelling, even in peacetime, was thought to have a destructive effect, as Dio told the people of Nicomedia.

183. Dio of Prusa, *Discourses* 38, 33-8; Greek

But you must also try to inculcate respect for you in the provincial governors by invariably making it clear that is is not enough in your eyes for you alone to be well-governed, but that you care for the entire Bithynian people and take wrongs done to others as much amiss as those done to you; and that if people place themselves under your protection and ask for help, your prompt support is given to all alike. All this is what will secure you genuine primacy, not your struggle with Nicaea over titles. (34) But I should like the Nicaeans to behave in the same way. So they will, if you are reconciled, and your power will be enhanced when it is combined: if you come together you will control all the cities, and if governors are bent on misconduct they will have more to fear from you and more to give them pause. But as it is now the other cities are excited by your quarrel: it makes you seem to need them, and the truth is that you do, because of your struggle with each other . . . (35) So that while you are fighting about primacy, the probability is that primacy lies with them, the people you are courting . . . (36) As for how things stand with the governors, what need is there to say anything when you know? Or don't you realise (I suppose it is possible) the autocratic power that your feud puts at the disposal of those who govern you? The man who wants to ill-treat the province comes knowing what he has to do to avoid paying the penalty: either he takes to the Nicaean clique and has that party on his side or he chooses the Nicomedians and is protected by you. And while he seems to care for one party or the other he cares for neither, but wrongs them all . . . (37) They have convicted you of folly in open court, and they treat you like children, who are often offered the most trivial things instead of what is worth most . . . So it is with you. You don't get justice, or protection for the cities from being plundered and for individuals from having their property confiscated, protection from their outrages against yourselves, from their drunken escapades; instead they offer you titles and have called you 'First', either orally or in writing, after which they can treat you last for the rest of time with no danger to themselves. (38) Things of that kind, on which you pride yourselves, are spurned by everyone who has a proper sense of values, but they are a particular source of mockery among the Romans and, what is even more insulting, they are referred to as 'Greek foibles'.

A governor who needed the protection of one city or group of cities would have to connive at the misdemeanours and oppression of the ruling circles in those cities.

184. Ulpian, Opinions, Book 1, in *Digest* 1, 18, 6, 2 and 5

It is part of the sacred duty of the provincial governor to ensure that men of superior power inflict no wrong on persons of lower standing; also that they do not persecute these men's defenders with malicious prosecutions when they are innocent . . . (5) The provincial governor shall ensure that persons of slender means are not harassed and ill-treated, as by the confiscation of their only means of lighting (or, only slave) or their scanty furniture for the use of others, on the pretext of the arrival of civil authorities or troops.

At the same time, as the provinces assumed greater importance in the eyes of Rome's rulers, supplying not only taxes but manpower at all levels (see **159ff.**), the status of their ruling classes increasingly became a matter of concern too, and the distinction between men of standing and those of inferior status as important as, if not more important than, that between citizen and non-citizen.

That citizens were subject to the capital jurisdiction of governors and could only appeal against it was argued by Garnsey 1968 (4), who cited a veto imposed by Hadrian on executions of members of city councils (*Digest* 48, 19, 15), except those guilty of parricide. They were exempt from all degrading punishments.

185. Ulpian, Duty of the Proconsul, Book 10, in *Digest* 48, 19, 9, 11f.

Those pretty well are the penalties that are normally imposed. But in fact it must be understood that there are distinctions between penalties and that the same penalty cannot be inflicted on all alike. Above all, members of city councils cannot be sentenced to work in mines, to labour connected with mining, to the fork or to burning alive. And if it should come about that they are being punished under a sentence of this type, they will have to be set free. This however cannot be effected by the authority who passed the sentence; rather he ought to refer the matter to the Emperor, so that the penalty may be modified or the man freed on his authority. (12) The parents and children of councillors are in the same legal position.

The sharp class stratification that obtained and was encouraged all over the Empire made oppression likely at all levels, each class taking out its wrongs on those below (the wives of Egyptian *fellahin* had nothing to beat but their donkeys). There were means of rising in the economic and social ladder, and certain pivotal positions, such as the centurionate and tribunate in the legion, that gave access to higher status in local and Roman life. But that was for individuals, and even then too speedy a rise (as of a freedman to political influence with the Emperor), caused resentment among their new peers. Classes kept a jealous hold on their privileges, wealth and power (cf. **150**).

186. Dio of Prusa, Discourses 34, 21-3; Greek

Leaving aside the council, popular assembly and the young men's and elders' associations, there is a body of no mean size which is virtually outside the constitution; some people have come to call them 'linen-workers'. And sometimes they find them a nuisance and say they are a mob that they could do without, responsible for the turbulence and disorder here, while at others they reckon them to be part of the city and reverse their judgement of them. If you think these people are doing you harm causing civil strife and upheaval, you ought to expel them altogether and not let them into the meetings of your popular assembly; but if you consider them in a sense to be citizens, not only in virtue of residing here but because most of them were born here and know no other city, then it is surely not right to deprive them of political rights or sever them from yourselves. (22) As things are it is inevitable that they should have become alienated from the interests of the community as a whole, when they are criticised and regarded as outsiders. There is nothing more damaging to cities than this, nothing more likely to provoke civil strife and discord . . . (23) 'What do *you* tell us to do, then?' Enrol them all as citizens, is what I say, and with the same privileges; not criticise them and disown them, but consider them as part of yourselves, which is what they are. If a man puts down 500 drachmas that can't mean that he is devoted to you and has instantly become worthy of citizenship; and if a man has failed to get the title of citizen, either because he is poor or because some registrar of citizens has omitted him, even when not only the man himself was born among you but his father and his forefathers too, that can't mean that he is incapable of affection for the city and of regarding it as his homeland, and if a man works in linen that he is worse than anyone else, his work should be thrown in his teeth and he should be abused for it, while if he is a dyer, leather-worker or carpenter it is quite wrong to criticise those activities.

The assembly is significant at Tarsus. De Ste Croix 1981 (11), 313f., remarks on the declining part it seems to have played in city life, with the last recorded activity of any significance coming from Pisidian Antioch at the end of the third century. He points out that no provision for an assembly is made in **23**; but there may have been informal meetings of the people at Tymandus before the desired council was set up. The decline of the assembly is certainly an index of the increasing exclusion of ordinary people from any formal role in politics.

The entry fee at Tarsus was high enough to keep out other than linen-workers; probably it was required only from citizens brought in from outside (Mackie 1983 (2), 90 n.7). The name 'linen-worker' was probably applied to members of a guild rather than generically to the lower classes at Tarsus. There is increasing evidence for organisations of workers elsewhere (see Jones 1978 (9), 81 with n.77). Guilds, of which the Ephesian silversmiths are the best known (*Acts of the Apostles* 19, 24ff., cited by Jones), could apply effective political pressure. How widespread restrictions on membership of the assembly were is uncertain: see Jones 1940 (1), 173f., with n.35, and Mackie 1983 (2), 48f., nn.4 and 7.

Not mere political privilege but actual survival was sometimes at stake. In time of famine it was the rich and powerful (city-dwellers too, as De Ste Croix 1981 (11), 13f., remarks) who controlled supplies of what grain there was (see **107**). Ruling circles were expected to invest surplus profits in benefits to their cities, very often of a substantial kind (**86f.**) But the obligation was often fulfilled half-heartedly, inefficiently, or even fraudulently, especially when public funds were being spent.

187. Pliny, *Letters* 10, 37f.

Gaius Pliny to the Emperor Trajan. The people of Nicomedia, my Lord, have spent 3,348,000 sesterces on an aqueduct that has been abandoned unfinished and is actually in ruins. In a second effort two hundred thousand sesterces have been allocated to another pipeline, and now that this too has been given up they need to spend more money so that the people who have misspent these enormous sums may have water.

(2) I have personally gone to inspect the extremely pure spring from which the water should evidently be carried, as in the original undertaking, on a construction of arches, so that it reaches beyond the flat, lower parts of the city. A very few arches are still in position; some can be built from the squared stonework that has been taken from the earlier construction; some of it in my opinion will have to be made in brickwork; that will be easier and cheaper.

(3) But my prime need is for you to send me a hydraulic engineer or an architect, so that the same thing that happened before does not recur. I can assure you of one thing: that the usefulness of the undertaking and its elegance are thoroughly worthy of your reign.

(38) Trajan to Pliny. Measures must be taken to ensure that water is brought to the city of Nicomedia. I have no doubt that you will tackle this work with the scrupulous care that it demands.

But I really must say that it is part of your job to investigate with equally scrupulous care whose fault it is that the Nicomedians have wasted so much money in the past. We don't want the fact that they have begun aqueducts and then abandoned them to hide mutual back-scratching. So whatever you find out, bring it to my attention.

If Pliny discovered any culprits in the closed ruling circle where there was nobody to check collusion between contractors and council officials it does not appear in the extant letters. His request for experts is ignored, and another in the following letter (on a theatre and gymnasium at Nicaea and bath at Claudiopolis) turned down on the grounds that experts were to be found in the eastern provinces. But, as Sherwin-White points out, aqueducts were developed in Italy and were only beginning to be provided in Asia Minor.

Further evidence that public money was not safe in the eastern half of the Empire is provided by a whole series of documents, beginning with the edict of Fabius Persicus (Smallwood, *Gaius-Nero* 380), that represent attempts to secure endowments by invoking governors and, eventually, the Emperor.

188. MW 500; Greek, from Acmonia

[- - -] and that six freedmen appointed by Praxias to his monument are to share in the distribution and to [?participate on an equal basis]; and that there are to be counted in the [place] of those deceased, persons who are of their descent to the number of six. The feast is to take place on the festal day of the month Panemus, and from the revenue from this endowment roses to the value of twelve *denarii* are to be borne to the monument of Praxias by the city magistrates and the secretary of the council. The council and all the persons appointed to the annual magistracies are to provide for the freedmen and are to make sure that no part of this monument or the plants or buildings round it are damaged or alienated in any way whatsoever.

This decree of the people has become law and is to be maintained for as long as the hegemony of the Romans shall last, and nobody shall have the power to change any part of what has been decreed or amend it or divert it to any other purpose in anyway whatsoever. All persons jointly and severally are to provide for the maintenance of the decrees passed by common consent and inviolate in accordance with the disposition made by Titus Praxias: 'and for me alone is it permissible to change anything inscribed in the decree or to correct anything or to make arrangements additional to those inscribed'.

It is particularly provided in all the decrees that only councillors who are present and taking part in the feast may have a share in this distribution, calling collectively and individually upon the deified Augusti and our ancestral deities, Zeus Stodmenus, Asclepius the Saviour, and Artemis of Ephesus, to witness and oversee and act as protectors of what has [thus] been decreed. The secretary of the council and priest Asclepiades is called upon also after his current year of office to take care in perpetuity of the [?gifts] and dispositions made by Praxias, just as he was called upon [by Praxias] to do.

The duty of drafting the decree fell on Ponticus the son of Diophantus, Hecataeus the son of Ponticus, and Alexander [- - -]. It was passed (or, validated) on 5 March in the eleventh (consulship) of Domitian Caesar Augustus Germanicus, in the [year 16]9 of our era, on the thirteenth day of the month Xandicus, [and was inscribed] by the hand of Hermogenes, public slave.

The date, carefully given in Roman and local forms, is 85 (the city used an era dating from Sulla's reorganisation of Asia, 85-4 BC; cf. **174**). Opinions differ as to the extent of the governor's (and even of the Emperor's) involvement in ensuring the security of Praxias' endowment; the former has been thought of as 'validating' the law: see Levick 1982, 53ff. But there is no doubt of the benefactor's anxiety. Governors and Emperors were certainly involved on other occasions (Smallwood, *Gaius-Nero* 380). Each city or provincial council acted on its own precedents; but it was natural for stronger sanctions to be brought in as weaker ones failed.

189. J.H. Oliver, *Hesperia* 21 (1952), 381ff.; 22 (1953), 966ff.; Greek, from Eleusis in Attica

Declaration of the prefect Severus: I too [approved] the public-spirited action [he performed] towards the gods. [If anyone] ventures to disturb any of the [consecrated] funds, a sum twice [the amount] shall be claimed for the Treasury from the person who committed this offence, as someone [liable to punishment] for sacrilege. The high priest and hereditary torchbearer in particular shall take overall charge to prevent this capital endowment from [ever] being put at risk and the quantity of money [consecrated] ever being diminished by a single denarius, on the clear understanding that if they overlook the [disturbance] of these arrangements it shall [by no means] be with impunity as far as they are concerned.

C. 135-40. Oliver explains this endowment as the gift of a wealthy Cretan benefactor of Athens and the shrine at Eleusis.

It was misuse of public money that led to the creation of a new office under Domitian (R. Syme, *JRS* 67 (1977), 38ff.), that of public curator: an occasional appointment held very often by a senator or other notable not connected with the city involved (Burton 1979).

190. Ulpian, Monograph on the Duty of the Public Curator, in *Digest* 50, 9, 4, Introduction and 1

Decrees of city councils passed for effect should be invalidated. (1) Accordingly, when then they have indulged in their usual practices, of discharging someone from a debt or enriching him, whether they have determined to confer either lands, buildings, or a certain sum on a person out of public property, nothing decreed along these lines shall be valid.

The failure of public enterprises is illustrated in **187**; gifts promised by dignitaries as a return for office or honour (**87**) might be withheld, and reneging was common enough to become the subject of a whole section of the *Digest* containing excerpts from the same monograph.

191. Ulpian, in the same work, *Digest* 50, 12, 1, Introduction and 1-3

If someone has undertaken to construct works for a community or to give it money the gift will not be subject to interest; but if the donor has begun to cause delays, interest accrues, as our Emperor, along with his deified Father, has replied. (1) It must be understood, however, that the man who has given the undertaking is not always bound by it. If indeed he has given it in consideration of some office which either has been or is intended to be decreed him or for another legitimate reason, his promise will be binding on him; but if he has no reason for his undertaking he will not be held to it. And that is a provision made in many imperial decisions both old and new. (2) Likewise if he has no reason for his undertaking but has begun to carry it out the man who has begun to carry it out is under an obligation. (3) We understand him to have 'begun' if he has laid the foundations or cleared the site. But even if the site has been set aside for him at his request, the balance is in favour of his being deemed to have begun; likewise if he has placed materials or funds in the public Treasury.

Distinguishing regular entry fees from sums offered in consideration of an appointment (theoretically voluntary and normally larger), Mackie 1983 (2) 93, n.19, argues that the latter too might be offered in response to informal pressure (she cites *Digest* 50, 12, 6, 3: attempts to intimidate men into providing statues), and that the survival of charges does not mean that individuals willingly undertook the office (she cites *Catalogue of Greek Papyri in the Rylands Library* 2 (Manchester 1915), 77).
Curators of lower rank were sometimes designated by cities to perform the same function for themselves and for villages within their jurisdiction.

192. Aphrodisias 57; Greek

Good fortune! Marcus Ulpius Appuleius Eurycles, designated high priest of Asia, of the temples in Smyrna, for the second time, sends greetings to the magistrates, council and people of Aphrodisias. It was your wish that I made provision also for the funds necessary for the contests, both because of your devotion to the most mighty Emperor Marcus Aurelius Commodus Antoninus Augustus, and to preserve the memory of those who made the bequest, and out of regard for the reputation of the city; members of the Synod had also already frequently approached me, and this department too I have not left unregulated, acting on the same principles as in my curatorship and with the same keenness.

Until the present time the institution of the contests has not been achieved: the sums provided needed to grow in order to meet both the intentions of the late founders and the scale of the fund from which the contests are due to be produced.

Now the contest provided by the will of Flavius Lysimachus has reached a capital endowment of 120,000, making it possible for the four-yearly musical contest to be provided from that sum as the testator wished. The resources beyond the 120,000, which are out on loan, and the interest that has accrued to these sums up to the beginning of the year make a total of 31,839 *denarii*. You can therefore put on this contest at the beginning of the year, with good fortune, on the basis of prizes worth one talent and competitions to match the prizes. The time appointed for the subsequent occasion and the next four-yearly event will be the period from the games of Barbillus [held] at Ephesus to those of the [?commune] of Asia. [Farewell].

Eurycles, a native of Aezani, had been president of Hadrian's Panhellenic League centred on Athens in 157, curator of the council of elders at Ephesus *c.* 162 (an appointment of the proconsul of Asia), twice high priest of Asia, and curator of Aphrodisias (*OGIS* 504-7); the present document dates to 180-90. He must have been well known in the Greek world and was presumably of equestrian rank. As Aphrodisias was a free city it should have been at its request that he was appointed curator (but cf. Pliny, *Letters*, 8, 24, 2). In a communication belonging to that appointment he found evidence of misapplication of funds (*Aphrodisias* 62); on the present occasion delay in instituting the games was due simply to the need to let the trust funds build up. That process was complete as far as Lysimachus' fund was concerned: Reynolds calculates at 6 per cent compound interest, with another small sum accounting for the 343 *denarii* additional to the 31,496 that four years would produce; that would make it possible to offer five prizes of a talent each (for celebrations of these contests, starting in 182 or 183, see *Aphrodisias* 59f., *MAMA* 8, 501 and 519). Eurycles also made sure that subsequent celebrations did not clash with other contests elsewhere.

Many failings illustrated in this chapter, Roman rapacity and brutality, the impotence or dishonesty of local officials, and collusion between the two, went back into the Republic. With the system unchanged, they could not be abolished, only checked. Three reforms in the system might have gone some way to remedy them: a speedy and permanent shift in the attitude of Emperors towards their 'sheep'; recognition of the responsibilities of cities and tribes in a widening of their freedoms; and a broadening of the base on which the constitutions of the cities themselves rested, so as to include a wider section of the population in running them.

As it was, the existing failings led to discontent and rebellion, which might be no more than a nuisance or might, in a time of crisis, endanger the existence of the Empire. Perhaps more serious was any threat to the income of members of the classes that were involved in government, if it made them find that the status that office conferred was beyond their means.

11

Resistance

The metamorphosis of the Roman Empire from an imperial into a class structure is noticed by Aelius Aristides, who is left to explain how the lower classes felt about it.

193. Aelius Aristides, *Oration* 26: Panegyric on Rome, 65f.; Greek

No envy sets foot in the Empire. You yourselves have set the example of how to avoid it by making everything available to all and providing those who are capable of it with a chance of taking their turn at ruling, not keeping them as subjects. Accordingly no hatred develops on the part of those who are outdistanced; since political life is open to all and it is as if it were being carried on in a single city, it is only to be expected that the rulers treat the ruled not as aliens but as their own people. Further, all the common masses in the Empire need have no fear of the powerful man among them: they can have recourse to you; but if they venture to cause a disturbance swift is the anger and vengeance visited on them by you. (66) So it is only natural that the present state of affairs is both pleasing and advantageous to rich and poor alike and there is no other way of life left.

For a minor instance of action taken against trouble-makers we may turn at once to an inscription dealing with bakers at Ephesus.

194. AJ 124; Greek, found near Magnesia on Maeander, Asia

(a) [- - -] and in accordance with agreements [- - - so that] it happens from time to time that the people are thrown into disorder and rioting by the reckless, [?misleading] rhetoric of the bakers' factions in the market place, for which they ought already to have been arrested and brought to justice. But since the city's welfare must be given higher priority than punishing these men, I have thought it best to bring them to their senses with an edict. Consequently I order the bakers not to meet as an association and not to become the ringleaders in reckless behaviour. They are in every respect to obey those appointed to defend the interest of the community and are to supply the city with a reliable baking service. Whenever from now on one of them is caught attending a meeting contrary to the proclamation or initiating any riot or factional disturbance he shall be arrested and punished with the appropriate penalty. If a person plotting against the city goes so far as to go into hiding he shall in addition be marked ?by branding with the word 'decuria' on the foot and the man who shelters such a person shall be subject to the same penalty.

(b) In the presidency of Claudius Modestus on the 4th day from the commencement of the month Clareon, at an ?extraordinary meeting of the council, Marcellinus said: 'A prime instance of the lunacy of the shop foremen was given yesterday by Hermias, the man attached to [- - -].'

Towards 200: edict of the proconsul of Asia and decree of the council of Ephesus. The main offence of the bakers was provoking riot; striking is inferred from the phrase about 'supplying a reliable service', but is only an inference (absence from work could have been incidental to the rioting). The cause of the trouble is uncertain: see Buckler 1923, 32. He explains the word 'decuria' as a reference to the corps in which the proconsul's lictors, who were responsible for the branding or (tattooing), were enrolled: *ILS* 1914.

With Rome and Italy primarily in mind, Augustus revived Caesar's law banning all but old-established and respectable associations (Suetonius, *Deified Augustus* 32, 1; Z. Yavetz, *Julius Caesar and his Public Image* (London, 1983), 85ff.). New clubs might be licensed by the senate, and those that were unlicensed were liable to be closed down. For *ad hoc* bans on potentially subversive associations in the provinces, see Pliny, *Letters* 10, 34 and 96, 7; the law was taken to apply throughout the Empire.

195. Marcianus, Institutes, Book 3, in *Digest* 47, 22, 1, Intro.

In the imperial instructions governors of provinces are enjoined not to allow the existence of fraternity clubs; nor are troops to have clubs in the camp. By decree of the senate persons of modest means are allowed to make monthly contributions, provided however that the meetings take place only once a month. But they are not forbidden to assemble for religious purposes, provided however that this does not result in anything happening in contravention of the senatorial decree banning unlicensed clubs (this is to prevent an unlicensed club meeting on a pretext of this kind). The deified Severus too issued a reply to the effect that this applied not only in the city but also in Italy and the provinces.

In *ILS* 4966 (Augustan) we have an association of Roman bandsmen claiming to be licensed by the senate, in 7190 (Antoninus Pius) a decree of the senate granting the petition of Cyzicus for its corps of young citizens to be recognised, and in Smallwood, *Nerva-Hadrian* 165 (136) the rules of a burial club at Lanuvium which quote from the senatorial decree on the subject in the same words as Marcianus; the text of the *Digest* is translated as arranged and supplemented by Mommsen (the clause in brackets may not be authentic).

Taxation and debt were constant factors in disaffection and rebellion in the Roman Empire, where the victims did not try to ease their difficulties by mere tax evasion, further borrowing or flight. But the Gallic revolt of 21 was overtly nationalistic and it was begun by leading men of the tribes concerned.

196. Tacitus, *Annals* 3, 40-6 (excerpts)

The same year the tribes of Gaul, who were heavily in debt, started on a rebellion. The keenest instigators of it were Julius Florus among the Treveri and Julius Sacrovir of the Aedui. (2) Both men were of high descent and their ancestors had performed good service; for that reason the Roman citizenship had long since been conferred on their families, at a time when that was an uncommon reward and given only for merit. (3) They held clandestine meetings to which they summoned the most aggressive men or those who, because of poverty and fear brought about by their vicious behaviour, had the strongest compulsion to crime. The agreement was that Florus should raise the Belgae, Sacrovir the less distant Gauls. (4) So at public gatherings and private meetings they began to deliver rebellious harangues about the unremitting taxation, the burden of debt, the brutality and arrogance of their governors, claiming also that the troops had been restive ever since they heard of Germanicus' death. (5) It was an excellent moment to reclaim their freedom: they need only consider how prosperous they were and how poor Italy, how useless the populace of Rome was in a war, with men recruited outside Italy the only sound element in the army.

(41, 1) There was hardly a tribe that was not contaminated by the germs of that outbreak, (2) but the first to burst into open revolt were the Andecavi and Turoni. The legate Acilius Aviola summoned the cohort stationed on garrison duty at Lugdunum and put down the Andecavi, (3) while the Turoni were suppressed by legionary troops, again under the command of Aviola, that Visellius Varro, the legate of Lower Germany, had sent, and by some Gallic chieftains who supplied reinforcements to hide their own disaffection and disclose it to greater effect later . . . (4) . . . (42, 1) Meanwhile Florus was pressing on with the plans by trying to induce a squadron of cavalry, which had been recruited from the Treveri and was being trained in Roman fighting methods and discipline, to open hostilities by massacring Roman business men. A few of the troopers were led astray, but the majority remained loyal to their duty. (2) Another mass of men, debtors or hereditary clients, took up arms. They were making for the mountain forest known as the Arduenna when the legions from both the armies, which Visellius and Gaius Silius had put in their way, blocking their route, kept them off. (3) Julius Indus, who came from the same tribe as Florus and, being a personal enemy of his, was the more eager to play an active part, was sent on ahead with a body of picked men and routed what was still a disorganised mob. (4) Florus gave his victorious opponents the slip and they could not find where he was hiding, but eventually, when he saw troops in position blocking his way of escape, he killed himself. That was the end of the disturbance among the Treveri.

(43, 1) The Aedui were a tribe with greater resources and the means of putting them down had to be brought from further away; their rising was on a correspondingly more massive scale. Sacrovir had occupied the tribal capital, Augustodunum, with units of armed men, so as to attach to his cause the flower of the young Gallic aristocracy, engaged there in acquiring a liberal education, and, through using them as hostages, their parents and kinsmen. He lost no time either in distributing to the men of an age to bear arms the weapons he had secretly forged. (2) They numbered forty thousand men, of whom a fifth were armed as legionaries, while the rest had spears, knives, and the other weapons that hunters use. (3) In addition there were men from the slave population, men intended for the profession of gladiator, who were clad from head to foot in steel after the national fashion: the Gallic word for them is 'crupellarii' and although they are ill-adapted to striking blows they are invulnerable when they are hit. (4) Those forces were increased by men from the neighbouring tribes; no open agreement had been reached between them, but there were individuals who were eager supporters . . . (44) . . . (45, 1) Meanwhile Silius was advancing with two legions. He sent ahead auxiliary units and devastated the country belonging to the Sequani, who lived on the outer edge of Gaul, shared a boundary with the Aedui, and were their comrades in arms. (2) His next target was Augustodunum . . . (3) Twelve miles out of the town Sacrovir and his forces put in an appearance on open ground. He had placed his steel-clad troops in the van, his regularly armed men on the wings, and the semi-armed in the rear. (5) He was among the leaders, going up to each of them on his magnificent horse, reminding them of the glorious achievements of the Gauls of old and all the defeats they had inflicted on the Romans, how splendid freedom would be if they were victorious, how much the more unbearable slavery if they were defeated again. (46, 1-5) . . . The Roman cavalry spread round the flanks while the infantry broke the van, not that there was much resistance on the wings. (6) The men in steel armour caused a minor delay while the plates held out against javelins and swords; but the soldiers seized axes and picks and cut through armour and bodies as if they were breaking down a wall . . .

(7) Sacrovir, accompanied by the men closest to him, went hastily first to Augustodunum then, afraid of being betrayed, to a house in the country not far away. There he died by his own hand, while his companions cut each other down. They set light to the house over their own heads and were all consumed in the flames.

Gallic social structure is clearly seen in this account: the noble still has his clients who are expected to be faithful unto death (Caesar, *Gallic War* 6, 13, 2; 19, 5; 7, 40, 7, cf. **173**). In the social changes that the Roman occupation accelerated (loans for capital development or to pay taxes were evidently an important factor, affording profits for Italian money-lenders), some nobles were ruined and took their dependants with them.

As social and economic conditions became more stable the lower classes are occasionally found acting on their own: they had least to gain from the supremacy of Rome.

197. Tacitus, *Histories* 2, 61

With the fates of great men hanging in the balance, I must apologise for relating the story of a person called Mariccus, one of the common people of the Boian tribe. He had the temerity to intervene in the course of events, claim divine powers, and challenge the armed might of Rome. In his character of Gallic liberator and god (that was what he made himself out to be), he had got together eight thousand men and was proceeding to terrorise the neighbouring country of the Aedui, when that soundest of tribes used the cream of its young men, along with reinforcements of a cohort from Vitellius, and routed the mob of fanatics.

Mariccus was taken in the battle, and when in due course he was thrown to the wild beasts and not torn in pieces the simple-minded crowd began to take him to be inviolable — until he was executed under the eyes of Vitellius.

An episode of the years of civil war and rebellion, 68-70; by 69 the nationalistic sentiments roused by the unsuccessful revolt of Vindex were beginning to stir. The Boians had been settled between the Loire and the Allier (Caesar, *Gallic War* 1, 28, 5); their conquerors, the young men from Augustodunum, were probably the successors of those who had been at work there in 21: they were aristocrats (evidently with arms at hand, cf. **41**) meting out punishment to a recalcitrant peasantry, and Mariccus' penalty was adapted to his class (see Paul in *Digest* 48, 19, 38, 2): a man of higher standing would have been deported to an island, in time of peace at any rate.

Aelius Aristides' rosy picture (**193**) must be rejected. In sporadic outbreaks of violence Roman citizens often fell victim, not surprisingly, as they represented two types of oppression; those of an upper class and of a ruling power (cf. **46**). But that does not mean that it is appropriate to apply the term 'class struggle' to the pre-industrial ancient world in any sense that is acceptable in common English, where it implies self-conscious classes.

The 'nationalist' element seen in Gaul often had a religious component, detectable not only in Mariccus' uprising but in the prophecies of doom made by the Druids in 70 (Tacitus, *Histories* 4, 54). The Druids had good reason to loathe Roman rule, under which their rites had first been forbidden to Roman citizens, then banned altogether (Suetonius, *Claudius* 25, 5). The pretext was the barbarity of its practices (human sacrifice), a more pressing motive perhaps its connection with the resistance and its hold on the lower classes, where it lived on after the upper classes had given it up as outmoded.

198. *The Augustan History, Life of Alexander Severus*, 60, 6

As he set out a Druid woman shouted at him in the Celtic language: 'On your way! But you needn't hope for victory! And don't trust yourself to your soldiers!'

This was one of the omens that led up to the assassination of Alexander Severus by his Rhine troops in 235. The anecdote shows the Druidical art of prophecy still alive, the prophecies unfavourable to Severus and couched in the native language.

Nationalism and religion were at one in the Jewish Zealot movement, with wealth, class and origin playing a dominant role in determining the membership. As the revolt of 66 got under way, insurgents occupied the Temple and excluded the sacrifices made there daily on behalf of the Emperor, while the upper part of Jerusalem was occupied by loyalists supported by members of the family of Herod the Great. Fighting went on for seven days.

199. Josephus, *Jewish War* 2, 425-7; Greek

On the next day it was the Feast of Wood-carriers, on which it was the custom for everyone to bring wood to the altar so that the fuel supply for the flame, which is kept perpetually burning, would never give out. They shut out their opponents from the ceremony, but enlisted a large number of *sicarii* (that is the name they gave to the brigands who kept knives concealed in their clothing), who had pushed their way in with the unresisting mass of people, and became bolder in their handling of the attack. (426) The royalists, who were inferior in numbers and morale, were forced to yield the upper city to their opponents, who stormed it and set fire to the residence of the high priest, Ananias, and to the

palaces of Agrippa and Bernice. (427) After that they began to carry fire
to the archives: they were keen to destroy the bonds of the money-
lenders and to bring debt-recovery to an end, with the double object of
winning over a mass of debtors to themselves and of setting the poor
against the rich, from whom they would now have nothing to fear. The
officials in charge of the record office had fled, and they set fire to it.

August 66. The *sircarii* were the followers of descendants of the Judas
who had organised resistance in AD 6 (**60n.**); these were the defenders
of Masada. The fact that they carried their weapons concealed (thus
keeping the element of surprise) does not lend support to the view that
the Romans disarmed their provinces. Other evidence is against that
view (cf. **196**), and the Romans would have found it difficult to enforce
such an order. The *sicarii* seem to have acted as urban terrorists, while
the Zealots operated in the country (E. Schürer, *The History of the
Jewish People in the Age of Jesus Christ* 2 (ed. G. Vermes, F. Millar *et
al.*, London, 1979), 598ff.).

200. The same, 4, 138-40; 147f.

Fresh brigands from the countryside came into the city and attached
themselves to the tougher men inside, after which there was no atrocity
that they left undone. (139) Mere raids and highway robbery did not
mark the extent of their audacity: they went as far as murder, not at
night or secretly or perpetrated on casual victims, but openly, in broad
daylight, and beginning with the most distinguished people. (140)
Antipas was the first that they arrested and imprisoned, a man who
belonged to the royal family and was one of the most powerful men in
the city, so much so that he was entrusted with the public treasury . . .
(147) The result was that the people reached such a point of grovelling
terror, and the insurgents of frenzy, that even the election of the high
priest fell into their hands. (148) They discounted the claims of the
families from which the high priests had successively been appointed and
set up undistinguished men of no family, so as to have accomplices in
their acts of sacrilege.

The Zealots under John of Gischala won control of Jerusalem in the
winter of 67-8 (Schürer, *History* 1 (1973), 496.

201. The same, 7, 437-42

The frenzy of the *sicarii* also took hold of the cities round Cyrene, like a
disease. (438) An utter villain called Jonathan, who was a weaver by
trade, had slipped through to Cyrene and persuaded a fair number of the
poor there to join him. He took them out into the desert with a promise
that he would show them signs and apparitions. (439) The only people

who noticed these transactions of the charlatan were the prominent Jews of Cyrene, who reported his 'Exodus' and the accompanying set-up to Catullus, the governor of the Libyan Pentapolis. (44) He sent soldiers, mounted and on foot, and easily overcame an unarmed crowd. Most of them were killed in the fighting, but some were actually taken prisoner and brought before Catullus. (441) The ringleader in the plot, Jonathan, got away for the moment, but there was a lengthy and extremely careful search all over the country and he was caught. When he was brought before the governor he contrived to escape retribution himself while providing Catullus with a pretext for injustice: (442) his lying story was that it had been the wealthiest of the Jews who had instructed him in his scheme.

This happened in the aftermath of the Jewish revolt, 72-3. Note Josephus' attention to the man's humble occupation. The end of the story was, according to him, that the governor executed 3,000 well-to-do Jews to have a 'Jewish war' of his own to win and confiscated their property to the imperial treasury to ensure that his action was acceptable to Vespasian. Josephus himself was incriminated alongside other reputable Jews of Alexandria and Rome on a charge of having supplied Jonathan with money and weapons, but Vespasian and Titus acquitted him. Catullus escaped with a reprimand (but died of disease), while Jonathan was tortured and burned alive (see **197n.**).

Egypt, where disruptive racial and economic factors reinforced one another, was also a place where revolt, when it was allowed to break out, took savage forms.

202. Cassius Dio, *History of Rome*, *Epitome of Book* 72, 4; Greek

And the people in Egypt known as Herdsmen rose in revolt and, under a priest called Isidore, made the rest of the Egyptians revolt as well. They began by dressing up in women's clothes and deceiving the Roman centurion into thinking that they were women of the district who meant to give him gold as ransom money for their husbands, and when he came up to them they cut him down. The man who was with him they sacrificed, took an oath over his entrails, and ate them; (2) but Isidore surpassed all his companions in courage. Next they defeated the Romans in Egypt in a pitched battle, and were not far from capturing Alexandria itself, but Cassius was sent from Syria against them. His strategy was to damage the good relations they had with one another and to separate one group from another: they were so desperate and so numerous that he did not dare to attack them when they were united. So he got the better of them by setting them at loggerheads with one another.

This revolt begun by natives of a district in the Delta belongs to 172-3. The trouble must have begun before the account opens, perhaps with non-payment of taxes; the people are not destitute, but the gold the 'women' had may have been their dowries in the form of personal ornament. The revolt must have reached considerable proportions to have defeated the Egyptian legion. Not only Roman authority was the target of their hostility; these *fellahin* were also bent on attacking Alexandria (for the contrast between that city and the countryside, see **135**, **167**), and their desperate need for unity is shown by their binding themselves together by committing the ultimate social crime — cannibalism (for another such act in Egypt, fifty years earlier, see Juvenal, *Satires* 15, 35ff.).

Aristides was right in one respect: there was no alternative way of life in the Empire, as Tacitus underlines when he sneers at the empty superstition of the Druids' prophecy (*Histories* 4, 54). Resistance took on the tinge of fantasy: bookish speculation among such sections of the upper class as were not reconciled to Rome; and hagiography and wishful thinking amongst the lower.

203. Livy, *History of Rome* 9, 18, 6

But there was another danger, which the most superficial of the Greeks made a habit of discussing (they even back the reputation of the Parthians against the fame of Rome!): that the Roman people would have been unable to hold out against the majestic name of Alexander — of whom in my view the Romans knew nothing, not even by repute.

Livy, in his account of the year 319 BC, written early in Augustus' reign, takes the opportunity to defend Rome against Greek ill-will (Bowersock 1965 (9), 109ff., suggests that it was the ill-will of other Greek intellectuals as well as that of Timagenes of Alexandria, an historian who fell foul of Augustus); the next item shows the defiance of a much later Greek of Alexandria, who is sustained by a sense of his own moral and social position.

204. Musurillo, *Acts of the Pagan Martyrs*, XI: The Acts of Appian (Greek)

((a), col. 2). Appian said, '[- - -] who, [- - -] sending (?) wheat to the rest of the cities, sell it for four times the price to recover what they have paid.' The Emperor asked, 'And who is it who takes the money?' 'You', replied Appian. The Emperor: 'And you are convinced of this?' Appian: 'No, but it is what we heard.' The Emperor: 'You ought not to have made this story public before you were convinced. Guard!' Appian caught sight of a corpse as he was led off and said, 'Corpse, when I get to my home country I'm telling Heracleianus ((b), col. 1) my father and [- - -]' As he was saying this he turned round, saw Heliodorus, and said,

'Heliodorus, not a word to say as I am led off?' 'Who is there to talk to', replied Heliodorus, 'when we have no-one to hear us? Go, my son; make an end. You have the glory of having met your death for your most beloved native city. Don't be distressed.' (Col. 2 [- - -] 'I charge you [- - -] The Emperor called him back. 'Don't you know now', he asked, 'to whom you are talking?' Appian: 'Yes, I do: I am Appian talking to a tyrant.' The Emperor: 'No, a monarch.' Appian: 'Don't tell me that! It was right and proper for your father, the deified Antoninus, to be Emperor: first of all, do you hear, he cared for philosophy, secondly he didn't care too much for money, thirdly he cared for everything good; you have the opposite qualities: you are dictatorial, care nothing for the good, and have no education.' Caesar ordered him to be led away. As he was being led off Appian said. 'Just this (col. 3) one request grant us, Lord Caesar.' The Emperor: 'What is it?' Appian: 'Give orders for me to be led to execution in the dress of my rank.' The Emperor: 'Granted.' Appian picked up his headband and put it on his head, and putting his special shoes on his feet he shouted out in the middle of Rome: 'Roll up, people of Rome! Have a look at a gymnasiarch in a million and envoy of the Alexandrians being led to execution.' The veteran officer in charge instantly ran and reported to the Emperor: 'My Lord,' he said, 'are you going to take this lying down? The Romans are grumbling.' The Emperor: 'What about?' The Consul: 'About the Alexandrian (col. 4) being led to execution.' The Emperor: 'Let him be brought back.' When Appian came in he said, 'Who is it who has called me back again just when I was paying my respects for the second time to my own death, and to those who died before me, Theon and Isidore and Lampon? Was it the senate, then, or you, you robber baron?' The Emperor: 'Appian, we do have some experience of bringing raving lunatics to their senses. You talk just as long as I want you to talk.' Appian: 'By your guiding star, I am not raving and not a lunatic: I am speaking up for my high rank and (col. 5) [for my privileges].' The Emperor: ['How so?'] Appian: 'I speak as a man of high rank and a gymnasiarch.' The Emperor: ['Are you claiming then that we] are not of high rank?' [Appian: 'That] I don't know; what I am speaking up [for is my own] high rank and [the privileges that belong to me.' The Emperor:] 'Don't you know now that [- - -]?' Appian: ['If you really don't know that, I shall tell you. [First Caesar] saved Cleopatra [- - -] took control of the monarchy and, as some claim, borrowed [- - -].'

This document is one of a series recounting the heroism of Alexandrian patriots in the face of Roman authority in episodes that stretch at least from the reign of Gaius to that of Commodus (Musurillo suggests that anti-Roman feeling among upper-class Alexandrians diminished when the city was granted a council by Septimius Severus (Cassius Dio, *Roman History* 51, 17, 3)). Appian, who may be related to the historian of the same name, accuses the Emperor Commodus (who is 'experienced' and in Musurillo's view close to the end of his Principate) of being involved in profiteering, in the grain trade if the text is correctly restored, but papyrus is another commodity that has been suggested. Heliodorus might be the son of the rebel Avidius Cassius (see **202**), while Isidore and Lampon were executed after a famous hearing under Claudius in which relations between the Greek and Jewish communities at Alexandria were the issue (Musurillo IV; and see **120**; for Theon, see his p. 103 and V.A. Tcherikover and A. Fuks, *Corpus Papyrorum Judaicarum* 2 (1960), 106). Appian's emphasis on his high birth and status as a gymnasiarch has suggested that, although he was not a Roman citizen, he was protesting against the summary execution of a person of standing; but he may be insisting only on the validity of Alexandrian rank in a Roman world, nationalism compounded by a sense of cultural superiority.

With Rome's power so great and no other way of life remaining (**193**), some fantasies involved Rome's only serious rival, Parthia.

205. *Sibylline Oracles* 4, 130-48 (Greek)

But when from cloven earth of Italy
Upswirling fire attains broad heaven above,
Consuming many cities, killing men,
When glowing cinders fill the spacious air,
And raindrops fall from heaven red as ruddle,
Then you may know the rage of God above
To slay the blameless race of men devout.
Then, war awakening, strife shall westward come,
And Rome's exile, his mighty sword aloft,
Shall cross Euphrates with his myriad hordes.
Doomed Antioch! City shall they never call
You, once you fall in folly to those spears;
By plague shall Cyrrhus die and direst battle.
Alas, unhappy Cyprus! Whirlwind-tossed
You'll sink below the sea's broad tidal wave.
Great wealth shall come to Asia, pillaged once
By Rome to stock a wealthy house; and more
Than twice as much shall she give Asia then,
And then there shall be war, a glut of war.

The reputation of the Sibylline oracles treasured at Rome attracted forgers. Fourteen books survive, Jewish-Hellenistic in inspiration. Book 4 was composed in about 80: It alludes to a disastrous earthquake in Cyprus of 76 or 77, and to the eruption of Vesuvius (79) as a punishment for the destruction of Jerusalem. The 'exile' is Nero; several imposters claiming to be him appeared in the east (Suetonius, *Nero* 57, 2; cf. Tacitus, *Histories* 2, 8, of AD 69). Nero was a philhellene, and if his rapacity made him an object of fear to the upper classes (in Tacitus Asia is 'terrified' of his return) that might make him more attractive to the lower.

Christians also dwelt on the return of power to the east and on the prophecies of the Sibyls and other authoritative sources.

206. Lactantius, *Divine Institutions 7: The Good Life* 15, 19

Hystaspes too, who was king of the Medes in very ancient times, and from whom the river now called Hydaspes took its name, passed on to generations to come a marvellous dream in which a boy with prophetic powers was involved: long before that race born of Troy was founded, he predicted that the Roman Empire and the Roman name would be swept off the face of the earth.

When the dream (or nightmare) of invasion from the east materialised in the third century, there were some ready to help the enemy.

207. Ammianus Marcellinus, *History* 23, 5, 3

What happened was this: an actor of mimes had been brought on at Antioch to give stage plays with his wife. He was presenting scenes from everyday life and there was total silence: the people were enthralled by the artistry of the performance.

'Either I'm dreaming,' his wife cried out, 'Or the Persians are here.' The audience turned their heads as one man and scattered in all directions to avoid the weapons flying down on them from the citadel. So the city was set alight and a large number of people who were wandering quite far afield, as they well might in peace time, were slaughtered, the neighbouring countryside was burned and plundered, and the enemy made their way home unscathed and laden with booty. Mareades, who had rashly brought them in to the destruction of his fellow-citizens, was burned alive. These events took place in the time of Gallienus.

In the Persian invasion which led to the capture of Valerian in 260 the Syrian Mareades, who was a member of the city council of Antioch, was made a puppet Augustus. According to an anonymous continuation of Cassius Dio (*Frag. Hist. Graec.* 4, 192), the respectable classes of Antioch fled the city, but the masses stayed: some of them were well-disposed towards Mareades, others were glad of any revolution.

12

Crisis

The fifty years 235-85 are presented by writers, ancient and modern, as bringing the Roman Empire close to destruction through a combination of invasion by Persians and Goths, internal political upheaval involving a rapid and violent turnover of Emperors, and economic decline, including uncontrolled inflation. Certainly these were years in which troubles came thickest, fastest, and in most striking forms — the capture of the Emperor Valerian by the Persians, for example. But allowances have to be made for the tone taken by ancient writers (see Alföldy 1974); the archaeological evidence does not tally with the black picture they paint (see King and Henig 1981). Further, the problems had been long in building up; and they were not all solved when the period came to an end.

In the eyes of one Roman senator, close to the centre of power in the first part of the third century, change had begun long before, in the reign of Marcus Aurelius.

208. 'Cassius Dio, *Roman History*, *Epitome of Book* 72, 36, 3f.; Greek

All the same, he was not as fortunate as he deserved to be; he was not physically strong and he encountered a host of problems practically all through his reign. But my own admiration for him is the greater for these very reasons: he both survived himself and preserved the Empire in extraordinary and untoward circumstances. One thing alone, then, marred his personal happiness: that having given his son the best possible upbringing and education, he was utterly disappointed in him. This must be the next subject of this narrative, as our history now falls away, as affairs did for the Romans of that time, from a realm of gold to one of iron and rust.

The difficulties that Marcus faced were primarily in his struggles with tribes on the Danube frontier (he died at Carnuntum), the Marcomannic wars arising from movements amongst the tribes (which were to culminate in the invasions of the Goths half a century later); but there was also a war with the Parthians and the plague brought back by troops who returned from it. His *Meditations* show his efforts to achieve personal tranquillity in the face of an Emperor's responsibilities (see Brunt, *JRS* (1974), 64, 1ff.). Dio, however, is more concerned with the failings of Commodus, especially in relation to the court and the senate: for a vivid incident of 192, in which Commodus as a gladiator threatened the senators among the spectators, while Dio suppressed his hysterical laughter by chewing leaves from his garland, see 73, 21, 1f.

Already in 222 the Emperor himself was pleading hard times.

209. *SP* 2, 216, with W. Schubart, Archiv für Papyrusforschung 14 (1941), 44ff.

(Col. 1) [Proclamation of Imperator Caesar Marcus Aurelius Severus Alexander, son of the deified Antoninus Pius the Great (Caracalla), grandson of the deified Septimius Severus Pius], Pious and Fortunate Augustus, [Supreme Pontiff, holder of tribunician power], consul, Father of his Country: [- - -], (col. 2) so that they are not forced into more than they can afford in order to demonstrate the joy they feel at my coming to power. That is how I came to conceive this plan. I was not without precedents, either, and among them my intention was to follow the example of Trajan and Marcus (Aurelius), who, besides being my own forbears, are Emperors who have proved themselves most particularly worthy of esteem; it is in order to claim precisely their position that I form my present resolve so that, if there had not been the obstacle of the inability of state funds to cope with current demands, I should have given a much clearer demonstration of my generosity and should even have had no hesitation in remitting both any revenue still owing from the past from this type of contribution and all the sums that we had previously been voted under the title of crown gold for my proclamation as Caesar or that we were still to be voted by the cities for this purpose. But these I think I cannot remit, for the reasons I have given a little above. On the other hand I have not failed to notice that they are all that the cities, as I see from present conditions, are able to pay [- - -].

For that reason let all persons in all the cities both in Italy and in the other territories know that I remit to the cities the sums of money due in lieu of golden crowns on the occasion of my coming to power as Emperor, an accession endorsed by the wishes and prayers of all men. They are to know too that I am doing this not because I have wealth and to spare but in pursuit of the policy I have adopted [- - -] ?in spite of my own difficulties, to make up the decline, not by ?devising new taxes (or, by acquisitions of territory) but by restraint, even though expenditures have virtually encroached on my private property: there shall be no desire on my part to demand funds, but rather to contribute to the advancement of the Empire by humanity and acts of beneficence, so that governors and those who have been sent to procuratorships by me, and whom I have sent only after the most rigorous process of scrutiny and selection, might likewise take the counsel afforded by my [station in life], to conduct themselves with the utmost moderation. For the governors of provinces are likely to understand more and more the full extent of their obligation to show unflagging consideration and care for the provinces of which they have been put in charge, if they are enabled to see the Emperor himself administering imperial affairs with such decorum, sobriety and self-restraint.

The magistrates in each city are to ensure that copies of this my edict are posted without fail in public so as to be visible to readers. (Year) 1, 30th day of Pauni.

24 June, 222. Alexander had already received crown gold (**75**) when he became Caesar the preceding summer (**128**): two charges in one year would have been excessive, and Alexander made the most of relief he had to grant.

In the third century incessant wars and civil struggles raised the cost of maintaining the army, always the main burden on imperial resources (**74 ff.**), beyond measure, and efforts to control the Empire and secure revenues added to expenditure by multiplying the numbers of officials active in the Roman world. That the army was perceived as the main burden is shown by the following passage.

210. *The Augustan History, Probus 22, 4-23, 3*

Let anyone who wishes now compare the twenty years of Trajan or of Hadrian; let him compare the era of the Antonines, which lasted about the same time — that is why I say nothing about Augustus, whose years in power can hardly be equalled by the human life-span; the wicked Emperors I pass over in silence. That saying of Probus, thoroughly well-known as it is, is enough by itself to show what he hoped to have achieved: he said that it would not be long before soldiers became redundant. (23, 1) Probus knew what he could do, he had no fear of barbarians or usurpers. (2) What a blazing outburst of joy there would have been if his reign had seen an end of the military! No provincials would be providing rations, no pay would be deducted from the largesse due to the people, the Roman state would keep its reserves indefinitely, no paying out for the Emperor, no tax demands for land-holders. In short, he was promising a golden age. (3) There were going to be no camps; nowhere was the sound of the trumpet going to impinge on us; the manufacture of weapons could come to an end. That mass of men under arms that now harasses the state with civil wars would be at the plough, or bent on scholarly pursuits, or learning a trade, or sailing the seas — with the bonus that none of them would be killed in war.

Probus was a disciplinarian who met his death after putting his troops to work planting vines: see Eutropius 9, 17, and Aurelius Victor, *Caesars* 37, 3f.

211. *RIC* 5, 2, 87 no. 652; Pl. 4, 3: Aurelianus of Probus

Obverse: Legend: Imperator Gaius Probus, Pious and Fortunate, Augustus. Radiate bust of the Emperor, left, holding sceptre surmounted by eagle.

Reverse: Legend: Concord of the Soldiers. The Emperor standing, facing right, clasping the hand of Concord; $\dfrac{\text{I}}{\text{XX I S}}$

Probus' well-founded nervousness about the troops is shown by this issue insisting on their acquiescence in his rule. The legend 'Concord of the Armies' had begun, significantly, on gold and silver of Nerva in 97 (*RIC* 2, 223, no. 2f.), the year in which he was joined in power by the military man Trajan; related legends had occurred, equally significantly, in the 'year of the four emperors', 69 (see B. Levick, *Scripta nummaria Romana*, eds. R.A.G. Carson and C.M. Kraay (London, 1978), 228).

The coin was struck at Siscia (S), a mint established by Gallienus after the invasions of Suebi and Sarmati and the rise of the Illyrian usurpers in the late fifties; it replaced the mint of Viminacium, south-east on the Danube. Siscia, situated at the confluence of the Sava and the Kulpa, had been a colony since Flavian times, had good communications with Italy through Emona, and was close to the mines of Dalmatia and Moesia (A. Mócsy, *Pannonia and Upper Moesia* (London, 1974), 208); it was to become one of the main imperial mints of the third and fourth centuries.

The mark XX I, 'twenty (sesterces) to one', like the radiate crown, distinguishes the coin as an '*aurelianus*', devised by the Emperor of that name and minted alongside the two *denarius* '*antoninianus*' originated by Caracalla; in spite of being tariffed at five *denarii* it was less than twice the weight of the *antoninianus*. MacMullen 1976, 110ff., sets the new coin in the context of the ending of the local eastern city small currency coinages in the seventies of the third century, by which time they were vastly under-valued against the imperial coinage; the imperial 'silver' took their place in supplying small currency. In MacMullen's view the importance of the *aurelianus* lay in the value stamped on it: the government had come to grips with the idea of fiduciary currency.

Ever-increasing costs led to debasement of the *denarius* and to inflation. The rate of debasement, negligible to *c*. 150, ran (with temporary leaps) at about $\frac{1}{2}$ per cent *per annum* until the death of Caracalla, was at 1 per cent until 238, and then rose to nearly 3 per cent (Walker 1978 (5), 142 fig.15). By the 260s there was runaway inflation.

Depreciation of the currency made taxation in kind preferable (from the collectors' point of view) to taxation in cash. In the following passage Brunt 1981 (5), 170, detects the origin of the regular tax of the late Empire, the 'military provisioning' (*annona*).

212. Modestinus, Replies to Queries, Book 6, in *Digest* 26, 7, 32, 6

Lucius Titius, joint heir with his sister, of whom he was also guardian, came from a community in which it had been the practice for the actual owners of estates, not the tenants, to meet the burden of provisioning and emergency contributions, and he himself had followed this established practice, which was a custom uniformly prevailing, when he provided grain both from the property he had inherited and from that which he shared with his sister. My question is whether it can be objected when he renders his accounts as guardian that he had been out of order in incurring expenses of this kind on his sister's behalf. Modestinus replied that the guardian of a grown woman may enter for the purpose in question up to a maximum of the amount the woman herself would be compelled to provide if she were administering her own affairs.

Modestinus was active in the first half of the third century, and the practice, originally intended only for emergencies, is made out to be well-established by the time he gave his reply. Indeed, this particular tax, or perhaps not a specific tax but simply supplies received as taxation in kind when they were intended for the army (see Birley in King and Henig 1981, 1, 43), seems to have been in operation since the reign of Marcus Aurelius, as MacMullen 1976, 272, n.3, argues from the following passage.

213. Scaevola, Digests, Book 5, in *Digest* 13, 7, 43, 1

Titius received a loan of money from Gaius Seius on the security of some wine skins. While Seius had the skins in his storehouse a centurion sent on provisioning duty carried them off as provisions and they were later recovered at the insistence of Gaius Seius, the creditor. My question is whether Titius the borrower or Seius the creditor ought to take responsibility for the incidental damage that arose out of the operations.

For the jurist and adviser to Marcus Aurelius Q. Cervidius Scaevola, see **157**; the names Lucius Titius and Gaius Seius are legal fictions, like the American John Doe.

214. AJ 199; Greek

Aurelius Ptolemy, also known as Nemesian, *strategus* of the Oxyrhynchite nome: since the public officials have met and have accused the bankers of the banks of exchange of having closed them because they are unwilling to accept the sacred currency of the Emperors, it has become necessary that an injunction should be issued to all owners of the banks to open them and accept all currency, except what is completely misstruck and counterfeit, and give change for it; not only to them but to all who are engaged in business transactions in whatever way. They are to know that if they do not obey this injunction they shall experience the penalty that the greatness of the prefect has ordained on previous occasions. Signed, in the first year, on Hathor 28th.

24 November, 260: the Emperors are probably the usurpers Macrian and Quietus in their first (and only) year; their coinage would be particularly dubious, but the prefect has dealt in the past with the same problem of banks closed by their owners.

Rising costs had a very serious consequence for the Empire: the running down of city life and a disinclination on the part of local dignitaries to play their part in sustaining the imperial apparatus. Their expenses had always been high, but so had been the rewards.

215. Smallwood, *Nerva-Hadrian* 215; Greek, from Ancyra, Galatia

Gaius Julius Severus, descendant of King Deiotarus and of Amyntas the son of Brigatus and Amyntas the son of ?Dyrialus the tetrarchs and of King Attalus of Asia; cousin of the consulars Julius Quadratus, King Alexander, Julius Aquila and Claudius Severus; kinsman of a very large number of senators; brother of Julius Amyntianus; leading member of the Greek community; he held the high priesthood and excelled in acts of largesse and the other forms of beneficence all who have ever sought honour by that means; during the same year he provided a continuous supply of olive oil in the concourse of the people; he also held office as priest of Augustus and was the first and only priest to make a gift of the resources traditionally belonging to the priesthood for the benefit of the city instead of using this fund for olive oil [as] all his predecessors had done; he also held the offices of archon, giver of games, and market supervisor, and made his wife a high priestess who likewise was outstanding for her acts of largesse; he entertained the armies that were wintering in the city and escorted on their way those that were passing through to the war against the Parthians; he lives a life of justice and equity and the tribe Paraca[- - -], the seventh, under the tribal presidency of Varus Logius, did honour to their benefactor.

Julius Severus was descended from the dependant rulers of Galatia who flourished in the late Republic and under the principate of Augustus and through them from Attalus II of Pergamum (220-138 BC). For his consular cousins see Halfmann 1979 (9), nos. 17 (Quadratus of Pergamum was consul in 94 and 105), 25 (the former king in Cilicia), 37 (Aquila, from Sardis, was consul 110) and 39 (Claudius Severus came from Pompeiopolis and was consul in 112). Severus himself entered the senate under Hadrian (Halfmann 62); his exceedingly high rank and wealth imposed the greatest obligations, even to entertaining Trajan's legions on their way to the east in 113-14. In the third century the incessant movements of the legions were a burden on the countries through which they passed which must have been hardly tolerable either to the lesser dignitaries who would have had to contribute to their support, or to ordinary people who could have found all they had carried off.

In Egypt, the last details of supplies for Caracalla's visit were prepared, and sureties had to be found for the men held responsible for supplying his entourage (cf. **75**).

216. *P. Got.* 3; Greek

To Aurelius Diogenes, *strategus* of the Panopolite Nome, from Aurelius Kolleetios, son of Akes and Senkales, fisherman of Phenebythus. I acknowledge that voluntarily and of my own free will I am standing surety for Psais, son of Psais and Sekos, fisherman nominated for the preparation of fish sauce, fine preserved fish, and fresh fish with a view to for (*sic*) the most glorious (or, much prayed for) visit of our Lord Imperator Caesar Marcus Aurelius Severus Antoninus, Greatest Parthicus, Greatest Britannicus, Greatest Germanicus, Pious Augustus, and I swear by the [Good Fortune] of our Lord to produce the aforementioned person. If [I do not] I myself shall be amenable [for all] that shall be required of him. In the 24th year of Imperator Caesar Marcus Aurelius Severus Antoninus, Greatest Parthicus, Greatest Britannicus, Greatest Germanicus, Pious Augustus.

The undertaking was given in 215-6 by a resident of Phenebythus, a riverside district of Panopolis. By an ironic slip, the writer misspelt the word for 'liable', making it mean 'rather cheerful', *hypeuthynus* becoming *hypeuthymus*; it is here rendered 'amenable'.

In the second century come the first signs that the price of office was too high. Already Plutarch could put forward the blessings of abstention.

217. Plutarch, *On Exile*, 12 (*Moralia* 604B); Greek

'We hold no office; we are not even members of the council, nor do we put on games.' Against that you can set this: 'We are not involved in political wrangles; we have no expenses; and we are not stuck to the doors of the governor; we don't care at all now who has been allotted the province, whether he is irascible or demanding.'

Eventually voluntary tenure of office became a thing to note.

218. *IGR* 4, 1525, from Sardis; Greek

The council and people and the council of elders honoured Tiberius Claudius Julianus, son of Tiberius, of the Tribe Quirina, the father, and his sons, the blessed Claudius Diomedes and Tiberius Claudius Chaereas; their father was a fine man who was twice general, garland-bearer, and master of the gymnasium, and who with eager generosity volunteered to perform the functions of the most important offices of state and the other public duties for his native city; the sons were fine men, unassuming, serious, self-restrained, cultivated and devoted to their native land and to their father; they honoured likewise Tiberius Claudius Crispus Tatianus: the men discharged the great majority of the offices of state and the public duties with brilliance and distinction, showed eager generosity in their tenure of the secretaryship and were responsible for organising the triumphal games.

The last-named man must be the uncle of the deceased youths. The inscription must belong to the late second century. Note that the magistracies are referred to as a kind of 'public duty'. ('Triumphal' games were those given high international standing by the Emperor, and the victors were allowed a triumphal entry into their native cities: see Jones 1940 (1), 232.)

Men qualified for office but unwilling to take it on found themselves under pressure. In Egypt the city councils granted by Septimius Severus were held responsible for the appointments and indirectly for the performance of the duties that the local officials had to discharge for the Roman government.

219. *P. Oxy.* 1415, lines 17-31; Greek, from Oxyrhynchus

When communications from [-]phesus concerning the [- - -] had been read, [- - - after the reading the president said], 'Men already committed to a public office were also assigned to others.' The councillors said, ['- - -'

The president said], 'Fill the office. Give [- - -]. Name the man you want.' Members of tribe [- - - spoke. Eudaemon the adviser said],

'Ptolemy [?cannot] cope with a public office; this for [- - -] refer all of it for something else with the most onerous [- - -] public offices', and [Ptolemy] the high priest, [son of Damarion], said 'I beg you, I cannot. I am a person of moderate means, I am living with my father.' [The president] said, 'Ptolemy still needs encouragement from you: like the others he [?is avoiding this duty], important as it is'. Eudaemon the adviser said, 'Ptolemy is also a person of moderate means, and he cannot [sustain] the burden.' [Ptolemy] the high priest, son of Damarion, said, 'The office is beyond me.' The president said, 'Even if [Ptolemy] is engaged in another office [he cannot] refuse you where that of the public banking is concerned. But it is clear that it is not permissible [- - -]'. The councillors said, 'Trustworthy, faithful Ptolemy! Sureties for him [- - -.' Ptolemy] the high priest, the son of Damarion, said, 'I beg of you, I can't [undertake two public offices] at one and the same time.' [Eudaemon the adviser said, 'Ptolemy] has often given proof of his good will.' The president said, 'I [put] him [forward] for your consideration.' The councillors said, 'Ptolemy will not refuse his tribe [- - -']. Eudaemon the adviser said, 'You chose him because you could rely on him.' (col. 2) The president said, [- - -].

Late third century. This attempt to elect the luckless Ptolemy to the position of banker (which other candidates had evidently avoided by pleading poverty) is discussed by Bowman 1971 (2), 101. The president (*prytanis*) rules that a man may hold two public offices simultaneously, then Ptolemy's tribe nominates him their candidate and eventually the president forwards the nomination, without any interval, as Ptolemy was present (cf. 26 section 51). Bowman points out that the question is not settled by the end of the fragment: Ptolemy's ally the adviser (exegete) is probably still alluding to his appointment as high priest, which Ptolemy had hoped would excuse him from further municipal burdens (for these duties, see also A.H.M. Jones, *Cities of the Eastern Roman Provinces* (2nd edn, Oxford, 1971), 481, n.26).

Even outside Egypt what comes to be called the curial class (*curia* is the word for the local council and its house) came to be hereditary and service obligatory.

220. Ulpian, Opinions Book 2, in *Digest* 50, 2, 1

As to members of city councils who are proved to have abandoned their home in the community to which they belong, the governor of the province is to ensure that they are recalled to their native soil and perform the appropriate duties.

There were legal grounds for exemption, including age or the cultivation of imperial estates, which were direct suppliers of the government (Callistratus, in *Digest* 50, 6, 6(5), 11). That helps in part to explain the way the peasants on an estate near Ağa Bey Köy in the province of Asia were treated in the first half of the third century.

221. AJ 142; Greek, from near Philadelphia, Lydia

[- - -] to see as they pass [- - -] and so that there might be some specious reason to be left behind as a justification for their outrageous behaviour, they arrested nine men and put them in chains. They said they were escorting them to your most excellent procurators, as the most excellent Aelius Aglaus is also acting as governor. And when they had exacted more than a thousand Attic drachmas as a price for his safety they set free one of the nine; the others however they kept in the chains and we have no clear knowledge, most divine of Emperors, whether they will escort these men alive to the most excellent Aglaus, (or) dispose of them too, very much as they did the previous ones. We therefore took the one course open to men in the miserable condition of having been deprived in this cruel way of their livelihood and their kinsmen, the one course open to us, made these events known both to your procurator in charge of the Registry, Aurelius Marcianus, and to your most excellent procurators of Asia. We present ourselves as suppliants, most divine of all Emperors that have ever been, to your divine and incomparable majesties, prevented as we are from attending to our labour in the fields, since the enforcement men and their deputies threaten with danger to our lives even those of us who remain — so we are unable, as a result of being prevented from working the land, to meet even the imperial tribute and other demands for the immediate future; and we ask that you show yourself (*sic*) favourable in receiving our petition and entrust the governor of the province and your most excellent procurators with the task of punishing the outrage, of ending incursions into the imperial estates, and the upset that is being caused us by the enforcement men and those who on the pretext of magistracies or public duties upset and pillage farmers, for the reason that everything we have from our forbears is subject to the prior claim of the most sacred Treasury under the regulations that govern cultivation: it is the truth of the matter that has been related to your Divinity.

If then some redress for these monstrous outrages is not accorded us, from your heavenly right hand, and support for the future, it is inevitable that those of us who remain, unable to bear the greed of the enforcement men and of ?our opponents, who use the pretexts we have already mentioned, shall leave even the hearths of our forefathers and our ancestral burial places and move to private land for our own preservation (the men who are carrying on this life of crime pass over those who live there in preference for your own farmers) (and) become refugees from the imperial estates in which we have been both born and reared and have continued since the time of our forefathers to farm in fulfilment of our undertaking to the imperial budget.

Some time in the first half of the third century when there were two Emperors (probably Septimius Severus and Caracalla), imperial officials had covered up their exactions on this estate by arresting some of their victims; on a previous occasion the arrested men had been made away with. The officials concerned are called *colletiones* in Greek, which is a word connected with Latin *collatio*, tax contribution, but spelt in Greek as if it were connected with the Greek word for glue. Whatever humour there may have been in this title originally had evidently vanished by the time the peasants of this estate wrote to the Emperors.

Their other oppressors were municipal officials who were wrongly forcing them to take on duties in the neighbouring cities, presumably accusing them of having left the cities to escape them (**220**), although they claim to be tenants of long standing.

Abbott and Johnson point out the power of great private landowners, who were evidently able to protect their tenants when imperial officials were unable to do so — or were in league with the oppressors.

The tenant farmers of the imperial estates threatened to leave. Aurelian is recorded as imposing on the governing bodies of communities responsibility for paying taxes on any deserted property.

222. *Codex of Justinian* 11, 59 (58), 1

The Emperor Constantine Augustus, to Capestrinus. Our parent the deified Aurelian has ordered that the governing bodies of communities be held liable for properties that have been abandoned and that on those estates which fail to attract owners as we had enjoined they should be accorded a three year period of exemption from tax and thereafter meet the usual obligations on these same properties; that being so, we keep to the same principle and enjoin that if it is established that the governing bodies are not capable of taking on those same properties, the burdens imposed on those same lands be divided between private properties and city territories. Received [- - -].

This measure (307-37) seems to show imperial concern for a general flight from the land and the taxes imposed on it, but Whittaker 1976, 147f., argues that it was intended only as a remedy for Egypt, where it had long been normal to assign uninundated land and irrecoverable taxes to those who could pay, and that this happened in the third century in the Fayum, after the Libyan invasions, the usurpation of Egypt by Palmyra, and the secession of Firmus. Constantine here extends the practice so that individuals as well as councils become liable, recognising that councils sometimes could not pay.

Economic stringency helped to shorten the vision of local ruling circles. In self-defence they looked to their own interests and (if they did not join in separatist movements) they welcomed or even actively sought an administration in which they would figure as more than one tiny unit.

223. *CIL* 13, 412; from Hasparren among the Tarbellians, Aquitania

Priest and likewise d(u)ovir and quaestor of his
District; quaestor, master, Verus went as envoy
To Augustus, winning for the peoples nine that
They should be distinguished from the Gauls. Back
Safe from town he dedicates this altar to the
Guiding Spirit of his district.

The date of this inscription is in doubt, but whether it belongs to the second or more probably to the third century it shows the people of Aquitania proper, the 'Nine Peoples' between the Garonne and the Pyrenees, very conscious of differing from the Celts who also belonged to the province established at the beginning of the Principate (Strabo, *Geography* 4, 1, 1, p. 177). The difference was acknowledged and they were treated as a separate unit for tax purposes; by 105 Lactora was appearing with Lugdunum Convenarum apart from the rest of Aquitania (**85**).

The rural district that Verus twice mentions as his home could not have been one of the type introduced into Spain by Augustus for census purposes (**63**; Mackie 1983 (2), 24), but is a pre-existing subdivision of tribal territory, coming into its own as the towns decline.

The division of the provinces was not welcomed by all.

224. Lactantius, *Deaths of the Persecutors* 7, 4

To spread universal terror, the actual provinces were hacked to pieces, and individual regions, in the end individual cities, almost, began to feel the weight of a multiplicity of governors and manifold departments, of tax officials, generals and deputy prefects.

Diocletian is held responsible for these impositions, but, as C. Roueché argues (JRS 71 (1981), 103ff.), some of the divisions belong earlier in the third century and, as A.H.M. Jones remarked (*The Later Roman Empire* (Oxford, 1964), 1, 42), the tendency to subdivide the provinces goes back to the beginning of the Empire; it was only accelerated in the third century.

Not only were provinces being divided. The status of personnel in charge of them was undergoing a change (cf. **85**, **221**).

225. Aurelius Victor, *The Caesars* 33, 33f.

Indeed, the insult offered to their own class was a provocation to the senators, apart from the wrong done to the world in general. For it was he (Gallienus) who was the first, out of fear that his own incapacity would lead to the transfer of control over the Empire to leading members of the nobility, to ban the senate from military service: they were not even to go near an army.

Senatorial legionary legates disappeared under Gallienus and their places were taken by equestrian prefects. Whether this entailed the exclusion of senators from imperial provinces is now disputed (see Pflaum 1976 and Osier 1977). A consular is found at Lambaesis in about 280 as governor of Numidia, for example (*CIL* 8, 2729).

Victor misrepresents the motive of Gallienus also: he was sensitive as other Roman historians were to the standing of the senate. The change ensured that legionary commanders were experienced soldiers (two appointments as leading centurion: *ILS* 2742), and Osier 1977, 686, sees Gallienus appealing to the equestrians of the Illyrian military elite who were his main support. However unacceptable to the senate, these men saw Rome through the military problems of the mid-third century.

Nor were the changes that Gallienus imposed the first sign of moves to replace senatorial with equestrian personnel in the army.

226. *ILS* 2771; Bostra

To the excellent Julius Julianus, prefect (rating two hundred thousand sesterces) of the First Legion, Parthica Philippiana, a most conscientious general: Trebicius Gaudinus, prefect of the New Reliant Armoured Cavalry Squadron Philippiana, to the best of commanders.

The three legions raised by Septimius Severus (**29f.**) had always been commanded by equestrian officers. Julianus commanded the legion when it was stationed at Bostra, 244-9, along with the cavalry unit. The mailed cavalry ('cataphracts', who wore scale body armour and carried a round shield and pike) were first added to the Roman army by Hadrian as part of the response to pressure on the Danube frontier from Dacians and Sarmatians (*CIL* 11, 5632, cited by J.W. Eadie, *JRS* 57 (1967), 167), but it was not until the third century and especially in the reign of Gallienus that cavalry overtook the legions as the main arm.

The Empire seemed to be in danger of breaking up. Its unity is emphasised in the following letter from Trajan Decius to Aphrodisias.

227. *Aphrodisias* 25; Greek

Imperator Caesar Gaius Messius Quintus Trajan Decius, Pious and Fortunate, Augustus, in his third year of tribunician power, twice consul, designated consul for the third time, Father of his Country, proconsul, and Quintus Herennius Etruscus Messius Decius, Supreme Pontiff, in his first year of tribunician power, consul designate, send greetings to the magistrates, council and people of Aphrodisias. It was to be expected, both on account of the goddess after whom your city is named, and on account of your close relationship with the Romans and your loyalty, that you should rejoice at the establishment of our monarchy and offer up appropriate sacrifices and prayers while we for our part preserve you the freedom which you already enjoy and all the other rights that you have obtained from Emperors before us, and are ready also to forward your aspirations for the future. Aurelius Theodorus and Aurelius Onesimus were on the embassy. Farewell.

The letter belongs to 250, probably to the last twenty days of the year. The traditionalist Decius responds to Aphrodisias' congratulations with a reference to Aphrodite/Venus, the mother of Aeneas.

It was Trajan Decius who sought to stamp out Christianity as a disruptive force in society, and to exploit hostility to it as a means of unifying the Empire, by issuing the edict of 250 that bound all free inhabitants of the Empire to sacrifice to the gods, pour a libation and taste sacrificial meat (W.H.C. Frend, *Martyrdom and Persecution in the Early Church* (Oxford, 1965), 407).

228. Eusebius, *History of the Church* 6, 41, 1f.; Greek

The same Dionysius, in his letter to Fabius, Bishop of Antioch, gives this account of the ordeals of those who bore witness in Alexandria under Decius: 'It was not as a result of the imperial edict that the persecution began amongst us: no, it had a start of a whole year, and the man who got in first was that prophet and practitioner of evils for this city, whatever his name was. He stirred up the pagan masses and egged them on against us, firing them with their native superstition again. (2) He worked them up into grasping every opportunity for wrong-doing, and they got the idea that the only form of religious devotion was this cult of devils, thirst for our blood. Their first victim, then, was an old man called Metras . . .'

Dionysius 'the Great' had been Bishop of Alexandria since 247, and left the city during the persecution: in the later persecution of Valerian he was banished (7, 11). Fabius had become bishop of Antioch for a short period in succession to Babylas, who had died in prison (6, 39, 2 and 46, 3).

As this passage suggests, there was genuine detestation of Christians and, now, fear of what their non-conformity might bring on the rest of society. Compare the anonymous denunciations that Pliny encountered in Bithynia, as well as his way of dealing with the problem (*Letters* 10, 96f.) Here as elsewhere (**208**, **212f.**, **218**) features of the third century were foreshadowed in the second.

Certificates issued to those who sacrificed insist that there had been no deviation.

229. *P. Michigan* 13, University of Michigan Studies 40 (1936), 157

To those appointed to supervise the sacrifices, from Aurelius Sakis, native of the village of Theoxenis, along with his children Aeon and Heras, we (*sic*) all lodging in the village of Theadelphia.

We have always continued to sacrifice to the gods and now, too, in your presence we have offered sacrifice in accordance with the regulations and poured libations and tasted the sacrifices and we ask you to sign below. May you continue to prosper.

(In a different hand) We, Aurelius Serenus and Aurelius Hermas, witnessed you sacrificing.

(First hand) In the first year of Imperator Caesar Gaius Messius Trajan Decius, Pious and Fortunate, Augustus, on Pauni 23rd.

17 June, 250.

It needed more than enforced paganism to save the Empire when regional and individual interests were combining with external threats to tear it apart and an Emperor could even drive a commander to revolt by seeking to anticipate it. The suspect Carausius of Menapia, commander of the fleet based on Gesoriacum, proclaimed himself Augustus and transferred his fleet to Britain in 287. He established a Franko-Roman Empire and claimed the status of co-ruler with Diocletian and Maximian (290).

230. *RIC* 5, 2, 496 no. 382; Antoninianus of Carausius

Obverse: Legend: Imperator Caesar Marcus Carausius, Pious and Fortunate, Augustus. Radiate draped bust of Carausius, facing right.

Reverse: Legend: Rome's Renewal. $\frac{\text{I}}{\text{C}}$ She-wolf standing to right, suckling Romulus and Remus.

The coin itself, minted at Camulodunum, as the mint-mark shows, was a token that the slogan on the reverse had a good chance of fulfilment. Carausius was a humbly-born native of the Low Countries, based in the most distant of Rome's western provinces, and with no hope of winning the whole. Yet he presents himself as a Roman Emperor on a coin that bears the wolf and twins, oldest symbol of Rome. Culture, ingrained habits of thought, political unity, self-regard, fear and economic interest (the break-up of the Empire would mean the disruption of trade), all made the Empire the only option for the upper classes, and even for many at lower levels of society, and helped to restore the Empire and keep it together.

Chronological List of Emperors

(Names in common use thus: *Octavian*.)

BC

31   Battle of Actium: M. Antonius (*Antony*) and Cleopatra defeated by Imperator Caesar (*Octavian*)

30   Death of M. Antonius and Cleopatra; *Octavian* in supreme power

27   Constitutional settlement: *Octavian* given title *Augustus*

AD

4   Caesar *Augustus* adopts Tiberius Claudius Nero as *Tiberius* Caesar

14   Death of *Augustus*

14-37   *Tiberius* Julius Caesar (Augustus: this becomes the regular designation of Emperors)

37-41   *Gaius* Julius Caesar (*Caligula*)

41-54   Tiberius *Claudius* Caesar Germanicus

54-68   *Nero* Claudius Caesar Germanicus

68-9   Ser. Sulpicius *Galba* Caesar

69   M. Salvius *Otho* Caesar

        A. *Vitellius* (Germanicus)

69-79   (T. Flavius) Imperator Caesar *Vespasian* (the prefixes Imperator Caesar now become normal)

79-81   *Titus* (Flavius) Vespasian

81-96   (T. Flavius) *Domitian*

96-8   (M. Cocceius) *Nerva*

98-117   (M. Ulpius) Nerva *Trajan*

117-38   (P. Aelius) Trajan *Hadrian*

138-61   (Ti. Aelius Hadrian Aurelius Fulvus Boionius Arrius) *Antoninus Pius*

161-9   *M. Aurelius* Antoninus and L. Aurelius *Verus*

169-76   *M. Aurelius* Antoninus

176-80   *M. Aurelius* Antoninus and (L.) Aurelius *Commodus*

180-93   (L.) Aurelius *Commodus*

193   P. Helvius *Pertinax*

        M. *Didius* Severus *Julianus*

193-8   L. *Septimius Severus* Pertinax

198-208   L. *Septimius Severus* and M. Aurelius Antoninus (*Caracalla*)

208-11   L. *Septimius Severus*, M. Aurelius Antoninus (*Caracalla*) and P. Septimius *Geta*

211-12   M. Aurelius Antoninus (*Caracalla*) and P. Septimius *Geta*

212-17   M. Aurelius Antoninus (*Caracalla*)

217-18   M. Opellius *Macrinus*
218   M. Opellius *Macrinus* and M. Opellius Antoninus *Diadu-
          menianus*
218-22   M. Aurelius Antoninus (*Elagabalus*)
222-35   M. Aurelius *Severus Alexander*
235-8   D. Iulius Verus *Maximinus*
238   D. Caelius Calvinus *Balbinus* and M. Clodius *Pupienus*
238-44   M. Antonius Gordianus (*Gordian III*)
244-8   M. Julius Philippus (*Philip the Arabian*)
248-9   M. Julius Philippus and his son of the same name
249-51   C. Messius Quintus *Trajan Decius*
251-3   C. Vibius *Trebonianus Gallus* and C. Vibius Afinius Gallus
          Veldumnianus *Volusian*
253   M. Aemilius *Aemilian*
253-60   P. Licinius *Valerian* and P. Licinius *Gallienus*
260-8   P. Licinius *Gallienus*
268-70   M. Aurelius *Claudius* (*II, Gothicus*)
270   M. Aurelius *Claudius* Quintillus
270-5   L. Domitius *Aurelian*
275-6   M. Claudius *Tacitus*
276   M. Annius *Florian*
276-82   M. Aurelius *Probus*
282-3   M. Aurelius *Carus*
283-5   M. Aurelius *Carinus*
283-4   M. Aurelius Numerius *Numerianus*

(For a list of pretenders see MacMullen 1976 (12), 93.)

Select Bibliography

Items are referred to in the text by author's name, date of publication and (in brackets) section of the bibliography in which the work is listed, if that does not correspond to the chapter in which the reference occurs: for a reference to Sherwin-White 1966 (1), 123, see the Bibliography for Chapter 1.

General and on Chapter 1

P.A. Brunt (1978), 'Laus Imperii' in P.D.A. Garnsey and C.R. Whittaker (eds.), *Imperialism in the Ancient World* (Cambridge)

T. Frank (ed.,) (1938-41), *An Economic Survey of Ancient Rome*, 5 vols. (Baltimore)

A.H.M. Jones (1940), *The Greek City from Alexander to Justinian* (Oxford)

D.M. Magie (1950), *Roman Rule in Asia Minor*, 2 vols. (Princeton)

F.G.B. Millar (1977), *The Emperor in the Roman World* (London)

F.G.B. Millar *et al.* (1981), *The Roman Empire and its Neighbours* (2nd edn, London)

M.I. Rostovtzeff (1957), *Social and Economic History of the Roman Empire* (2nd edn by P.M. Fraser, 2 vols., Oxford)

A.N. Sherwin-White (1966), *The Letters of Pliny: a Historical and Social Commentary* (Oxford)

On Chapter 2

A.K. Bowman (1971), 'The Town Councils of Roman Egypt', *Amer. Stud. in Papyrology* 11 (Toronto)

G.P. Burton (1976), 'The Issuing of Mandata to Proconsuls and a new Inscription from Cos', *ZPE* 21, 63ff.

S. Frere (1961), 'Civitas — a Myth?', *Antiquity* 35, 29ff.

Chr. Habicht (1975), 'New Evidence on the Province of Asia', *JRS* 65, 64ff.

A.H.M. Jones (1960), 'Procurators and Prefects in the Early Principate', *Studies in Roman Government and Law* (Oxford), 115ff.

N. Mackie (1983), *Local Administration in Roman Spain A.D. 14-212*, British Archaeological Reports, International Series 172 (Oxford)

F.G.B. Millar (1966), 'The Emperor, the Senate and the Provinces', *JRS* 56, 156ff.

—— (1967), 'Emperors at Work', *JRS* 57, 9ff.

On Chapter 3

E. Birley (1969), 'Septimius Severus and the Roman Army', *Epigraphische Studien* 8 (Düsseldorf), 15ff.

D.J. Breeze and B. Dobson (1978), *Hadrian's Wall* (Harmondsworth)

B. Campbell (1975), 'Who were the "Viri Militares"?' *JRS* 65, 11ff.

G.L. Cheeseman (n.d.), *The Auxilia of the Roman Imperial Army* (Oxford, 1914; repr. Chicago, paperback)

B.M. Levick (1967), *Roman Colonies in Southern Asia Minor* (Oxford)

E.N. Luttwak (1976), *The Grand Strategy of the Roman Empire from the First Century A.D. to the Third* (Baltimore-London)

H.M.D. Parker (1958), *The Roman Legions* (Oxford, 1928; repr. with bibliographical additions by G. Watson)

G. Webster (1974), *The Roman Imperial Army of the first and second centuries A.D.* (London, 1969; repr. with corrections)

On Chapter 4

P.A. Brunt (1966), 'Procuratorial Jurisdiction', *Latomus* 25, 461ff.

G.P. Burton (1975), 'Proconsuls, Assizes and the Administration of Justice under the Empire', *JRS* 65, 92ff.

F. De Visscher (1965), *Les Édits d'Auguste découverts à Cyrène* (réimpression sur l'édition de 1940 avec réproduction complète du texte grec, Osnabrück)

P. Garnsey (1966), 'The *Lex Iulia* and Appeal under the Empire', *JRS* 56, 167ff.

—— (1968), 'The Criminal Jurisdiction of Governors', *JRS* 58, 51ff.

—— (1970), *Social Status and Legal Privilege in the Roman Empire* (Oxford)

A.H.M. Jones (1960a), 'Imperial and Senatorial Jurisdiction in the Early Principate', *Historia* 3 (1955), 464ff. (repr. in *Studies in Roman Government and Law* (Oxford), 67ff.)

—— (1960b), 'I appeal unto Caesar' in G. Mylonas and D. Raymond (eds.), *Studies Presented to D.M. Robinson*, 2 (St Louis, 1953) 918ff. (repr. in *Studies*, 51ff.)

A.N. Sherwin-White (1963), *Roman Society and Roman Law in the New Testament* (Oxford)

On Chapter 5

P.A. Brunt (1966), 'The "Fiscus" and its Development', *JRS* 56, 75ff.

—— (1981), 'The Revenues of Rome', *JRS* 71, 161ff.

D.J. Crawford (1976), 'Imperial Estates' in M.I. Finley (ed.), *Studies in Roman Property* (Cambridge), 35ff.

S.J. De Laet (1975), *Portorium: Étude sur l'Organisation douanière chez les romains* (Bruges, 1949; repr. New York, 1975)

D. Flach (1979), 'Die Bergwerksordnungen von Vipasca', *Chiron* 9 (1979), 399ff.

P. Garnsey (1971a), '*Honorarium Decurionatus*', *Historia* 20, 323ff.

—— (1971b), '*Taxatio* and *Pollicitatio* in Roman Africa', *JRS* 61, 116ff.

K. Hopkins (1980), 'Taxes and Trade in the Roman Empire (200 B.C.-A.D.400)', *JRS*, 101ff.

E. Lo Cascio (1981), 'State and Coinage in the Late Republic and Early Empire', *JRS* 71, 76ff.

D.R. Walker (1976-8), *The Metrology of the Roman Silver Coinage*, 1 (*Augustus-Domitian*); 2 (*Nerva-Commodus*); 3 (*Pertinax-Uranius Antoninus*), *Brit. Arch. Reports* Suppl. 5, 22, 40 (Oxford, 1976, 1977, 1978)

On Chapter 6

R. Duncan-Jones (1982), *The Economy of the Roman Empire: Quantitative Studies*, 2nd edn (Cambridge)

D. Flach (1978), 'Inschriftenuntersuchungen zum römischen Kolonat in Nordafrika' *Chiron* 8, 441ff.

K. Hopkins (1978/9) 'Economic Growth and Towns in Classical Antiquity' in P. Abrams and E.A. Wrigley (eds.), *Towns in Societies* (Cambridge, 1978; paperback 1979), 35ff.

A.H.M. Jones (1974), *The Roman Economy: Studies in Ancient Economic and Administrative History* (ed. P.A. Brunt, Oxford)

S. Mitchell (1983), 'The Balkans, Anatolia, and Roman Armies across Asia Minor' in S. Mitchell (ed.) *Armies and Frontiers in Roman and Byzantine Anatolia*, *British Archaeological Reports*, *International Series* 156 (Oxford), 131ff.

H.-G. Pflaum (1940), 'Essai sur le Cursus Publicus', *Mémoires présentés à l'Académie des Inscriptions et Belles-Lettres* 4

H.W. Pleket (1983), 'Urban Elites and Business in the Greek Part of the Roman Empire' in P. Garnsey *et al.* (eds.), *Trade in The Ancient Economy* (London)

G. Rickman (1980), *The Corn Supply of Ancient Rome* (Oxford)

On Chapter 7

A.J. Christopherson (1968), 'The Provincial Assembly of the Three Gauls in the Julio-Claudian Period', *Historia* 17, 351ff.

J. Deininger (1965), '*Die Provinziallandtage der römischen Kaiserzeit*', *Vestigia* 6 (Munich)

J.F. Gardner (1974), *Leadership and the Cult of the Personality* (London-Toronto)

E.W. Gray (1970), Review of Herrmann (1968), *Gnomon* 42, 390ff.

P. Herrmann (1968), '*Der römische Kaisereid*', *Hypomnemata* 20 (Göttingen)

K. Hopkins (1978), *Conquerors and Slaves* (Cambridge, 1978), esp. Ch. 5, 'Divine Emperors', 197ff.

S.R.F. Price (1980), 'Between Man and God: Sacrifice in the Roman Imperial Cult', *JRS* 70, 28ff.

K. Scott (1975), *The Imperial Cult under the Flavians* (Stuttgart-Berlin, 1936; repr. New York, 1975)

L.R. Taylor (1931), *The Divinity of the Roman Emperor* (Middletown, Conn.)

On Chapter 8

L. Harmand (1957), *Un Aspect social et politique du monde romain: le Patronat sur les collectivités des origines au Bas-Empire* (Paris)

J. Nicols (1980a), 'Pliny and the Patronage of Communities', *Hermes* 108, 365ff.

—— (1980b), '*Tabulae Patronatus*: a Study of the Agreement between Patron and Client Community', *ANRW* 2, 13, 535ff.

R.P. Saller (1982), *Personal Patronage under the Early Empire* (Cambridge)

On Chapter 9

G.W. Bowersock (1965), *Augustus and the Greek World* (Oxford)

—— (1969), *Greek Sophistis in the Roman Empire* (Oxford)

P.A. Brunt (1971), *Italian Manpower 225 B.C.-A.D. 14* (Oxford)

—— (1976), 'The Romanization of the Local Ruling Classes in the Roman Empire' in *Assimilation et Résistance à la culture gréco-romaine dans le monde ancien: Travaux du VIe Congrès internationale d'Études classiques* (Bucharest-Paris)

G. Forni (1953), *Il Reclutamento delle legioni da Augusto a Diocleziano* (Milan-Rome)

—— (1974), 'Estrazione ethica e sociale dei soldati delle legioni nei primi tre secoli dell'impero', *ANRW* 2, 1, 339ff.

M.T. Griffin (1982), 'The Lyons Tablet and Tacitus', *CQ* 32, 404ff.

H. Halfmann (1979), *Die Senatoren aus dem östlichen Teil des Imperium Romanum bis zum Ende des 2 Jh. n.Chr.*, *Hypomnemata* 58 (Göttingen)

M. Hammond (1957), 'Composition of the Senate A.D. 68-235', *JRS* 47, 74ff.

C.P. Jones (1971), *Plutarch and Rome* (Oxford)

—— (1978), *The Roman World of Dio Chrysostom* (Cambridge, Mass.)

J.C. Mann (1983), *Legionary Recruitment and Veteran Settlement during the Principate* (ed. for publ. by M.M. Roxan), *Inst. of Arch. Publ. 7* (London)

H.-G. Pflaum (1950), *Les Procurateurs équestres* (Paris)

A.N. Sherwin-White (1973), *The Roman Citizenship*, 2nd edn (Oxford)

R. Syme (1958), *Colonial Elites: Rome, Spain, and the Americas* (Oxford)

On Chapter 10

T.D. Barnes (1968), 'Legislation against the Christians', *JRS* 58, 32ff.

P.A. Brunt (1961), 'Charges of Maladministration under the early Principate', *Historia* 10, 189ff.

—— (1975), 'The Administration of Roman Egypt', *JRS* 65, 124ff.

G.P. Burton (1979), 'The Curator Reipublicae: towards a Reappraisal', *Chiron* 9, 465ff.

B.M. Levick (1979), 'Pliny in Bithynia — and What Followed', *Greece and Rome* Ser. 2, vol. 26, 121ff.

—— (1982), 'Domitian and the Provinces', *Latomus* 41, 50ff.

H.W. Pleket (1961), 'Domitian, the Senate and the Provinces', *Mnemosyne* Ser. 4, 14, 296ff.

On Chapter 11

W.H. Buckler (1923), 'Labour Disputes in the Province of Asia' in W.H. Buckler and W.M. Calder (eds.), *Anatolian Studies presented to Sir W. Ramsay* (Manchester), 27ff.

G.E.M. De Ste Croix (1981), *The Class Struggle in the Ancient Greek World* (London)

S.L. Dyson (1975), 'Native Revolt Patterns in the Roman Empire', *ANRW*, 2, 3, 138ff.

H.M. Last (1949), 'Rome and the Druids: a Note', *JRS* 39, 1ff.

R. MacMullen (1970), *Enemies of the Roman Order* (Cambridge, Mass.)

H.A. Ormerod (1978), *Piracy in the Ancient World* (Liverpool, 1924; repr. with paperback 1978)

V.A. Tcherikover and A. Fuks, *Corpus Papyrorum Judaicarum*, 2 vols. (Cambridge, Mass., 1960)

On Chapter 12

G. Alföldy (1974), 'The Crisis of the Third Century as seen by Contemporaries', *Greek, Roman and Byzantine Studies* 15, 89ff.

P. Callu (1969), *La Politique monétaire des empereurs romains de 238 à 311* (Paris)

M. Crawford (1975), 'Finance, Coinage, and Money from the Severans to Constantine', *ANRW* 2, 2, 560ff.

P. Garnsey (1974), 'Some Aspects of the Decline of the Urban Aristocracy in the Empire', *ANRW* 2, 1, 229ff.

A. King and M. Henig, (eds.) (1981), *The Roman West in the Third Century*, 2 vols., *British Archaeological Reports, International Series* 109 (Oxford)

R. MacMullen (1976), *The Roman Government's Response to Crisis A.D. 235-337* (New Haven-London)

F.G.B. Millar (1969), 'P. Herennius Dexippus: The Greek World of the Third Century Invasions', *JRS* 59, 12ff.

P. Oliva (1962), *Pannonia and the Onset of Crisis in the Roman Empire* (Prague)

J. Osier (1977), 'The Emergence of Third Century Equestrian Military Commanders', *Latomus* 36, 674ff.

H.-G. Pflaum (1976), 'Zur Reform des Kaisers Gallienus', *Historia* 25, 109ff.

C.R. Whittaker (1976), '*Agri Deserti*' in M.I. Finley (ed.), *Studies in Roman Property* (Cambridge), 137ff.

Index of Passages Cited

Aurelius *Arcadius Charisius*; jurist of the third-fourth centuries; see *Digest*.

Flavius *Arrian*; second-century native of Bithynia; consul *c*. 130, he governed Cappadocia under Hadrian and defeated the Alans. He preserved the *Discourses* of Epictetus, the Stoic philosopher. Epictetus, *c*. 55-*c*. 135, was a slave of Nero's freedman Epaphroditus, later killed by Domitian, and a pupil of Musonius. Freed by Epaphroditus, Epictetus began to teach philosophy at Rome and, after the philosophers had been expelled by Domitian, at Nicopolis in Greece.
Tr. W.A. Oldfather (2 vols., Loeb, 1925-8).

> *Discourses of Epictetus* 4, 1, 91-8   **146**

The Augustan History; title given to a collection of biographies of Emperors, Caesars and pretenders, 117-285, after *Suetonius*. Authorship and purpose of the work are debated, its evidential value uneven.
Tr. D. Magie (3 vols., Loeb, 1922-32).

Hadrian 15, 12f.	**2**
Pertinax 1, 4-2, 11	**132**
Alexander Severus 60, 6	**198**
Probus 22, 4-23, 3	**210**

Augustus; 63 BC-AD 14; the first Roman Emperor. He left a summary account of his achievements to be set up at Rome; it is known to us from three sites in Galatia: Ancyra (the Latin, with a Greek paraphrase, was inscribed on the walls of the temple of Rome and Augustus), Antioch (Latin) and Apollonia (Greek); the appendix was added for the benefit of provincials.
Tr. F.W. Shipley (Loeb, 1924); ed. (Latin) and tr. P.A. Brunt and J.M. Moore (Oxford, 1967).

> *Achievements of the Deified Augustus*, Appendix (EJ p. 30f.) **77**

Sextus *Aurelius Victor*; senator from Africa, governor of Pannonia Secunda 361, Prefect of the City 389; his biographies of Emperors from Augustus to Constantius were composed from 360, after *Suetonius*.
Ed. E. Pichlmayr (Leipzig, 1911).

> *Caesars* 33, 33f.   **225**

Callistratus; jurist of Greek origin active in the first half of the third century; see *Digest*.

Cassius Dio Cocceianus; senator from Nicaea, Bithynia, consul for the second time with Alexander Severus, 229. He wrote a biography of *Arrian* and a *Roman History* from the foundation of the city to 229.
Tr. E. Cary (9 vols., Loeb 1914-27).

Codex of Justinian; codification of imperial legislation promulgated under Justinian.
Ed. P. Krueger (Berlin, 1888).

Comparison of Mosaic and Roman Law; an essay of the fourth century, comparing Old Testament and Roman legal codes.
Text *FIRA* 2, 543ff.
Digest; collection of authoritative statements on Roman law promulgated in 533 under *Justinian*.
Ed. Th. Mommsen (Berlin, 1889).

Dio Cocceianus (*Chrysostom*), *of Prusa*, c. 40-after 112; rhetorician and philosopher, pupil of Musonius, expelled from Rome by Domitian; a friend of Trajan, he returned to political life in Bithynia.
Tr. J.W. Cohoon and H. Lamar Crosby (5 vols., Loeb, 1932-51).

Eusebius, c. 260-c. 340; Bishop of Caesarea from c. 315; his *History of the Church* is the principal source for the early history of Christianity.
Tr. G.A. Williamson (PC, 1965).

Eutropius; campaigned with Julian, 363; published a survey of Roman history from Romulus to 364.

Marcus Cornelius *Fronto*; c. 100-c. 166; born at Cirta, suffect consul 143; tutor to Marcus Aurelius and Lucius Verus, and leading orator.
Tr. C.R. Haines (2 vols., Loeb, 1919-20).

Herodian; third-century native of Syria, official in Rome and author of *Imperial Histories from the Death of Marcus Aurelius* (180-238).
Tr. C.R. Whittaker (2 vols., Loeb, 1969-70).

Hyginus; Trajanic land-surveyor, author of works on boundaries, land-tenure and land-disputes, and imperial land-regulations. The *Establishment of Boundaries* is thought to be the work of a later author. Ed. F.

Blume, K. Lachmann and A. Rudorff, *Die Schriften der römischen Feldmesser*, 1 (Berlin, 1848, repr. 1962).
Establishment of Boundaries 205L (achmann) **61**

T. Flavius *Josephus*; born into an aristocratic Jewish family in 37-8, a priest and a Pharisee, he took part in the Jewish revolt of 66 and was captured. After the war he was made a Roman citizen and received a pension from the Flavians, whose accession to power he had prophesied. The Greek translation of his *Jewish War* appeared between 75 and 79, his *Antiquities of the Jews* in 93-4.
Tr. H. St J. Thackeray, R. Marcus, A. Wikgren and L.H. Feldman (10 vols., Loeb, 1926-65). *Jewish War*, tr. G.A. Williamson (PC, 170, rev. E.M. Smallwood) 1981).

Jewish War 2, 266-9	**39**
Jewish War 2, 352f.	**88**
Jewish War 2, 425-7	**199**
Jewish War 4, 138-40; 147	**200**
Jewish War 7, 437-42	**201**

Justinian; Emperor of the East, 527-65, responsible for the codification of Roman law which included the *Codex of Justinian* (imperial legislation) and *Digest* (jurists' opinions).

Lucius Caelius (or Caecilius) Firmianus also known as *Lactantius*, *c.* 240-320; a native of north Africa, summoned to Nicomedia by Diocletian to teach rhetoric, he lost his post in 303, having been converted to Christianity. He moved to the west in 305. The *Divine Institutions* (303-13) commends Christianity to literary men and the *Deaths of the Persecutors* (?318) shows how persecutors came to a bad end.
Ed. S. Brandt and G. Laubmann, *Corpus Scriptorum eccles. latin.* 19 and 27

Divine Institutions 7: the Good Life 15, 19	**206**
Deaths of the Persecutors 7, 4	**224**

Livy (Titus Livius), *c.* 59 BC-AD 17, a native of Patavium, whose *History of Rome from its Foundation* closed in 9 BC; of the original 142 books 1-10 and 21-45 are extant; others survive in epitomised form or underlie the work of other writers such as *Aurelius Victor* and *Eutropius*.
Tr. B.O. Foster, E.T. Sage, A.C. Schlesinger and R.M. Geer (14 vols., Loeb, 1919-59); A. De Sélincourt (1-5), B. Radice (6-10), H. Bettenson (31-45) (PC, 1960-82).

History of Rome 9, 18, 6	**203**
History of Rome, Epitome of Book 139	**121**

Lucian, a native of Samosata, *c.* 120-after 180, he spoke not Greek but probably Aramaic as his first language; he was successively a pleader, a

rhetorician and, at Athens, a philosopher, and he accepted a minor treasury post in Egypt. His *Alexander* is an attack on a charlatan of Abounoteithus.
Tr. A.M. Harmon, K. Kilburn and M.D. Macleod (8 vols., Loeb, 1921-67).
    Alexander 57   **141**

Aelius *Marcianus*: jurist active in the period after Caracalla, the author of manuals and monographs, see *Digest*.

Martyrs, Acts of the: some are based on official reports of the trials, others on eye-witness accounts, but with fictional elements, some are purely legendary.
    Musurillo, *Christian Acts* 1, 6, 1-7, 2 Martyrdom of Pionius   **43**
    Musurillo, *Christian Acts* 6 The Scillitan Martyrs   **48**

Herennius *Modestinus*: jurist, pupil of Ulpian, Prefect of the Watch between 226 and 244; wrote handbooks and a collection of his *Replies*; see *Digest*.

Aemilius *Papinian*: enjoyed a brilliant career, and became prefect of the Guard in 203, but was executed in 212 in the aftermath of Geta's murder. He published 37 books of *Queries*, 19 of *Replies*, a work called *Definitions*, and another on adultery. His work as a jurist was much admired. See *Digest*.

Julius *Paulus*: jurist, fl. c. 210; a pupil of *Scaevola*; he was banished by Elagabalus, recalled by Alexander Severus, and nominated prefect of the Guard; he may have held office jointly with Ulpian. He wrote nearly 320 books, including a commentary on the praetorian Edict, 26 books of *Queries* and 23 of *Replies*. See *Digest*.

Pausanias: mid-second-century native of ?Lydia, author of a *Guide to Greece*.
Tr. W.H.S. Jones, H.A. Ormerod and R. Wycherley (5 vols., Loeb, 1918-35); P. Levi (2 vols., PC, 1971).
    Guide to Greece 10, 34, 5   **41**

Philo Judaeus: c. 30 BC-AD 45, a native of Alexandria and head of the Jewish community there, he represented them on an embassy sent to Rome to ask exemption from the duty of offering cult to Gaius (39-40); the *Embassy to Gaius* and *Against Flaccus* showed the evil fate of persecutors and influenced *Lactantius*.
Tr. F.H. Colson, G.H. Whitaker and R. Marcus (10 vols., Loeb, 1929-53); *Embassy to Gaius* ed. and tr. E.M. Smallwood (Leiden, 1961)
    Embassy to Gaius 299-302   **170**

Flavius *Philostratus*, *c.* 170-reign of Philip I, of a Lemnian family, became a member of Julia Domna's philosophical circle, writing the *Life of Apollonius* at her request; later, at Athens, he wrote the *Lives of the Sophists*.
Tr. F.C. Conybeare and W.C. Wright (3 vols., Loeb, 1912-52)

Pliny the Elder (Gaius Plinius Secundus), *c.* 23-79. A native of Comum, he was uncle of *Pliny the Younger*. He served as an equestrian officer in Germany and under Vespasian held a series of procuratorships and the command of the fleet at Misenum which he held at the time of his death in the eruption of Vesuvius. His works included a lost history in 31 books, a work in 20 books on the wars against the Germans, also lost, and the *Natural History*, a compilation in 37 books.
Tr. H. Rackham, W.H.S. Jones and D.E. Eichholz (10 vols., Loeb, 1938-62).

Pliny the Younger (Gaius Plinius Caecilius Secundus), *c.* 61 to *c.* 112; a senator from Comum, he reached the consulship in 100. The tenth book of his *Letters* is a dossier of his correspondence with Trajan when he was governor of Bithynia, *c.* 110 until his death.
Tr. B. Radice *Letters* and *Panegyric on Trajan* (2 vols., Loeb, 1969); *Letters* (PC, 1963).

?Lucius Mestrius *Plutarch* of Chaeronea, born before 50, died after 120; philosopher and biographer, he numbered influential Romans among his friends. Of the essays cited here, *On Peace of Mind* is to be dated after 107, *On Exile* after 96 and the *Precepts* between 96 and 114 (see C.P. Jones, *JRS* 56 (1966), 72f.).
Tr. of *Moralia* by F.C. Babbitt, W.C. Helmbold, P.H. De Lacy *et al.* (16 vols., Loeb, 1927-69).

Rutilius Claudius Namatianus: pagan poet, probably a native of Tolosa, who held the City Prefecture in 414. His poem, written in 'accomplished elegiacs' (F.J.E. Raby), celebrates a journey to his estates in Gaul. Tr. J.W. and A.M. Duff, *Minor Latin Poets* 2 (Loeb, 1934).

Quintus Cervidius *Scaevola*, leading jurist of the later second century, prefect of the Watch 175, adviser to Marcus Aurelius and teacher of *Paulus*; he was the author of 20 books of *Queries*, 40 of *Digests*, 6 of *Replies* and 4 of *Rules*. See *Digest*.

Sibylline Oracles: written in imitation of the official collection of Sibylline oracles kept on the Capitol at Rome, they claim to be genuine utterances of the Greek sibyls; they are the work of Jewish and Christian authors, the former dating from the mid-second century BC to the time of Hadrian, the latter to the second century AD onwards. Fourteen books are extant.
Ed. J. Geffcken (Leipzig, 1902); A. Kurfess (Tusculum, 1951).

Strabo, *c*. 63 BC-AD 21 at least, a native of Amiseia. He wrote *Historical Sketches* in 47 books (now lost) and a *Geography* in 17, perhaps for the use of men in public life.
Tr. H.L. Jones (8 vols., Loeb, 1917-32).

Gaius *Suetonius* Tranquillus, *c*. 70-after 121; secretary to Hadrian, dismissed in 121. Wrote biographies of literary men and *Lives of the Caesars* (Julius to Domitian).
Tr. J.C. Rolfe (2 vols., Loeb, 1914); R. Graves (PC, 1957).

?Publius Cornelius *Tacitus*, *c.* 56-reign of Hadrian; senator of Gallic origin, consul 97. He published a biography of his father-in-law Gnaeus Julius Agricola, ethnographical work *Germany* (both in 98), *Histories* covering the period 69-96 (first decade of the second century) and *Annals*, which, if completed, covered 14-68.
Tr. M. Hutton, R.M. Ogilvie, E.H. Warmington, C.H. Moore, J. Jackson *et al.* (5 vols., Loeb, 1914-70); H. Mattingly, *Agricola* (PC, 1948); M. Grant, *Annals* (PC, 1956); K. Wellesley, *Histories* (PC, 1964).

Domitius *Ulpian*; a native of Tyre, assessor to Papinian as prefect of the Guard, along with Paul; he was prefect of the Grain Supply and of the Guard in 222, but was murdered by the guardsmen in the following year. He is known to have been the author of nearly 280 works, including a commentary on the Praetorian Edict in 81 books, *Laws*, *Institutions*, *Rules* and *Replies*. He summed up earlier writers and nearly a third of the *Digest* is taken from him. See *Digest*.

Venuleius Saturninus: mid-second-century jurist, active in the provinces, the author of works on *Guarantees* (19 books), *Interdicts* (6) and the *Duty of the Proconsul* (4). See *Digest*.

Documentary Sources: Inscriptions

Papyri

AJ 199 (= *SP* 230 = *P.Oxy.* 1411) Banks close their doors against the currency **214**
EJ 117 (= *P.Oxy.* 240) Brutality of soldiers in Egypt **168**
R.O. Fink, A.S. Hoey and W.F. Snyder, *The Feriale Duranum* (Yale, 1940) A military calendar **128**
Musurillo, *Pagan Acts*, XI (= *P. Yale Inv. 1536* + *P.Oxy.* 33) *Acts of Appian* **204**
P. Got. 3 Guarantee of fish supplies for Caracalla **216**
P. Michigan 13, 157 Certificate of sacrifice to pagan gods **229**
P.Oxy. 1415, lines 17-31 Attempt to force a man to take office **219**
P.Teb. 2, 289 Letter of a *strategus* to a toparch **169**
Smallwood, *Gaius-Nero* 370 (= *P. Lond.* 1912) Claudius' letter to the Alexandrians **120**
SP 2, 216, cf. *Archiv für Papyrusforschung* 14 (1941), 44f. Alexander Severus renounces crown gold **209**

Coins

EJ 49 (= *RIC* 1, 105 no.19) Cities of Asia restored **78**
RIC 5, 2, 87 no. 652 Probus and the acquiescence of the troops **211**
RIC 5, 2, 496 no. 382 Carausius as Augustus **230**
Smallwood, *Nerva-Hadrian* 30 (*RIC* 2, 229, no. 93) Italy exempted from supplying the imperial post **92**

Index and List of Ancient and Modern Geographical Equivalents

Most classical sites indexed may be found on the maps. Towns and districts are indexed under their classical names, rivers and other geographical features by their modern names. Celebrated figures (Emperors and their families, literary men, etc.) are indexed under the names most familiar to English readers, other Romans under their gentile names.